RODEO

RODEO

An Anthropologist Looks at the Wild and the Tame

Elizabeth Atwood Lawrence

The University of Chicago Press
Chicago and London

The University of Chicago Press, Chicago 60637
The University of Chicago Press, Ltd., London

© 1982 by The University of Tennessee Press, Knoxville

All rights reserved. Published 1982
University of Chicago Press edition 1984
Printed in the United States of America

91 90 89 88 87 86 85 84   1 2 3 4 5

Library of Congress Cataloging in Publication Data

Lawrence, Elizabeth Atwood, 1929–
    Rodeo, an anthropologist looks at the wild and the
tame.

    Bibliography: p.
    Includes index.
    1. Rodeos—Social aspects—United States.
    2. Rodeos—Social aspects—Canada.   I. Title.
GV1834.5.L38   1982b   791'.8   83-18176
ISBN 0-226-46955-7

TO MY FATHER
  whose memory is part of all endeavors
AND FOR BOB, PRISCILLA, AND MARK
  companions on Western trails of discovery and enrichment

PREFACE

THE IMMENSE POPULARITY of rodeo and the marked preoccupation with it throughout the American Great Plains is a phenomenon which commands the attention of the social scientist, for here is an event which obviously holds deep meaning for a large segment of the regional population. The contests and performances of rodeo are remarkably patterned and repetitive, comprising a kind of ritual event which serves to express much that is significant not only in the lives of its participants and audiences, but also within the society that endorses it.

I first developed an interest in the sport of rodeo in the summer of 1975 while in Montana studying the significance of the horse among the Crow Indians. As a researcher who had turned from the clinical practice of veterinary medicine to anthropology in order to make human-animal relationships my primary focus, it became immediately apparent that rodeo held rich potential. In my work with societies which have significant associations with livestock, my goal is to expand the traditional ethnographic perspective by including, as far as possible, the input of the animals themselves in these associations. Rodeo provides an ideal context in which to observe the interactions between members of a certain society and their animals, interactions which, though reflecting many phases of actual cowboy and ranch life, are intensified and dramatized for sport and display. Rodeos provide valuable information about the ways people perceive of and participate in relationships with animals and also with nature and the wild. On a deeper level rodeo offers insights into the manner in which a given socio-cultural group may deal with the universal dilemma of man's place in nature.

At the heart of rodeo is the West—the land itself as the original setting for this unique event. The region holds interest not only because of its physical characteristics and its noteworthy human and natural history, but also because of the symbolic meaning with which it has become imbued. The West as myth and symbol came into being out of people's perceptions of its wild elements and their reactions to its vastness and awesome splendors. A study of Western Americana—the regional history, literature, film, folklore, and legend —provides a rich source of insights into what the West has come to stand for. Rodeo, I discovered, is a complex and articulate performance, related to these other forms of expression and incorporating many of the same themes, yet in a sense going beyond them in not only stating what the West was and is, but what the present society wishes it to continue to be.

ELIZABETH ATWOOD LAWRENCE

Westport Harbor, Massachusetts
March 24, 1979

ACKNOWLEDGMENTS

To THE OFFICIALS of the Crow Fair, whose friendliness and hospitality first made me welcome behind the scenes at their rodeo, I will always be grateful. My heartfelt thanks go to the Professional Rodeo Cowboys Association for their many courtesies, and especially to the managers of the Calgary Stampede and Cheyenne Frontier Days. Dave Allen provided valuable help, as did Buddy and Judy Vernon, Deb Leatherberry, Ann Secrest, Howard Harris, James Ward of the Alamo Chapter of the American Diabetes Association, the Hollidays, Winston Bruce, Neal Gay, and that family of outstanding horsemen, the Real Birds. Phil South, ecologist with the United States Forest Service, was particularly cooperative and enthusiastic in sharing his experience and insight. I also want to thank the United States Fish and Wildlife Service for the assistance of many of its officials.

Countless numbers of unnamed individuals along the way took time out from their busy lives to give me the help that was so important to my field work, and I am grateful to them. With sincere regard I want to thank the rodeo people who graciously allowed me to become a part of their exciting world; those days of "going down the road" are among the most memorable of my life. In keeping with the spirit of rodeo, one who follows the circuit, even as an observer, must show some of the same tenacity, endurance, and self-reliance that the sport exalts. So I am thankful for all that is represented by the rodeo adage "when the going gets tough, the tough get going."

For permission to quote lyrics from rodeo songs, I want to thank the following:
Groper Music (BMI) for "Night Rider's Lament," © Michael Burton, 1975 by Groper Music (BMI). Used by permission. All rights reserved; Greenhat Music for "Rodeo Gypsies," "Ol' Time Fan-

dango," and "The Dalharted Cowboy," by Michael S. McGinnis
1973, 1977; Texas Red Songs for "Freckles Brown," by Red Steagall;
Peso Music for "Up Jumped the Devil," by James S. (Sandy) Pinkard
and Irving Dane, © 1976; Rocker Music/Richard O'Bitts for "Dad-
dy's Biggest Dream," by Lealand Dwayne Pack and Duke Benson
Pack; Peso Music/Composium Music for "King of the Rodeo," by
Denise and Christopher Crockett, © 1976; American Cowboy Songs,
Inc. for "Jod'e the Rodeo Clown," by Chimp Robertson and Gary
McMahan; Owepar Publishing Company and Porter Music Company
for "The Rodeo Fan," by Frank Dycus, (Copyright 1975 by Owepar
Publishing Company. International Copyright Secured—All rights
reserved. Used by permission. Copyright assigned 1980 to Porter
Music Company); Otter Creek Music, Inc., for "Tight Levis and
Yellow Ribbons," by Glenn Sutton and Red Steagall; Tree Publish-
ing Company, Inc., and Sugarplum Music Company for "Mammas
Don't Let Your Babies Grow Up to Be Cowboys," by Ed and Patsy
Bruce, © 1975 Tree Publishing Company, Inc., and Sugarplum
Music Company; Jack and Bill Music Company c/o The Welk Music
Group, Santa Monica, CA. 90401 for "My Heroes Have Always Been
Cowboys," by Sharon Vaughn, (Copyright © 1976 Jack and Bill
Music Company, c/o The Welk Music Group, Santa Monica, CA.
90401. International Copyright Secured. All Rights Reserved. Used
By Permission); Curley Fletcher for "Bad Brahma Bull" (Public
Domain); Song of Cash, Inc. for "All Around Cowboy" by Jack
Routh and Len Pollard, © 1975, All Rights Reserved; and American
Cowboy Songs, Inc., for "Copenhagen," "Rodeo Rose," "Rodeo's
New Breed," "Rodeo Life," "The Yellow Stud," "I'm Country,"
"Mighty Lucky Man," "Rodeo, You've Cast A Spell," "Lord, I've
Got to be A Rodeo Man," "Born to Follow Rodeo," and "Bull
Rider," all by Chris LeDoux. Grateful acknowledgment is made to
Alfred H. LeDoux, President of American Cowboy Songs, Inc., for
his warm friendliness and the generous spirit with which he shared
the lyrics of Chris LeDoux's expressive rodeo songs.

Permission was kindly granted by Harper & Row Publishers, Inc.,
to quote from the poem, "The Cowboy," and by the Liveright
Publishing Corporation to quote from e.e. cummings' poem about
Buffalo Bill.

To the Nocona Boot Company go my thanks for supplying the
illustration of their advertisement and giving their permission to
reproduce it in this book. Photographers Robert Ridley, Randy
Huffman, and James Svoboda, Jr. (J.J.J.) deserve credit for their
excellent photographs.

I want to express appreciation to Professors Robert R. Jay and Robert C. Padden, who were influential in my graduate studies, and thanks to Professor William Beeman for his encouragement. I am indebted to the memory of the Donaldson's. And to Robert, Priscilla, and Mark Lawrence belongs my deepest gratitude for their help in making this project possible.

CONTENTS

ILLUSTRATIONS

RODEO

1

INTRODUCTION

RODEO IS NOT MERELY what the multitudinous and ever-prevalent posters, bumper stickers, and buttons proclaim it to be—"number one sport" in the American Great Plains. As its participants readily admit, it is more a way of life than a way to make a living. In most areas of the rural West, and in many cities as well, the sport involves a good share of the population, directly or indirectly, at some time in their lives. Wholehearted support is generally evident, whether it comes from a six-year-old backyard buckaroo practicing bronc riding astride a barrel, or a merchant from Cheyenne who has a share in the $3 million that the Wyoming city estimates its Frontier Days Rodeo brings to local businesses (P.R.C.A.:7). Pervasive in its influence and steadily gaining in popularity, the sport of rodeo permeates the very fabric of life in the West, as exemplified particularly in the Great Plains states of Montana, Wyoming, Nebraska, Oklahoma, Texas, and the Canadian province of Alberta, where most of the field work for this study was undertaken.

Statistics showing the extent of the population's involvement in the sport are virtually impossible to obtain. The Professional Rodeo Cowboys Association (P.R.C.A.), the official organization for professional rodeos, sanctions over 600 performances each season, which an estimated 14 million spectators pay to attend (P.R.C.A.: Denver Office, 1978). Inclusion of those sponsored by the International Rodeo Association raises the number of annual rodeos to about 1,000. This figure, however, represents only a fraction of all the rodeos actually held; unsanctioned rodeos and those sponsored by other organizations are numerous. Many communities throughout the ranching country hold their own rodeos all during the season. One small city in southeastern Montana, for example, stages im-

3

promptu or "jackpot" rodeos once or twice weekly from June to September in addition to several larger performances. Throughout the Western states during the spring, summer, and fall there are rodeos almost every day: 4-H, youth, and old timers' rodeos, all-girl, all-Indian, high school and college rodeos, and countless others. Virtually every Western town has its big annual rodeo, planned many months in advance and advertised by huge banners which arch over the main street. Often such a rodeo is the central event of a fair, a carnival, or a series of festivities, and is a widely publicized and eagerly anticipated seasonal celebration. Over the years some of these develop their own traditions and distinct flair, building up a prestigious reputation with the participants and drawing large audiences.

Visitors to the Western states invariably plan to attend a rodeo, for the sport has come to be closely associated with the particular complex of qualities that is identified as "Western" by Americans, and indeed as "American" by the rest of the world. A highlight of the 1979 visit of China's Vice Premier, Teng Hsiao-ping, for example, was his attendance at a Texas rodeo. Those who arranged his travel schedule to acquaint him with the United States felt that "if the idea was to show that the Chinese visitors were just folks, the rodeo was the place to put it across." As part of the East-Meets-West rodeo festivities, the Vice Premier and his entourage were presented with cowboy hats and treated to a ranch-style barbecue and a concert of country-western music. Just before embarking on his ride around the rodeo arena in a stage coach, the Chinese dignitary received the gift of a pure-bred Brahma bull (Lelyveld 1979:10). In the same spirit, the cowboy hats recently worn by the members of the United States Olympic Team served to distinguish the American contenders from those of other countries.

The star of the rodeo is the cowboy, and the one symbol which has come to represent the American Western frontier, and even America herself, most completely is the cowboy. A complex figure who partakes of both the reality of the rugged life he lived on the frontier and of the myth that has grown up around it, it is he who has captured the imagination of the world. The cowboy and his original occupation, that of being a mounted herder, are of course, inextricable. He has spanned the days from the Texas trail drives, through the time of the open range, down to the present era of modern ranching.

Today ranchers in the Great Plains remain as a specific group, generally well-defined and distinguishable from surrounding societies (see, for example, Bennett 1969). Ranching society has remained close to its heritage and has preserved much of its original character. Even in our mechanized age, ranch hands in daily work may still experience direct contact with horses, cattle, with the wild and their own perceptions of it, and with what remains of wilderness. For this reason, and because of its universal appeal, cattle ranching has come to represent the American westward movement and to typify the nation's frontier experience. Rodeo is the direct outgrowth of the cattle industry and, as will become evident in this study, serves to reflect and preserve that heritage. It is precisely the working cowboy's daily preoccupation with his stock and the attendant values that grew out of his work which are being recapitulated in rodeo. The American cowboy has given his name and image to his inheritors in the sport, for every contestant is called a cowboy.

This study is concerned with the ways in which rodeo is used by the ranching society—and by the population which shares that ethos—as a ritual event which serves to express, reaffirm, and perpetuate its values, attitudes, and way of life. As Edmund Leach has stated, "ritual action and belief are alike to be understood as forms of symbolic statement about the social order" (1965:14), and "the individuals who make up a society must from time to time be reminded, at least in symbol, of the underlying order that is supposed to guide their social activities" (1965:16). Victor Turner gives as a "major function" of ritual that it "adapts and periodically readapts the biophysical individual to the basic conditions and axiomatic values of a human social life" (1974:43).

My theoretical approach to the data as an anthropologist looking at the wild and the tame is an interpretive one. It is my assertion that rodeo picks up the main themes from the pastoral life of the cowboy, both past and present, identifies and exaggerates them, and makes them explicit through patterned performances. As Clifford Geertz has written of the Balinese cockfight, so it may be said of rodeo that the sport "renders ordinary, everyday experience comprehensible by presenting it in terms of acts and objects which have had their practical consequences removed and been reduced (or, if you prefer, raised) to the level of sheer appearances, where their meaning can be more powerfully articulated and more exactly perceived." He goes on to state, again with relevance to rodeo, that the cockfight "catches up" certain themes, "and, ordering them into an encompassing structure, presents them in such a way as to throw into relief a particular view of their essential nature. It puts a construction on them, makes them, to those historically positioned to appreciate the construction, meaningful—visible, tangible, graspable—'real,' in an ideational sense" (1974:23).

My view is that rodeo may be seen as an important collective "text" in the sense that "the culture of a people is an ensemble of texts which the anthropologist strains to read over the shoulders of those to whom they properly belong" (Geertz 1974:29), a text in which certain aspects of a culture's ethos are "spelled out externally" (Geertz 1974:27). In rodeo performances, which possess remarkable structural uniformity both at the level of the individual events and in the order of their succession on the program, the anthropologist may identify and interpret recurring themes as meaningful expressions of the supporting society's attitudes and concerns.

The method of analysis used, for example, by Paul Bouissac (1976) for the circus is also in some ways applicable to my investigation of rodeo. Bouissac considers the circus a "language" which is used to convey certain messages between the performers and the audience. "This process of communication obviously can take place only because of the existence of a code shared by the performers and the public" (1976:5). In the case of rodeo, with its contest aspect, as opposed to the circus as pure performance, it is of course essential to realize that communication between the participants themselves (not only contestants but all who are involved in its production) is just as important as that between the performers and the audience.

In a similar way Louis Dupree, believing that the "sports and games of a people reveal something of the ethos of their culture," shows how the Afghanistan horseman's sport of buzkashi is related to its cultural context. In the modern version of this rough event, a goat or calf carcass which is torn to pieces by the players replaces the live prisoner of war who was formerly its victim. Dupree interprets buzkashi as "a game which epitomizes Central Asian nomadic cultural patterns—fierce individual competition within a framework of loose cooperation" (1976:2). The Afghan sportsman who participates in this national game is the "product of a harsh, inward-looking, group-oriented society" (Dupree 1970:19). "The games are an important reminder to the sedentary folk of their former heroic nomadism and the greatness of historic cavalry victories" (Dupree 1976:2).

Also relevant to my study of rodeo is the work of Richard Schechner, who deals with the convergence between the study of various dramatic forms and the interests of social science under the rubric of "performance theory," and includes such events as "sports, ritual, play, and public political behaviors" as examples of "communicative behavior" (1973:3–4). The aim of this drama scholar, who draws on the work of such anthropologists as Turner and Geertz, is to elucidate the close connection that exists between a society and its dramatic forms (Schechner 1969, 1973, 1976). Performance as the subject for serious and indepth analysis by social scientists is a relatively recent phenomenon, and is only now becoming established as an exciting and productive field for scholarly investigation. Geertz calls attention to the fact that in anthropology the idea that such "cultural forms can be treated as texts, as imaginative works built out of social materials, has yet to be systematically exploited" (1971:27). The work of Lévi-Strauss is not an exception here, because "he [Lévi-Strauss] does not seek to understand symbolic forms in terms of how they function in concrete situations to organize perceptions (meanings, emotions, concepts, attitudes); he seeks to understand them entirely in terms of their internal structure" (Geertz 1974:36). My work proceeds from the observable events of the rodeo, and the concrete interactions they exemplify, toward an interpretive analysis, for the symbolic stems from the concrete. Historian Henry Nash Smith referred to this process when he wrote of events in the American West that "men cannot engage in purposive group behavior without images which simultaneously express collective desires and impose coherence on the infinitely varied data of experience" (1971:ix).

The sport of rodeo, like the duties of the working cowboys from which it was derived, deals with the relationships between man and animals, both domesticated and undomesticated, and on a deeper level with the human relation to the land—the wilderness and the wild. Brought into focus by means of the various contests and displays of rodeo, these man-nature relationships are dramatically delineated, categorized, and manipulated. As an outgrowth of ranching, rodeo embodies the frontier spirit as manifested through the aggressive and exploitative conquest of the West, and deals with nature and the reordering of nature according to the dictates of this ethos. It supports the value of subjugating nature, and reenacts the "taming" process whereby the wild is brought under control. This can be thought of in terms of the force of "culture" reaching out to dominate "nature"—the culture/nature dichotomy here representing two opposite conceptual categories or contrasting poles.

The work of Lévi-Strauss (especially 1969, 1975) which deals with the nature/culture opposition is well known in anthropology but does not make use of it in a way which is directly applicable to my study. In order to make clear the meaning of nature and culture as I am using these terms, I quote from Sherry Ortner who, acknowledging "due respect" to Lévi-Strauss, explains that:

> Every culture, or, generically, "culture," is engaged in the process of generating and sustaining systems of meaningful forms (symbols, artifacts, etc.) by means of which humanity transcends the givens of natural existence, bends them to its purposes, controls them in its interest. We may thus broadly equate culture with the notion of human consciousness (i.e., systems of thought and technology), by means of which humanity attempts to assert control over nature.
>
> (1974:72)

It is important also to emphasize the concept that culture "at some level of awareness asserts itself to be not only distinct from but superior to nature, and that sense of distinctiveness and superiority rests precisely on the ability to transform—to 'socialize' and 'culturize'—nature" (Ortner 1974:73).

The process of American pioneer expansion, with its conquering of nature and its bringing of "the wild" into the domination of "civilization" as the frontier was pushed westward, exemplifies what has been called "culture's ongoing dialectic with nature" (Ortner 1974:87). Rodeo is essentially concerned with this opposition, as it comes to terms with nature in the form of cattle, horses, and other beasts incorporated as elements of the sport, and proceeds to align and realign the human relationship with them. Thus the various elements of rodeo events act as counterparts of the natural objects—the land and the living creatures, and all that was once wild—which are brought under man's dominion.

I believe that human relationships with animals merit more precise attention at the level of concrete observable mutual interactions as opposed to their more remote consideration—regarding animals as mere representations of totems, for example. From this basis the investigator can go on to explore and interpret such interactions and to determine the ways in which they may be related to the sociocultural systems in which they occur. Close observation of these dynamic relationships does not preclude the analysis of resultant data in an interpretive or symbolic way. On the contrary, it forms a far more secure base for valid interpretation than would be the case with a more abstract approach.

Much of the anthropological work previously done in the sphere of man's association with animals has virtually discounted the contribution of the animal as a living creature with certain distinct characteristics of its own that influence its role in the relationship. Clark Wissler's (1914) classic work on the horse in Plains Indian culture is a case in point. Considering the horse as a "tool," his theoretical position took negligible account either of the influence of the animal's requirements as a large herbivore or of the psychological and spiritual effects of human interaction with an animal of its particular nature. Recent studies often focus on the role of certain animals in human cognitive systems with little regard to those animals' physical interrelationships with people. Neville Dyson-Hudson, in discussing the study of pastoral nomads, has expressed the current need in anthropology for more data on animals:

> It is equally clear that if understanding a pastoral society involves understanding its herding operations, then understanding the herding operation in turn involves understanding the species herded. In short, for pastoral societies "socially significant phenomena" comprise a far wider category than "social phenomena," and the present unsatisfactory state of nomadic studies must in part be attributed to the slowness with which social anthropologists have come to terms with the results of veterinary and pasture research.
>
>   (1972:14)

Because of limitations imposed by the species barrier, perhaps no one can "get inside" an animal to the extent that a field anthropologist attempts to do when studying people of an alien culture. Yet I believe that I have gained a sensitivity in relation to animals that is akin to this empathy through my close association with them, my training in veterinary medicine, and my years of experience practicing in this field. I trust that such professionally acquired knowledge for elucidating the nature of animals will contribute to the validity of this study in anthropology, and provide an example of the way in which two disciplines may complement each other.

My choice of rodeo as a subject for analysis is the result of the convergence of several factors in my own development as a social scientist. Initially, a deep interest in the expanding science of ethology was the natural outgrowth of my work with and concern for animals. This led me further on a path of my own—research not on either animal behavior or human behavior alone but on the interactions between people and animals. As a veterinary practitioner I had observed that a great deal of private information about the inner nature of an individual was revealed to me through that person's interaction with, and relationship to, animals. In a corresponding way, I came to feel that in the study of society equally relevant insights regarding the nature of a particular group could be gained through a study of that group's relationships with animals and their shared attitudes which result in certain characteristic types of interactions. These concerns were complemented by my longstanding interest in nature and in human relations to the natural world and to the earth itself, particularly that portion of it which has thus far escaped man's domination and may be called wild.

Although during field work it was not possible to become an actual rodeo contestant, I did approach this perspective by becoming an "insider" of the rodeo circuit in some respects. After overcoming initial obstacles, I succeeded in gaining admission behind the chutes, even at the largest and most prestigious professional rodeos. I was able to obtain introspective data and ultimately established the rapport with informants that made it possible to empathize with them. It was very helpful, also, that I had a sense of personal familiarity with the sport of rodeo because of my own past experience as a horse show exhibitor. Though the similarity between the two events is superficial, and more differences than likenesses become evident under analysis, nevertheless a background of participation in this type of livestock show was advantageous.

It should be pointed out that throughout much of this study I am concerned with the informants' own perceptions of how things are rather than "facts" as they might be interpreted by someone outside the rodeo or ranch group. Because of this, and due to the insights they reveal which would be lost by paraphrasing, I feel it is important to retain the language that people used in expressing themselves and have used direct quotes when possible. Also, I do not claim in this work to present "the real West" but only to show that the rodeo is a quintessential part of that complex (and perhaps indefinable) mystique which we call the American West. As the cowboy sport of rodeo developed out of frontier experience, so it also shaped and continues to shape our perceptions of all that the Western frontier has come to symbolize.

In perpetuating the frontier spirit, rodeo is expressing something relevant, not just for Westerners but for Americans, concerning the way they see themselves and their past. Though Westerners generally draw sharp contrasts between themselves and Easterners, the two regions can be understood as complementary parts of a larger whole which in one sense reflect the historical unfolding of the country. Westerners in the Great Plains no doubt hold more tenaciously to values that are related to the frontier because they may still experience some elements of it directly. Easterners, in large measure separated from those wilder elements, have tended to lose sight of some of these values and to question their continued utility in a developed world. As the East, where the wild is no longer a threat, looks to the West for understanding of the antagonisms which were once a part of their common frontier heritage, so the West must look to the East to visualize the changes in outlook that take place when the land becomes domesticated. The relationships of people with nature and animals are of greater universal concern today than ever before as the sphere of the tame inexorably expands at the expense of the wild. The dilemma associated with the balance that human societies establish between the wild and the tame in ordering their world is increasingly crucial. Rodeo, at its deepest level, addresses these issues, giving assurance that there are still wild elements to tame while at the same time expressing ambivalence concerning the nature-to-culture trans-formation which is symbolized in the various events.

Field research for this book was carried out during the years of 1975 through 1978. My analysis of rodeo deals with the sport as observed in the Great Plains, and is limited in scope to those areas where there is historical continuity between cattle ranching and rodeo. Data from rodeos in other areas of the country are used for purposes of comparison. The major portion of my study relates to standard rodeo, which follows the almost invariable pattern set forth by the rules and guidelines of the P.R.C.A. Observations from variant types such as women's, youth, and old-timers' rodeos, for example, are used to add supplementary and contrasting dimensions. Throughout the text cross-cultural comparisons with other herding societies help to clarify certain characteristics of the American cowboy and rancher, by means of both differences and similarities.

2

THE SPORT OF RODEO

—Rodeo. Sure as Bobcats are ornery, it's no tea party. Ask any cowboy who explodes out of a chute biting off a sunfishin' chunk of fury . . . and then chews it. That, though, is his life . . . skinned raw from the living flank of adventure. He takes it, tames it and loves it.

(Calgary Exhibition and Stampede Brochure, 1978).

FOR THE READER who may not be completely familiar with rodeo, a general description of the sport and an explanation of each event ordinarily included in the program should be helpful. This will provide a framework of information for the forthcoming analysis and theoretical discussion of rodeo. The aim in this overview is not just to present a catalogue of facts, but also to convey some of the feeling and flavor of a rodeo performance.

GENERAL DESCRIPTION OF RODEO

Rodeos are held in arenas in which the basic elements remain about the same whether they are small local shows or large professional performances, whether they take place in the city or the country, whether they are held outdoors or have a modern indoor amphitheater for a setting. Arenas may vary in size but are usually oval in shape. Typically located about half-way across one of the long sides of the oval are the chutes, usually about eight to twelve in number, strong metal-framed pens that confine the rough stock just before their release into the arena for the bucking events, and from which the riders climb down to mount their animals. Broncs and bulls are herded into the chutes through runways leading from fenced-in areas behind the chutes, where vans unload them. These chutes are

12

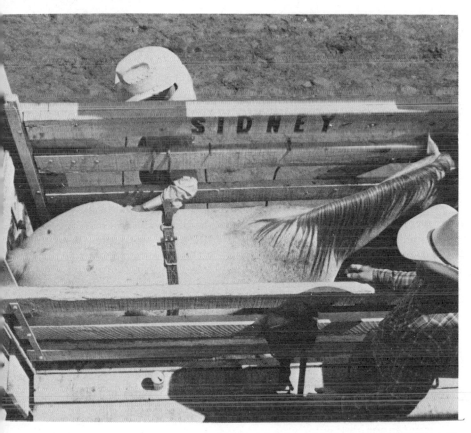

Just before being released into the arena, bulls and broncs are confined in chutes where the contestants mount them.

(Robert Ridley Photo)

engineered in such a way that when a contestant gives the nod that he is mounted and ready, the chute gate may be swung open, catapulting man and beast sidewise into the arena in view of the audience. Opposite the chutes, on the other long side of the oval arena, is the grandstand where the spectators sit for the performance. Only rarely are there seats behind the chutes; if available, tickets for these are sold for a very high price or are distributed only to officials or celebrities. The area immediately behind the chutes is strictly reserved for contestants and officials. Members of the press, photographers, or an anthropologist can gain access only by special permit,—a pass given when credentials have been validated and purposes approved. This exclusiveness is rigidly enforced by rodeo committeemen, or at larger performances by the police. Sometimes a rough plank allows those admitted to stand just behind the chutes, but often one must stand directly on the bars making up the structure of the chutes themselves in order to view the inner workings of the bucking contests. At best, gymnastic ability and a willingness to be bumped and bruised, kicked and ignored are the price of first-hand knowledge of rodeo. A woman is taboo here and if she gains admittance is treated as a nonperson.

At one small end of the oval, usually to the right of the chute area, are located the entrance gates for the participants in the "timed" events. These consist of special chutes from which the steers or calves are released, and a structure called a "box" where each mounted contestant waits his turn to perform. At the opposite end of the arena are penned areas in which animals leaving the arena after each event are caught.

For a typical rodeo performance there are two judges, though more than this number officiate at the national finals, and only one is present at some of the smaller shows. These men who evaluate each participant's ride in the rough stock events are hired from the ranks of contestants or former contestants, often injured ones. There are two mounted pickup men in the arena for the bronc riding events; their function is to help riders get safely off the animals after their rides are completed. The pickup men are usually engaged by the stock contractor, who is hired by the rodeo committee to supply all of the animals used in the rough stock events as well as the cattle for the timed events. The pickup men typically wear chaps on which the stock contractor's name, monogram, or trademark is boldly emblazoned. The stock contractor or rodeo director, usually mounted on a showy Quarter Horse fitted with an ornate tooled leather or silver-decorated saddle bearing his name, often remains in the arena

Contestant jumps on behind mounted pickup man, who has ridden up
beside him to help get him off the bronc.

(JJJ Photo)

to supervise the proceedings. For the timed events, the timers and the flagmen, who signal the moment when a feat has been completed, are the counterparts of the judges.

A very important role in every rodeo is assigned to the announcer, who usually occupies an elevated booth or "crow's nest" above the arena near the chutes, which is sometimes shared with television cameramen or newspaper reporters. It is he who sets the tone for the entire performance, interprets the sport for the spectators, proclaims the scores and times, banters with the clowns, encourages the contestants, puts words into the mouths of the animals, and tries to make the members of the audience feel they are participating with the contestants. His announcement of the name of each rider, followed by the city or town and the state of his origin, as well as the name of each bronc or bull performing in the rough stock events, establishes the pace for the rodeo and keeps the spectator's attention fixed on the show. He gives data on famous or especially accomplished contestants such as those who have previously qualified for the national finals. Also, he repeatedly urges the audience to applaud for the losers—those who are bucked off or receive a "no time,"—pointing out that such encouragement is a way of "paying them off," and is the only recompense they will receive for their efforts in the arena and the many miles they have travelled to get there.

"Going on down the road" is the contestants' phrase for being on the rodeo circuit. Many of them travel for most of the year, living in campers or motels. Top contenders, and others as well, become confirmed nomads, and may enter four or five rodeos a week and even two different rodeos in one day during the height of the season, in an attempt to accrue the greatest possible number of wins. This means they are driving or flying between rodeos for much of their time. A large percentage of contestants come from ranching or livestock-raising backgrounds, though a few are from cities, and it has recently become possible to learn the skills of rodeoing by attending schools run by champions and former champions. With very few exceptions, the contenders on the Western rodeo circuits come from the Western states.

Professional rodeo, and indeed every standard adult rodeo, is almost totally a man's world. A spirit of male camaraderie and mutual helpfulness is prevalent. Contestants travel and live together, and may place their entries for rodeos according to a "buddy system." Some bring their families for part of the year, but this is the exception rather than the rule. No women, save for an occasional photographer, newspaper writer, or television filmer, go into the chute area or in the section where the contestants "warm up." Nor are any children ordinarily seen there. Women generally do not serve as officials other than rodeo secretaries, and I was told in 1978 that a woman had been barred from a professional rodeo judging seminar that year. In the steer wrestling event at a professional rodeo, a woman cannot act as hazer (rider who keeps the steer running straight) for her husband, though she might do so in a small country setting. One woman, a highly skilled pickup rider, told me she is not eligible to obtain a P.R.C.A. card permitting her to officiate in this role. Rather, she must get individual approval for each show in which she is asked to work, and these are usually unsanctioned. Contestants are typically young men in their late teens or twenties, especially those in the bull riding and bareback bronc riding events. Older men are often seen in other events, particularly the ones involving roping skills, and it is common to see participants in the timed events who are in their thirties and forties, with a few rugged individuals competing into their fifties.

Most rodeo contestants present a clean-shaven, conservative image which is at the opposite pole from "hippie." Recently, however, a few have deviated from this norm by adding a certain contemporary flair to their clothing and lifestyles. Many of these followed the lead of the celebrated rodeo star who holds the record in the sport, having been six times champion all-around cowboy of the world. His donning of a flamboyant beaver cowboy hat set at a rakish angle, with his hair showing conspicuously below it, and his wearing of his Levis inside his boots, were a milestone. Gifted with a great deal of charm and charisma in addition to exceptional athletic ability, and doubling as a country-western singer, this versatile hero of the movie "The Great American Cowboy" and producer of his own line of Western clothes has become a legend in his own time.

Despite the outward conformity exhibited by most contestants, one of the salient characteristics of the sport of rodeo is the individualism built into its structure. Participants are not members of a team, have no managers or coaches, pay all their own expenses, keep their own winnings, and guide their own careers. No salary or subsidy supports them when they do not win—which, for most, is a good deal of the time. Even the top winners, who receive large sums of money, often find it difficult to make ends meet because of the expenses of travel and the high entry fees in professional rodeo—up to $100 per event for the larger shows.

It is important to emphasize that male rodeo contestants are without exception referred to as cowboys in the arena. I do not ordinarily use this term here to designate rodeo participants because of the confusion which might be created later when I describe the working cowboys of the trail drives and ranches. But nevertheless, men who compete in rodeo are called cowboys, think of themselves as cowboys, and have indeed inherited the cowboy image with all that its complex mystique implies. Rodeo contestants dress in cowboy hats, Western-tailored yoked shirts, Levis, leather chaps, cowboy boots, and whatever type of spurs is specified for their particular event.

In addition to money, a winning contestant receives a large, showy silver belt buckle. Usually this item depicts the event in which it was won and has the title of the event imprinted on it, as well as the name of the rodeo, its location, and the date; often the name of the contestant is added later. Trophy buckles are always worn by participants, and signify varying degrees of prestige. A buckle won at Cheyenne, distinctively embossed with five circles of laurel leaves, I was told, will usually be worn by its possessor in preference to any other—even a world's champion buckle.

Among the sponsors and promotors of rodeo is the Winston Cigarette Company, which is responsible for the scoreboards used at professional rodeos, provides the official numbers worn by contestants in the arena, and donates large amounts of prize money, in addition to giving gala parties for rodeo personnel. In return, most smokers in the sport use Winstons. This company's counterpart in the Little Britches Rodeo circuit is the Kool-Aid Company, whose slogan "Enjoy Kool-Aid" appeared along with the contestant's number on the back of each youngster who qualified for the organization's finals in North Platte, Nebraska in 1978. In addition to Winston, the Skoal and Copenhagen Tobacco Companies provide financial support for professional rodeo, and almost every contestant chews their bitter leaves and spits tobacco juice. The pockets of their shirts often display a permanent circle, like a trademark, where the cans have made an impression. The Levi-Strauss Company contributes money and trophy buckles, and the Lee Company follows suit in providing support for the men who prove daily that their jeans are tough. The Black Velvet Whiskey Company sponsors "Miss Black Velvet," a voluptuous cowgirl dressed all in black, who rides a black horse in the grand entry and parade of some of the larger rodeos and attends the accompanying festivities. This company also donates money toward any rodeo horse who is given a name including the word "velvet," as, for example, "Smooth Velvet," or "Deep Velvet."

Rodeo is indisputably rough, violent, and dangerous to man and

Above: Silver buckles are awarded to winners of rodeo events. The Cheyenne Frontier Days buckle is especially prized.   *(JJJ Photo)*

Below: The saddle bronc event, "cornerstone of rodeo," is felt to be directly related to ranch work. Note feather in rider's hat.   *(Photo by Randy Huffman)*

beast. An ambulance is always in attendance and often in use throughout a performance. Bandages are the rule and casts are commonplace. Contestants often continue to ride after sustaining severe injuries, or return to the arena before old wounds and fractures are healed. Deaths resulting from rodeo injuries are not rare, nor are permanent disabilities. The show goes on in any weather, and the fabled Great Plains extremes, often extolled in regional folklore, become a reality for both participant and spectator. July of 1978 in Casper, Wyoming, for example, found me unable to take notes in the 30° weather, whereas within the next few days the thermometer soared to 100°. In Nebraska in August 1978, neither a blinding dust storm nor warnings of an imminent tornado could cause the cancellation of the Ogalalla Roundup. And that same evening a full-capacity audience remained enthusiastic throughout hours of a torrential downpour. The announcer keynoted the show by saying that the two things Nebraska never gets enough of are hay and rain. Arena officials donned ponchos and plastic covers for their white Stetson hats, but contestants wore only their usual clothing, and battled in the mud with the same nonchalance with which they so often faced the blowing dust and searing heat.

Rodeo holds fast to the image of its origins in the historic Texas trail driving days and in the open range cattle era which superseded them, and preserves a strong tie with the American frontier ethos. It is tightly interwoven with today's ranching life in the Western states. Frequently billed as "A Legend Walkin' Tall," as it was in the 1978 Calgary Stampede brochure, rodeo advertises itself as "American Legend in Action," and explicitly attempts to recreate, exaggerate, and dramatize the violence, color, and agonistic action that have served to romanticize the Old West and its conquest. Rodeos take their names from cattle driving and ranching terms—hence, the Calgary "Stampede" and the Pendleton "Roundup." During the annual "Frontier Days" celebration in Cheyenne, Wyoming, this city with an historic past rooted in the cattle industry demonstrates its pride in that heritage by recreating for nine days each July the excitement of its early times as a cowtown. "The Daddy of 'em All" is a festival of gigantic proportions, centered on rodeo, and planned over an eleven-month period every year. The Cheyenne Chamber of Commerce film on Frontier Days boasts that "Wyoming is today what America was yesterday," and extends an invitation to all to attend the rodeo that helps keep it that way. The area, just another quiet Western city at other times, goes wild and literally explodes with visitors during the celebration. Motels, reserved a year in advance, are filled to overflowing. Restaurants, and particularly bars, are jammed, and the cowboy hangout, the Mayflower, revels in its yearly spree of rowdiness and riot, with its floors slippery from thrown drinks, its walls resounding with shouts from recurring fistfights, and its concrete entrance ramp likely to be invaded by a drunken cowboy riding his horse into the interior of the bar to relive a legend of the Old West.

Although the structure and order of the rodeo program remain remarkably constant no matter what type of show it is and where it is held, the total effect generated by a given rodeo can be felt by a sensitive observer to vary according to context. I say sensitive observer because I attended a rodeo in New Jersey with the express purpose of contrasting it with those in the West. While I was carefully noting all the differences that I felt existed, I met one of the officials from the Denver office of the Professional Rodeo Cowboys Association, who had just flown in to witness this Eastern show. I asked him what differences he found here, and his response was that the only variation he saw was the foreign-sounding names listed in the program! (Most of the contestants here were from the East and reflected its ethnic diversity.)

Nevertheless, differences do exist, though it may be difficult to precisely define them. A rodeo like the one in Big Timber, Montana, a long way from the nearest city and deep in the heart of ranching country, reflects an atmosphere that harks back to the early days of rodeo when it was purely a cowboy's holiday, and had not yet taken on its performance aspect. Vast stretches of space with vistas of distant mountains serve to make it remote from the modern world. One feels here that same timelessness that contributed to the impact of the West itself upon the pioneer emigrants, shaping their percep- tions as well as their lives and destinies. Contrasted to this, the International Rodeo Association Finals performance in the Tulsa Coliseum was affected by its urban surroundings, and seemed to belong less to the heritage of cowboy contests and more to the realm of Saturday night entertainment. The crowd was interested, but in some indefinable way, detached, and, enclosed within the building's walls, it had lost touch with the very essence of the West—the landscape and the sky. The Calgary Stampede, on the other hand, reflects the dual nature which arises out of a contradiction. It is set in a large modern city, yet a city that is not far removed from a past rooted in the Canadian Great Plains cattle frontier. The result is a strange combination of sophistication, as shown in entertainment acts that arise out of Alberta's diverse cultures and technological progress, with the most elemental of frontier themes as evidenced by "wild cow milking" and "wild horse racing."

Returning again to the Cowtown, New Jersey rodeo, it was a vital proving ground for the ideas I had been formulating regarding the relevance of context. For here was a professional rodeo that included all the standard events of the sport and was run and managed in exactly the same way as its Western counterparts. Yet it seemed far different, and I can only describe it as "muted" in comparison. The edges of the sport seemed dulled. The rodeo owner and manager of Cowtown is the eighth generation in his family to carry on the cattle business in that location, his forebears' brand having been registered in 1706, and so Cowtown is advertised as "Cow Capital of the *First* Frontier." The manager explained that the frontier had originally moved West from here, and now he was trying to bring it back to the East again by means of his rodeos, which are held weekly from June to September. "It's a novelty for the people here," he pointed out, and his words revealed insight, for a novelty is a far-cry from a way of life! Frontier memories had long ago faded from this region—pride in the Cowtown cattle brand notwithstanding—and they now seem too dim to give life and spirit to rodeo. The marsh birds circling above the rodeo arena belie the presence of the nearby New Jersey salt flats. Traffic on the Jersey Turnpike roars by only a few miles away, and as the rodeo owner puts it, he would have preferred Indians and coyotes as enemies rather than traffic and mosquitoes. The air is humid in Cowtown, and the animal odors, usually mild and pleasant in the open plains, become acrid when not diluted by prairie winds.

Reflecting on the Cowtown experience, I realized that here was a "textbook case" in which rodeo had been completely removed from its cultural context. And in being cut off from its appropriate social and physical surroundings it had lost much of its significance as a ritual. It could provide entertainment and competition, but it could not communicate meaning where there was nothing to receive and respond to its messages. Now I could relate this to a conversation with an informant during the Casper, Wyoming, rodeo the previous month. This man, the world's champion saddle bronc rider, in his race to acquire points to retain his title, told me he had travelled all the way to New Hampshire to enter a sanctioned rodeo. I asked him if the rodeo was the same there. "Yes," he said, "a rodeo is a rodeo, and they're all the same to me." But then he thought for a moment. "The only difference," he went on, "is that people there are not familiar with rodeo like they are here. They don't understand it."

Audiences, of course, are a very important part of rodeo. They demonstrate enthusiasm in cheering for the contestants, and their participation is essential to the performance. Though tourists are often among them, most of the spectators at the typical Western rodeos are area residents, who look forward with pleasure to attending a certain number of rodeos during the year. A few devoted fans may follow the circuit. A large percentage of audiences are composed of families, many with babies and children. Some people bring picnics, but most make frequent trips to concession stands for food and drink. A typical rodeo spectator holds a Pepsi in one hand and a hot dog in the other. Cotton candy, popcorn, and ice cream bars are available, and adults may partake of beer, usually a brand that supports rodeo. Sometimes snuff, called "snuice" by stockmen, is sold at the food booths. Rodeo does not command full attention from its audiences for all of its three- to four-hour duration; often people walk around, eat, and visit, especially during the events that are not their favorites. For example, a man may go out to get coffee during the girls' barrel racing event, saying "There isn't enough action in this for me."

Spectators readily communicate their feelings about performances, particularly at those rodeos which take place in the country or where the setting seems informal. They encourage the roughstock riders with shouts of "stay with 'im, ride 'im!" They verbalize their disappointment when a rider is bucked off. They scream vindictively at a contestant's horse that does not perform properly in the calf roping. Some "boo" the judges for a score they feel is too low and cheer when a re-ride is granted to a contestant whose animal failed to buck. They shout insults at a pickup man who does not rescue a rider fast enough or a stock contractor they feel is too bossy.

Audiences vary as to which type of events they prefer, the roping contests or the bucking events, and rodeo people say that this is determined by regions—Northwesterners favoring the former and Southwesterners the latter. One thing is agreed upon, however, that the bull riding event is the greatest crowd-pleaser. Some say it is bloodlust which makes this event the avowed favorite. It has been suggested by psychologists that people want to experience vicariously the danger of the participants who are risking death, without having to be personally affected by it. This is said to make them feel secure and give them a feeling of elation. Whatever the reasons (some will be suggested in this study), people are fascinated, and keen anticipation builds up throughout the entire rodeo performance, for bull riding is ordinarily the last on the program.

But whether the man-animal contest within the sport of rodeo involved a bull, bronc, or other form of livestock, there never was an audience in my experience who cheered for the animals or whose sympathy outwardly appeared to be with the beast as opposed to man. With one exception I never found an individual at a Western rodeo whose attitude varied from this norm. The particular person I mention as an exception was a college girl from Massachusetts who had travelled West for the summer to work on a Wyoming cattle ranch, and had come to Sheridan with the ranch workers for a Saturday night's outing. The episode is worthy of mention because at that crucial stage in my field work her observations of ranch/rodeo people's views of animals, and the sudden interposition of her articulation of dissident "Eastern" perceptions in that Western setting, helped me to crystallize the contrasts involved. For as we sat together among the huge crowd in that packed grandstand, our shared impotence intensified by being enveloped in an alien culture, I became aware of the power that the surrounding and supporting society exerts as a profoundly influential force in the ritual itself.

The members of this supporting culture, as native Westerners, were attuned not only to their region's physical dimensions, but to its complex and dynamic mystique which includes all that rodeo epitomizes. For them the performance represented the expected, and their response was the natural outgrowth of their ethos. It is the uninitiated, however, who are able to see with full clarity the particular characteristics that make an event unique. Often it is by means of the impact made possible by sharp contrast that the essence of a situation, taken for granted by a native, is made to stand out in bold relief. The Eastern historian, Francis Parkman, for example, saw and recorded his impressions of the untamed Western frontier with a freshness and sensitivity of perception that only a newcomer could bring to it. As A.B. Guthrie, in his foreword to Parkman's classic *The Oregon Trail* (1950:xi), recognized, "no man accustomed to the ways of the wild" could have communicated it so vividly. It was Easterners like Owen Wister (1902) with his literary creation of the archetypal horseman of the Plains, Frederick Remington with his painstaking artistic depictions of range life, and Theodore Roosevelt with his characterization of ranching as an invigorating and adventuresome life, who had gone West and, by means of heightened awareness to their new surroundings combined with special talent, were able to fix for all time the image of the American cowboy.

THE PROGRAM OF EVENTS IN RODEO

"How the West was fun—and still is."
(Slogan from the 1978 Calgary Stampede)

Since a knowledge of the events which constitute the sport of rodeo is necessary to an understanding of discussions which follow, a synopsis of each of these events is in order. Every rodeo begins with a display of the American flag by a rider in cowboy dress, described by the announcer as "presentation of the flag Western-style," followed by the playing and/or singing of the Star-Spangled Banner. The audience is reminded to stand as the flag passes by and is requested to remain standing for the national anthem. Then there is usually a recitation of "The Cowboy's Prayer" which, using rodeo metaphor throughout, asks God to "guide us in the arena of life," and to give "help in living our lives in such a manner that when we make that inevitable ride to the country up there . . . that you, as our last judge, will tell us that our entry fees are paid" (Hall 1973:199-200). Next comes the grand entry parade, during which the stock contractor, pickup men, rodeo queen and members of her court, and other officials ride around the arena and are introduced individually as they gallop to the center and bow, wave, or doff their hats.

The competitive events which make up the rodeo program are divided into two basic categories: the rough stock and the timed events. There is a prescribed order for these which is approximately the same in most rodeos. The rough stock events are those which pit a man against an untamed animal that he attempts to ride according to certain rules and for a specified length of time, ordinarily eight seconds. In this sense, rough stock events too are "timed," but the time interval is fixed for all contestants, and is signaled by a horn or buzzer (at Cheyenne by a gunshot). Standard rough stock events are saddle bronc riding, bareback bronc riding, and bull riding.

THE ROUGH STOCK EVENTS

Saddle Bronc Riding   Saddle bronc riding is considered the cornerstone of rodeo, and is invariably referred to by each announcer as "the classic event" of the program. It is perceived of as directly related to the era of cattle drives and open range ranching, when one outfit would match its top rider against that of another, using a couple of unbroken horses. Common belief holds that a ranch background with experience in breaking and training rough horses is a prerequisite for a successful competitor, and that this event requires more practice and experience than either the bareback bronc or bull riding event. In these latter two events, in contrast, it is believed that men with the proper build and athletic ability can come from any background and learn to master them. In the saddle bronc event a regulation saddle is used, which resembles a trimmed-down Western saddle but lacks the horn. The horse also wears a halter, to which is attached a single braided rope rein that is held in the hand of the rider on the same side of the halter to which it is attached. To make a qualifying ride, the contestant must have his spurs over or in front of the break of the shoulders and touching the horse when the animal's front feet hit the ground on the first jump out of the chute. This is called "marking him out." Throughout the ride the judges score on how well the rider uses his feet in spurring from the horse's shoulders to the saddle's cantle in a rhythmic stroke. Riding with only the rope rein in his hand requires exceptional balance, and the opposite hand must remain free at all times. Riders attempt to get in tune with the bucking motion of the horse and coordinate their spurring action with it. A contestant is disqualified for being bucked off before the eight seconds, for changing hands on the rein, losing a stirrup, touching the animal, equipment, himself, or the rein with the free hand, or for wearing spurs with locked rowels (revolving disks with sharp points). A bucking strap made of leather covered with sheepskin is tightened around the horse's flank just before the animal is released from the chute. This is said to be an added inducement for the horse to buck, and rodeo personnel are adamant in their assertions that it is not painful to a bronc, but merely annoying, and that it does not in itself cause the animal to buck, but rather enhances his tendency to do so. The flank strap is abruptly released as soon as possible after the ride has been completed by one of the pickup men galloping up beside the bronc. The animal generally stops bucking at the very moment this strap is undone.

The pickup men help the rider to get free of his bronc as soon as the eight-second horn has sounded, usually by riding up beside him and allowing him to jump on the back of their horse and from there to the ground. Some contestants prefer to jump off their broncs themselves, and learn to do it with flair. Each of the two judges marks the contestant on how well he rides—whether he is in rhythm with the horse, and how well he spurs and maintains control—scoring him from one to twenty-five points. At the same time the horse is scored from one to twenty-five according to how hard he bucks and how difficult the judge feels he was to ride. Then the two judges' markings are added to make up the contestant's score. Thus, in this event, as in the other two rough stock events, the combined score represents the performance of both man and animal. No matter how skilled the contestant, he cannot earn a high score without a good performance on the part of the animal. Since a rider must accept whatever animal is drawn for him by officials, "the luck of the draw" plays a big part in determining success. A score in the seventies or eighties is considered good.

The depiction of a saddle bronc rider represents the sport of rodeo, and is used in the logo of the Professional Rodeo Cowboys Association. It stands for Wyoming on the state flag and appears on automobile license plates in that state and on "Welcome to Wyoming" signs at its borders. The figure of this rider on an untamed horse has come to be used all over the nation, and internationally as well, as a symbol for the American West and its conquest.

Bareback Bronc Riding   Bareback bronc riding is the most recently added event on the program, having become a standard part of the show about thirty years ago. It was developed by the sport of rodeo specifically for competition in the arena, and is regarded as having no direct connection with ranch work. Contestants ride with a "riggin'," a leather circingle fitted around the horse's body just behind the withers with an attached handhold like that of a suitcase. No stirrups, halter, or reins are used. One gloved hand of the rider grips the handhold during the ride, while the other hand must remain free. Bareback riding is noted for being the wildest of the bronc events and the most physically demanding for the contestant, often being described as "bone-jarring." To perform in it the rider must have a powerful grip and a body that can absorb the shock of being whipped back and forth over the back of the horse, sometimes to the extent that the back of his head appears to touch the animal's rump. Good balance is a special prerequisite, for bareback horses are generally smaller and "shiftier" than those of the saddle bronc competition, and without the restrictions of saddle, halter, and rein, they are freer to jump, kick, and even spin. The rider tries to lean back and maintain a spurring rhythm along the animal's neck and shoulders in a narrower arc than that of the saddle bronc rider, raking his legs in an up and down motion rather than front to back. As in the previously described event, the contestant must have his spurs over or in front of the break of the shoulders and touching the animal, when the horse's feet hit the ground on the initial jump out of the chute. Wild spurring is the hallmark of this event, with the rider who spurs the highest and hardest receiving the greatest number of points. Riding with rowels too sharp or locked, however, disqualifies a contestant. Higher scores are also given on the basis of a difficult horse and a rider who is judged to be in control. During the eight-second ride which a contestant must make to qualify, he cannot touch the horse or himself with his free hand. The rider is disqualified if his hand becomes "hung up" in his rigging. Because of the tight fit of his gloved hand in the handhold, this inability to remove the hand is a real danger. If it happens the rider must try to keep pace with the bronc, often by running beside it, until a pickup man can ride over and help to free him. This mishap occurs fairly often and results in frequent injuries. The flank strap on the bareback bronc is the same as described for the saddle bronc event and the procedure for its use is identical.

Bull Riding   Bull riding is considered to be at once the most popular event for the spectators and the most dangerous for the contestant. Unlike the situation in the bronc events, and arising out of differences between the equine and bovine nature, the greatest potential hazard to the participant stems from the bull's actions after the rider is on the ground. Bull riders are often regarded as "a breed apart" in the rodeo world. Since there are more crippling injuries and deaths resulting from bull riding than from bronc riding, bull riders need not only great courage and endurance, strength and fitness, but another quality as well: even those rated at the top in this event feel they must bring to it a positive mental attitude in order to win consistently. Many of them study psychocybernetics or practice what they call Zen bull riding. Contestants "psych themselves up" before their ride with various exercises and often practice deep concentration. An elaborate pre-ride ritual usually takes place in which their bull ropes are repeatedly readjusted, and rosin is applied to make the grip more secure. A rider may slap his own face and body, or his comrades may give encouragement like "Try, Willie, don't quit. The bull might correct your mistake if you do. Don't let him beat you out there." These same procedures are also part of bronc riding, but they are more pronounced in bull riding. Luck, always an important factor in rodeo, is believed to play an even greater role in the bull riding event. Luck is felt to determine success or failure not just in the process of drawing the rank bull which is necessary in order to make a high-scoring ride, but also in not getting one's legs "mashed" in the

Above: No saddle, halter, or reins are used in bareback riding, the wildest bronc event. Note Winston scoreboard. *(JJJ Photo)*

Below: Bull riding is considered the most popular event for spectators and the most dangerous for contestants, who are a "breed apart."
(Photo by Randy Huffman)

chute prior to the ride, or being slammed into the arena fence by the maddened beast, in not being drawn into the "well" created around the center of his body by a spinning bull, and, especially, luck in not being stomped on or gored after "bucking off" the bull. Good and bad breaks seem magnified in bull riding, and more directly determine the difference between life and death.

For bull riding a contestant uses a rope encircling the animal's body behind the hump region, inserting his gloved hand in a loop of this rope. There must be a bell, or bells, attached to the rope in such a way as to hang below the bull during the ride. The flanking device on a bull is also made of rope, and is tightened just before the ride as with the broncs. In many cases the bull is jabbed with an electric cattle prod, termed a "hot shot," just before being released from the chute, or repeatedly during a varying interval prior to that time.

Since it is held to be common knowledge that a bull will attack a horse, the structuring of this event usually differs from that of the bronc events. Mounted pickup men are not ordinarily used, and their role is carried out by clowns. Sometimes a rodeo clown has a dual role as bull fighter and entertainer, but often, especially at larger shows, the roles are separate. At Cheyenne, for example, the man who is acclaimed as the most highly skilled bull fighter in the sport dresses in tattered rags and dons a frazzled wig but is dead-serious about his work of helping the bull riders. He does not attempt to be humorous at all. "I'm about as funny as a funeral in the rain," is his way of stating it, as he dashes off to do the handstands and jumping exercises that keep him in shape for his demanding job. Rodeo clowns in general wear many variations of classic harlequin apparel, usually choosing a preponderance of red, but track shoes are a must for fast and nimble escapes from an angered bull. A bull fighting clown is a top athlete, and must be fearless as well as agile to successfully perform the function of protecting the contestant from injury once he is off the bull. The clown rushes to the bull and tries to distract the animal's attention so that the rider will not be gored or stepped on. With wild antics he attempts to attract the bull's attention to himself, and he then carries on sparring actions with the animal that are somewhat reminiscent of a matador's. Frequently a clown will jump into a barrel that has been placed in the arena, and the bull will butt the barrel with his horns and roll it. Quite often a bull without a rider is sent into the arena for a clown to fight, and the animal is goaded to knock over a dummy (to which the announcer gives the name of an unpopular person), or to butt a large rubber tire. Contestants sometimes have to be helped by a clown to extricate their hand if it gets hung up in the rope, as frequently happens. At the beginning of a ride, a clown may make waving motions in front of the bull to try to make it buck harder and thus increase the likelihood of a higher marking from the judges.

A bull rider must hold his rope with only one hand, and is disqualified not only for being bucked off before the eight-second interval, but also for touching the animal with his free hand or for using sharp spurs. Balance is important, and he tries to move his body with each jump and keep in time with the creature's thrusts. The event is scored like the bronc events, with the important exception that the rider does not lose points for failing to use his spurs. It is considered much more difficult to spur on a bull ride, as many of these animals will jump, kick, and spin themselves around, and just staying on their backs is a feat. The contestant wears longer-shanked spurs with larger rowels than those in the bronc events, and he will receive extra points for using them. The judge's evaluation of how well a contestant stays in control of the ride contributes to a winning score, as does the bull's rank behavior; a spinning bull is marked higher.

THE TIMED EVENTS

The standard timed events are calf roping and steer wrestling; two more—steer roping and team roping—are often added to the program. Timed events differ from rough stock events in many ways which are obvious even to a superficial observer. They all require well trained saddle horses which help the riders to perform certain difficult tasks involving cattle, and thus are highly suggestive of ranch life. The horses used in these events, unlike the broncs and bulls which are furnished by a stock contractor, are ordinarily owned by the contestants, having been arduously trained by them over long periods of time in order to perfect their performance. The cattle for the timed events are furnished by the stock contractor or rodeo producer. Times for the same event in different rodeos cannot always be meaningfully compared because of variation in the size of arenas.

Calf Roping   Calf roping is an explicitly ranch-born event which depends largely on the harmony between a contestant and his mount, whose performance as a roping horse is felt to make up at least 75 percent of the success formula. The event directly reflects the days when branding of calves was done on the open range, and a quick horse with good "cow sense" and a cowboy with skill in roping

Calf roping, a ranch-born event, depends upon harmony between man and mount. "Piggin' string" is carried in roper's mouth.

(JJJ Photo)

formed a working partnership. The goal in this event is to rope from horseback a running calf which has been given a headstart from the chute, secure the rope to the saddle horn, then dismount and run down to the calf, throw him to his side, and tie three of his legs with a short piece of rope called a "piggin' string" which the contestant has carried in his mouth. It is a race against time, and sometimes skillful contestants can do it in less than ten seconds. The contest begins behind a rope barrier where the rider and his mount wait in the "box" for the calf to be released. The barrier is automatically released when the calf reaches a certain distance into the arena. If the contestant should ride through the barrier, a ten-second penalty is added to his time.

Once the calf is roped, the horse should stop quickly, and while the rider proceeds to get the calf on its side and tie it securely, the horse tries to keep the rope taut by moving backwards away from it. This helps the roper make the tie; in order for him to do it well, the horse has to keep just the right amount of pressure on the rope. If there is too little pressure the calf can get up and get away; if there is too much the rope will start to choke the calf, causing it to fight and struggle, thus adding seconds to the contestant's time. The key to a good roping horse is thought to be consistency, allowing the rider to know what to expect, but the mount must also possess speed and the all-important ability to "rate cattle"—that is, pull up behind them and keep the distance between himself and the calf constant so that the rider can throw his loop.

The factor of luck again plays a part in the calf roping event, mainly through the contestant's drawing of a certain calf. Though these animals are sorted for conformity in type and weight (usually between 200 and 350 pounds), still in every group there may be a few rank ones. Such calves have more spirit and will consequently kick and fight and even run toward the roper before the tie can be made. A contestant cannot win with a calf of that nature, so the luck of the draw influences his performance. Needless to say, a man's own skill in roping and tying with no wasted moves is essential to winning. A roper is disqualified if he misses the calf, although he may throw twice if he carries two ropes. There is also the qualification that the roper's tie must hold for six seconds after he has remounted, called for time, and slackened his rope. The contestant with the shortest time wins the event.

Steer Wrestling Steer wrestling is the second of the two timed events which are standard in rodeo, and it differs from the first in being a

contest invented strictly for rodeo, having little ranching application. The event is also referred to as "bulldogging," and the
contestants as "doggers," terms which stem from the origin of the
event. The contest was invented by the celebrated black cowboy, Bill
Pickett, who, as a youth on a Texas ranch in 1881, watched bulldogs
being used to catch and hold cattle by the upper lip until a cowhand
could rope them (Hanes 1977:25). Impressed by the fact that such a
dog could keep a captive animal submissive by this tooth-hold on its
sensitive membranes, Pickett determined to try the procedure himself. He succeeded in perfecting it and gained fame for his remarkable
ability to throw a steer by sinking his teeth into its upper lip.
Eventually he "turned pro," exhibiting his spectacular and highly
acclaimed feat as part of the famed 101 Ranch Wild West Show
throughout the early decades of the twentieth century.

The procedure has changed now, and a dogger no longer bites his
quarry, but the contest is similar in its essence—that is, in pitting
one man, without a device or appliance, against one steer. The
contestants are usually big, powerful men who must stay in superb
physical shape in order to wrestle steers that may weigh up to 700
pounds. A bulldogger enters the arena mounted, must leap from his
horse at top speed, grab one horn and the jaw of the running steer,
stop him, and then throw the animal flat on its side or its back with
all four feet and head straight. Time is called at the moment when
this is accomplished, and a score of ten seconds or better is ordinarily
needed to win. The steer wrestler's horse plays a significant part in his
success, and is carefully trained to run up next to the steer, enabling
the rider to make the jump. The horse must pass the steer and veer off
to the left, permitting the contestant's feet to drop in front of the
steer. At the start of his event the dogger has the assistance of the
hazer, who rides into the arena on the other side of the steer, trying to
keep him running straight, thus enabling the steer wrestler to jump.
The hazer, who usually gets a percentage of the winnings, must be
skilled, for if he leaves the box too soon he can cause the steer to veer
off to the left in front of the steer wrestler's horse, causing the steer to
get out of position for the wrestler; if he leaves too late, the steer may
move away from the contestant. In this event the man who quickly
and consistently gets a steer off balance while staying in control of
himself is the one who places in the money. Fractions of a second
often determine the winner. Rules state that the steer must be caught
from the horse, and if the animal gets loose, no more than one step
may be taken to catch him.

Above: In steer wrestling, or "bull dogging," the contestant must leap from his horse and wrestle the steer to the ground. *(Photo by Randy Huffman)*

Below: In team roping the header and the heeler work together to rope a steer. Close cooperation and timing are essential. *(JJJ Photo)*

Team Roping   Team roping is an event for two contestants who work together as they might do on a ranch, to rope a steer. Coordination is its hallmark, and the two mounted participants must have well-trained horses and be accustomed to working together. The "header" throws the first loop, catching the steer by the head and turning him back so the "heeler" can then lasso him by the hind legs with his rope. For this event, ropes are initially loose from the saddle horns, and after making the catch each roper must take a wrap around the horn, a procedure known as "dallying." Time is taken when both ropes are tight and the two horses are facing the steer. In a head catch, rules require the rope to be around the horns, neck, or one horn and the neck. There is a five-second penalty for a head catch that includes a front foot and for a heel catch with only one hind foot in the rope.

Steer Roping   Steer roping is also called by the descriptive terms "steer jerking" and "steer tripping." This event is considered to require the most "scientific" skill of any roping contest. It calls for a perfect partnership between a contestant and his horse, as the roper aims to tie down a big steer singlehandedly against time. Some states do not allow this event to be held at all because of the rough treatment of steers that it entails, and a rodeo arena must be extra large to permit its maneuvers. Witnessing steer jerking may have a shocking effect upon an uninitiated or sensitive spectator, evoking a gasp (or, interestingly, a laugh), and even some Western stockmen who are inured to the work of the range indicated they are critical of the event because many steers are injured and killed during its performance. Rodeos in the ranching areas of states like Wyoming and Nebraska, however, are apt to include steer roping, and prestigious shows like Cheyenne Frontier Days feature it with all its roughness. It is an extremely difficult and challenging activity, which requires long hours of practice. One of the most prominent contestants in steer roping, a Wyoming veterinarian, retired from a successful practice in his early forties partly because he wanted to spend more time training for this demanding sport.

Steer roping is considered a ranch-oriented contest, entailing skills used when a lone cowboy riding the range came across a steer that needed doctoring, so that it was necessary to rope and restrain him. The procedure, which is hard to describe because of its intricacy, is as follows: the rider first ropes the steer around the horns (the only legal catch), pitches the "slack" in his rope over the steer's right hip, and then turns his horse off to the left, hitting the steer with the rope and making him fall to the ground on his side. The steer is usually at this point dragged across the arena by the horns for a varying interval, often with the result that its horns are broken off or other injuries are sustained. A well-trained roping horse keeps applying pressure to the rope as the rider dismounts and runs back to tie the steer. Again, the expert schooling of the horse is a key to winning, for if the mount slacks off on the rope, the steer will jump up before the contestant can get there to tie the animal's feet. The horse must also be big and powerful to carry out this procedure and still keep his footing. The steer roper throws up his hands when his tie has been made, signalling for time.

BARREL RACING

There is one event included in most, but not all, rodeos, which stands in a class by itself because it is the only event in a standard rodeo in which girls and women are allowed to enter. This is the barrel race, which, as its name implies, is a race against time. Horsewomen compete for the honor of racing in a clover-leaf pattern around a pre-set course marked by barrels and then making a mad dash out of the arena in the shortest possible interval. The object is to cut close enough to the barrels to decrease one's time without incurring the ten-second penalty that is given for knocking over a barrel. Rigid rules about costume govern the dress for this event in professional rodeo. No jeans are allowed, but rather the participants usually wear brightly colored and smartly tailored suits, with matching cowgirl hats that often blow off from the breakneck speed of the ride and the sharp turns that are required. The galloping mount is jerked to a sudden halt at the end of the run.

At the most prestigious shows like Cheyenne and Calgary this event is not a part of the standard program in a strict sense. Rather, the Calgary committee structures the barrel race into its night show, making it seem more like entertainment than rodeo contest. At Cheyenne only one performance, the championship go-round, is held within the regular afternoon rodeo performance, on the concluding day of the show. There, unlike the men's events, all the preliminary barrel race competition is held outside of the actual rodeo. Girls or women in barrel racing are usually called "gals" by announcers. Riders told me they are subject to a rule not applicable to men contestants that requires them to ride in the grand entry if the stock contractor requests it. A participant in barrel racing brings her own highly trained horse to each rodeo for this competitive event, and horse and rider work as a team to win the race for the shortest time.

Above: A horse gallops at break-neck speed in the barrel race, the only event for women in standard rodeo. Crop is carried in rider's mouth.
(*Robert Ridley Photo*)

Below: Teams of three men compete in the wild horse race to subdue, saddle, and ride an untamed horse in the shortest time.　(*JJJ Photo*)

There is no ranch connection exhibited here, unless one considers general horsemanship as a ranch skill.

OTHER EVENTS THAT MAY BE INCLUDED IN RODEO PROGRAMS

Other events frequently included in rodeos throughout the West include the wild horse race, a raw spectacle often billed as "a rodeo unto itself." Differing from the bucking stock used in the standard riding events, horses that participate in this contest are claimed to be truly wild, never having been handled, ridden, or even saddled. They are indeed termed "outlaws" and live up to this name by putting up a fierce and violent struggle against the men who attempt to subdue them in the arena. Rules call for a pair of "muggers," who must hold the horse long enough to saddle him and allow a third man who is the principal contestant to mount him and ride around the track in a specified direction. That trio wins whose rider first completes this course. The event involves much wild plunging and rearing and sounds of the whinnying of terrified horses as the men try to hold them, and most contestants resort to the practice of "earing the horse down" to subdue them. This involves first grabbing the bronc's ear with the hand and then reaching up and biting it with the teeth until the pain causes the animal to stand and allow a man to saddle him. Some rodeos prohibit ear-biting, but most allow it and anticipate it as a regular feature. Crowds attending the rodeo are encouraged to shout and help make the horses wilder; at Cheyenne there is an old tradition of firing guns in proximity to the animals to make them fight more furiously.

The chuckwagon race is a feature of some of the larger rodeos, notably Cheyenne and Calgary, where it is held in a large racetrack surrounding the arena. In this event, called the "rangeland derby," teams of four thoroughbred type race horses pull stripped-down chuckwagons. These are flanked by two or three mounted men known as outriders, who must complete the course with their chuckwagon in order for their driver to win. At the sound of the starting gun, one outrider throws a fifty-pound cook stove and some tent-poles and canvas into the back of his outfit's wagon, and the horses begin their mad dash. Each team must complete a dangerous figure-eight course in the arena, demarcated by barrels, and then take off around the track, racing for the finish line. It is an action-packed event, thrilling to audiences and dangerous to man and beast. It has a tenuous connection with cattle trail driving days, when the chuckwagon was a vital part of each outfit and cooks may have vied for the honor of arriving at camp first.

Wild cow milking is a humorous contest in which participants try to get milk from the udders of beef cows. The one who turns in a specified amount of milk first is the winner. There is always a clown involved who attempts to get milk from the sexual organs of a similarly marked beef bull which has been unobtrusively turned into the arena with the cows, and the clown is rebuked for his ignorance. A little more serious, but still along the same lines, is the occasional mare and colt race, or "dinner bell derby," an event for horses only, which takes place in a stretch of the track. Prior to this contest nursing colts have been kept from their dams for an interval long enough to have made them hungry, and a race is set up for them to run to their mothers on the other end of the track.

Other extra events may be wild cow riding or Shetland pony bucking contests for children, bucking contests involving exotic animals such as yaks and buffaloes, boys' or old-timers' steer or bronc riding, Quarter Horse races, Roman riding races, various types of relay races, and rookie or novice saddle bronc riding. Some country rodeos feature breakaway roping for old men or girls, in which the rope comes apart as soon as it has encircled the calf's neck and the contestant does not have to tie the calf.

Children's rodeos in the youth circuits and the Little Britches contests provide "junior dally ribbon roping," a race against time for pairs of children, one of whom rides into the arena and ropes a calf, after which his helper must run on foot to the calf to retrieve a ribbon from the animal's tail. There are mounted flag races for boys, and trail-riding events including obstacle courses for girls. Pole-bending, in which the rider tries to guide her mount around a series of poles in the shortest possible time, is also open to girls. The usual animal-oriented events in which girls may participate at nonprofessional rodeos involve goats. In goat tying, a girl springs off a galloping horse and ties up a goat which has been tethered in the arena. In goat tail tying, a female contestant must tie a ribbon on a goat's tail. Both events are competitions for the fastest time. At rodeos approved by the Girls Rodeo Association (recently renamed the Women's Professional Rodeo Association), which are held relatively infrequently and at vast distances from each other throughout the West, girls have a "steer undecorating" event, in which a ribbon taped to a steer's back must be retrieved by the mounted contestant, with the aid of a hazer, in the shortest possible time. It is exclusively at such all-female shows that women may enter the rough stock events, and these include only

Men past their prime can still compete in rodeo. Here a sixty-three-year-old contestant rides in an old timers' bareback bronc event. (*JJJ Photo*)

the bareback bronc riding and bull riding, never saddle bronc riding. The girls ride for six rather than eight seconds and, unlike male contestants, have the option of using one or both hands on the handhold or bull rope. Their choice of one or two hands must be consistent, however, for the duration of their ride.

VARIETY ACTS

Often interspersed throughout all types of rodeo programs are various clown acts. A large percentage of these involve the clown with many different types of animals, both domestic and wild, and are of particular interest to this study. Most clowns ride a mule or have a trick horse, and many carry with them into the arena a suckling pig which they feed from a nursing bottle. Often trained dogs are used, and frequently monkeys perform, usually as cowboy-clad riders of the dogs. Certain clowns have a jalopy as the focus of their act, representing a kind of machine-age counterpart to the animal acts. Many center on explicit sexual ribaldry which ridicules women in general or their wife or mother-in-law in particular. Some use animals, especially monkeys, to make fun of current politicians. Virtually all seem concerned with biological phenomena—excretory functions, nasal discharges, blood, sweat, nursing from the breast, or dying.

Trained animal acts which do not involve clowns are sometimes included, as well as various trick riders and performing horse exhibitions. Indian dances may take place between events, and special entertainment in the form of currently popular country-western singers is frequent. The rodeo queen may be featured during the rodeo, and statistics about her are cited while she gallops around the arena. She smiles beneath her typically pink or turquoise cowgirl hat, and her shapely tight-jacketed chest is draped with a banner bearing her title, as she leans out of her saddle to wave to fans around the arena, and then sharply curbs her horse.

PARADES

Parades are an important part of rodeos, and typically occur along the main street of the town during the morning of a day when a rodeo is to be held in the afternoon or evening. The stock contractor usually takes part, as do the queen and her court and possibly the royalty from the rodeos of nearby towns. People in the parade may dress as famous Western characters, such as mountain men or Pony Express riders, and the cavalry is often represented. Rodeo clowns and their various animals take part, and local or state business and civic or religious organizations provide floats, mounted participants, or auto caravans. Politicians wave from cars labelled with their names and offices, and law enforcement posses, firefighters, and men's fraternal organizations pass in review. Bands march with drum majors and majorettes, and military displays are included. The parade is the prelude to the excitement of the rodeo in a Western town, and keynotes many of its motifs and themes.

This general survey of rodeo has been intended to familiarize the reader with the cowboy sport. In the next chapter we will look at the beginning and early development of both its performance and contest aspects, bringing to light much that is relevant to a deeper understanding of the essential nature and significance of rodeo. Though the beginnings of the competitive aspect antedate the performance aspect, the Wild West phenomenon is described first. In this way, after discussing the Wild West Show, material on cowboy life may be immediately followed by that on rodeo so that correlations between them may stand out more distinctly.

3

THE ORIGIN AND DEVELOPMENT OF RODEO

THE PERFORMANCE ASPECT: THE WILD WEST SHOW

> Buffalo Bill's
> defunct
> > who used to
> > ride a watersmooth-silver
> > > stallion . . . .
> > > > e.e. cummings (1978:7)

THE ORIGIN OF RODEO is traceable to two sources—the sports and contests first indulged in by early-day working cowboys for their own amusement and that unique American form of outdoor entertainment, the Wild West Show. One cannot consider the latter without linking it to the name of one of the most fabulous figures in the history of performance, William Frederick Cody, better known as "Buffalo Bill." All other shows of this type may be considered imitations or outgrowths of this man's original extravaganza, for it was he who started the Wild West Show and he who dominated it (Russell 1970:105). Although he has been the victim of a recent trend toward the "debunking" of heroes in the United States, this extraordinary man was not the charlatan created by modern myths, as exemplified by his portrayal in the 1976 Robert Altman film, "Buffalo Bill and the Indians, or Sitting Bull's History Lesson" (Rudolph & Altman 1976). For in his early years Cody actually did live many of the exciting and colorful frontier exploits which were later dramatized in his show. He had worked for a freighting firm on wagon trips across the wild plains, had been a Pony Express rider, battled Indians, fought in the Civil War, and succeeded in making an

44

unusually commendable record as a frontier and army scout (Russell 1960).

Due to a fortuitous combination of authenticity and personal charm, this flamboyant man was able to present to the American people vivid scenes and demonstrations, characteristic of the fast-disappearing Western frontier which they could never experience. Though there had been similar acts presented for entertainment prior to his Wild West, it was Cody who first combined them into a "formula that spelled success" (Russell 1970:5). So great was his commitment to authenticity that he considered the word "circus," and even "show," anathema, and called his production simply the "Wild West," or referred to it as an "exhibition."

The start of Buffalo Bill's Wild West can be dated from the summer of 1882. In that year, after a decade of show business background in melodrama, Cody returned to his hometown of North Platte, Nebraska, and became chairman of its Fourth of July celebration. There, to the delight of the townspeople, he staged what has become known as the "Old Glory Blowout." Cody persuaded local businessmen to offer prizes for various roping, shooting, riding, and bronco-breaking events. He expected to attract about a hundred cowboy contestants, and actually got a thousand. This unprecedented and unexpected success gave him the impetus for his future enterprise (Russell 1970:2). Thus 1882 marks the beginnings of both the Wild West Show and one part of the dual origin of its successor —rodeo.

For among the events displayed so realistically in the Wild West —such as the attack on the Deadwood Mail Coach, a Pony Express ride, a buffalo hunt, horsemanship demonstrations by riders from all parts of the globe, and the traditional finale of "Custer's Last Stand"—were performances called "Cowboy Fun." These included attempts to ride wild broncos and mules, and a record of such events has been preserved on a film that can be viewed at Buffalo Bill's Ranch in North Platte, Nebraska, now an historic landmark. In the movie one can see that the cowboys had to mount their animals in the open, with no chutes, and usually the unfortunate beasts were thrown to the ground in order to permit the cowboys to get on their backs. Then the bucking contests continued until the broncos tired or the riders were dislodged. Additional demonstrations included steer wrestling, roping and riding of "Texas Wild Steers," and other skills of the range. The 1897 program lists under Cowboy Fun, "Picking up objects from the ground, lassoing wild horses, riding the buckers, etc." (Buffalo Bill's Wild West:3). The cowboys here were salaried show performers, in contrast to their future counterparts, the rodeo contestants, who would receive pay only by winning.

It is historical fact that before Buffalo Bill the American cowboy was far from being considered a hero. It was largely due to the influence of the Wild West that he was given that status (Russell 1960, 1970:117; Smith 1971:109). Owen Wister's landmark novel, *The Virginian* (1902), which would cast him in the heroic mold for all time, had not yet been published, and cowboys were considered at worst as armed desperadoes, and at best rough, rowdy, uncouth, and irresponsible laborers. Their image in the public mind was that of hired men on horseback who led monotonous lives of unenviable drudgery, and had no romantic connotation (Frantz & Choate 1955:73–75; Smith 1971:109–111; Adams 1946:41). Buck Taylor, "King of the Cowboys" in his Wild West Show, was Cody's creation; he later became the fictional hero of Prentiss Ingraham's dime novel of the same title. Thus was the figure of the cowboy hero born—the strong, handsome man, as daring and courageous as he was noble and generous, with his unswerving chivalry, personal code of honor, and almost courtly manner. It was this image that was epitomized by Wister's taciturn Wyoming plainsman, and which became forever influential, even in shaping the future behavior of the working cowboy himself (Russell 1970:118). Like Wister's, though, Buffalo Bill's creation was a cowboy without cows, yet he was stamped indelibly upon the popular imagination. The dull routines involved in the occupation of cattle herding had been transformed almost overnight into a bold and free, colorful and individualistic way of life that would become the dream and envy of virtually every time-bound and machine-oriented worker who felt imprisoned by the newly industrialized American society.

Not only did Buffalo Bill create the rangeland hero, but he is also credited with originating the style of ten-gallon Stetson hats for cowboys (Russell 1960:171)—no small accomplishment, if true, considering the importance of that trademark. No doubt it was the popularity of Cody's show that transformed such things as "cowboy," "roundup," and "stampede" into common household words. And by being the first to bring cowboys and spectacle together in combination, it was he who paved the way for rodeo as it is known today.

It is evident that the Wild West Show and the informal cowboy contests that were later to develop into rodeo had a close connection from the start. For often a cowhand who had performed in the Wild West returned home to demonstrate his skills at the local roundups and roping and riding contests which were becoming part of Fourth of July and other festive celebrations throughout the range country. Some Wild West performers had been recruited from such competitive get-togethers which were not yet known as rodeos. In 1890, Buck Taylor, already mentioned as a star of Buffalo Bill's Wild West, was manager of Denver's Cowboy Tournament, thus linking the two phenomena. Also Cheyenne Frontier Days, held continuously since 1897, had an original purpose remarkably similar to Cody's, stating that it wished to "revive the thrilling incidents and pictures of life that may be reproduced in form by those who were once actors in that period" (Russell 1970:59). Its program that first year, as well as its aim, was close to that of the Wild West. Out of eight contests, six were cowpony, wild horse, and free-for-all races, and two were roping and wild bronco riding (Hanesworth 1967:19–20). But other events still included in that early day were such typical Wild West acts as sham battles, and spectacles like stage coach holdups and Pony Express rides, which have since been eliminated from rodeo. Another interconnection between the two is the fact that it was Guy Weadick, a noted past-performer in the 101 Ranch Wild West Show, who was responsible for staging the first Calgary Stampede in 1912.

Rodeo is not the only development that originated in the Western pageantry of Buffalo Bill's Show. The Wild West is credited with being the first large-scale event to dramatize the American West and transform the entire region into a place of romance and glamour. It is also true that the antecedents of the many stories, comics, novels, plays, radio and television scripts, and films included in the genre known as "the Western" were originally derived from the spirit which made the Wild West so ostensibly a part of Americana. And it was not only in the young nation itself that Buffalo Bill achieved great popularity and acclaim; the show was considered a great sensation by royalty and commoner alike as it travelled and played in London and throughout Europe, for about six years near the turn of the century (Russell 1970:46).

The real American Wild West that Buffalo Bill's Wild West was commemorating had passed into history by 1893. That was a peak year for the show, in which it played to sellout crowds in Chicago, only a few miles from the World's Columbian Exposition. By a strange turn of events, the historian Frederick Jackson Turner, first scholar to give serious theoretical consideration to the American frontier, was the speaker at the American Historical Association meeting that year at the Columbian Exposition. There, a short distance away from the location of Buffalo Bill's vivid frontier dramatizations, he presented his now-famous thesis, *The Significance of the Frontier in American History* (Turner 1894). A few years previously, the United States Census Report of 1890 had declared that the "frontier of settlement" in this country no longer existed. And so it happened that the scholar, as well as the showman, had reacted to the official closing of the frontier.

Briefly summarized, Turner's thesis embodied his assertion that the frontier had been the most important factor in shaping American character and history. From the wild and rugged land itself, Turner argued, had come the main stimulus for the development of the strength, self-reliance, and individualism that characterize Americans and formed the basis for the growth of American democracy. Thus, it was a coincidence as to place, but not of time, for both Cody's show and Turner's thesis reflected the fact that attention was now turning to the frontier for the very reason that it had disappeared. Nostalgia was the common feeling, as the existence of boundless land for the taking, which had been the frontier's greatest treasure, was now a thing of the past. Free land was, of course, the essential element for the range cattle industry, and the key to its unprecedented prosperity. Now that the rugged and adventurous frontier life as epitomized by the cowboy on the open range was jeopardized, it was natural that it be not only dramatized, but analyzed, as each man in his own way sought to clarify the nature of what it was that was disappearing. Scholars would debate Turner's thesis for many decades—and on into the present—but they would be forever stimulated and enriched by his ideas and the issues he raised regarding the frontier (Billington 1977; Taylor 1972).

Like Turner, those who planned Wyoming's first "Frontier Days" celebration in 1897 had noted that "the frontier line of advancing settlements has already disappeared like misty shadows vanishing before the Sun's Rays" (Hanesworth 1967:11). It is not by chance that this festival of the West at Cheyenne, destined to become one of the greatest rodeos in the country, began very early in its history to focus almost entirely on the activities of the cowboy. For, of all those pioneer figures associated with the American frontier, it has been from the beginning the cowboy who has most clearly exemplified its spirit. The cowboy has gained universal acceptance as the predominant image of the frontiersman. Neither the explorer, mountain man, miner, trader, or soldier who preceded him into the Western wilderness left a legacy as pervasive and enduring as this mounted herdsman who was master of such a vast domain. He seemed to overshadow, yet somehow to embody, them all. In his classic work on the cowboy, Philip Ashton Rollins wrote:

> These men rode out into a vacant empire; met the traditions and the customs of the hunters, trappers, and traders, the primal pioneers; with unanimity adopted all of the traditions and the usable part of the customs, added to them, crystallized the whole into a code of compulsory usage. . . .
>
> (1973:343)

It is the cowboy who is considered to express the essence of the West, and who has come to symbolize for the world not only this country's westward expansion, but ultimately even America herself.

The popularity of the sport of rodeo today reflects the nation's continued preoccupation with the cowboy and all that he represents. An understanding of rodeo requires an understanding of the characteristics of the unique man who originated it—the American cowboy—out of whose lifeway this ritual of the West was created and perpetuated.

THE CONTEST ASPECT: THE AMERICAN WORKING COWBOY

> Now a rodeo is not to be confused with traveling Wild West Shows where hired hands in cowboy boots and three-dollar hats ride crowbait horses around inside a tent. A rodeo is a cowboy contest, the gents you see in the arena are genuine bronc-stompin' cowboys—brass-bound, copper-riveted throughout, with iron backbones and tails screwed on—not a carnival hand in the lot.
>
> (Rounds 1949:11)

Though obscured by myth, the nature of the working cowboy and his way of life can be reconstructed, at least partially, from a study of various sources. Though first-hand accounts are relatively scarce, some cowboy writings in the form of autobiographies, letters, diaries, and descriptive articles are available. In addition, there are biographies, collected life histories, journals, and books written by contemporary travelers, soldiers, and other observers who spent time on the cattle frontier and recorded their experiences and impressions. Even during the heyday of the cowboy era, a few of the more perceptive participants sensed that it represented a type of epic life destined to be of brief duration and were impelled to preserve their memories of it.

And fleeting it was, this period when the mounted herder rode as a monarch over the grassy expanses of the Great Plains. The cowboy reign began in about 1867, just after the end of the Civil War, and was already drawing to a close by 1892. The cowboy's vocation was created in the Texas trail drives, when he was hired to escort large herds of feral Longhorn cattle northward from Texas to the Kansas railheads for shipment East, or up as far as Wyoming and Montana to supply ranchers with stock. Through this process a $4.00 cow became a $40.00 beef animal, and the American cattle industry had its start. The fabulous open range era followed the trail driving period, and success was overwhelming, while free land for the taking seemed limitless. But the end came swiftly, hastened by diverse enemies—among them overstocking, the invention of barbed wire, the influx of homesteaders and small farmers, and climatic disasters in the form of blizzard and drought. Fortunes were made and lost by the barons of the cattle frontier, but the cowboy had no share in them, for, despite his tendency toward haughtiness, he was technically a hired hand. As such, he was entirely distinct from his boss, the entrepreneur cattleman.

The American cowboy, also termed "cowhand" or "cowpuncher," has often been the subject of treatises written from various perspectives. My examination of the cowboy here stresses his relationship to the natural environment, and focuses on the ways in which some of his characteristic attitudes, perceptions, and traits may have developed as a result of his interaction with the forces of nature. For the primary environment of the Great Plains and the particular domestic animals that became part of it created the herders' work, and their work in turn created the cowboys' lifeway and ethos. A distinct society resulted, often referred to as a breed apart. It was said that a person "would know a cowboy in hell with his hide burnt off" (Abbott & Smith 1939:268).

Cowboys partook of a life which, though differing in detail from that of classic Old World nomads, suggests that they are an American counterpart. Like most pastoralists, it was their animals which shaped the lives and movements of these mounted New World cattle herders. The triple complex of man-horse-cattle interacting with the environment of the Great Plains created a society unlike any other, yet with certain resemblances to some of the world's pastoral peoples. Frederick Jackson Turner, whose frontier thesis, as mentioned, deals with the impact of the physcial environment in molding American character, called the cowboys' experience on the cattle frontier "the greatest pastoral movement in recorded history" (Frantz & Choate 1955:12).

In order for such a phenomenon involving the interaction of man, animals, and the Western wilderness to take place, early concepts of the land itself had to be changed. For centuries before the cowboys began to use it, the Great Plains had been considered uninhabitable for white men, a wasteland unfit for human civilization, a desert whose harshness and aridity, in the words of trailhand Andy Adams, previously "had baffled the determination of man" (1903:64). White men had been slow to associate the great herds of buffalo which had lived off these grassy plains with the potential for pastoral riches which existed there. They had not yet acquired the wisdom expressed by Chief Arapooish of the Crow Indians, a horse-pastoralist people whose mounts grew strong on this nutritious native herbiage alone: "The Crow country is a good country. The Great Spirit has put it in the right place" (Medicine Crow 1939:vii). Instead they had listened to opinions like that of Daniel Webster who asked in 1838:

> What do we want with this vast worthless area?
> This region of savages and wild beasts, of
> deserts, shifting sands, and whirlwinds of
> dust, of cactus and prairie dogs?
>
> (Forbis 1973:19)

and of Horace Greeley who remarked in 1859 that in the Great Plains "we seem to have reached the acme of barrenness and desolation" (Forbis 1973:19).

Yet it was destined that once its former occupants, the Plains Indians, were mostly subjugated and the teeming herds of buffalo destroyed, the vast stretches of unclaimed land populated now only by such native forms of wildlife as antelope, prairie dogs, and meadowlarks, would be exploited by man. Two things were needed for the conquering: transportation to overcome its huge expanses, and someone with the courage to meet its harsh conditions. Then came "a man with guts and a horse"—for that is said to be the true definition of the cowboy (Adams 1967:5). The opportunity was seized; the challenge was met: hardy wilderness-adapted horned cattle, vast in numbers but unmarketable in Texas, would be driven north for sale. The Texas Longhorns had been a legacy from Spain to the New World, as were the smart tough little mustangs ridden by the cowboy herders. So, too, was much of the cowboys' clothing and equipment derived from Spain, through the Mexican vaquero.

But the exploitative spirit, the will to make this land yield, the drive for profit which motivated the barons of the cattle empire, were American. Yankee ingenuity and determination would make it possible for meat to come out of the "desert," in spite of the difficulties. In the Old World, beef was the diet of lords and kings, or for others, a holiday treat. In the new continent, through nature's bounty and man's endurance, Americans would eventually become the greatest beef-eaters of modern times (Boorstin 1974:5). One resource was the key to vast riches—grass, stretches of grass seemingly as endless as the ocean. The conditions provided by nature in the Great Plains were nearly perfect for grazing large herds of cattle—if a man could be found to get them there.

The Longhorns were particularly well-suited to the Great Plains environment. Toughened by natural selection during their years in Texas as feral animals untended by man, they required little of the care and attention that are necessary for domestic breeds. They possessed long sharp horns for defense, their water requirement was lower than that of domesticated cattle, and they could endure harsh extremes of weather (Dobie 1941). Only a rough, wiry, longlegged breed like the Longhorn could have endured the rigors of the trail drives.

It has been said that "in Texas cattle live for the sake of man, but in all other countries, man lives for the sake of his cattle" (Boorstin 1974:7). The reference is to Old World cattle which, in contrast to the animals the cowboys herded, are in certain cases cherished and protected. In some of the African cattle-complex societies, for example, the care and concern they receive would cause them to be called "coddled" in cowboy lingo. Often the bovine animals within those cultures are guarded, petted and groomed, sung to, and revered as objects of elaborate ceremony. Cattle are valued for symbolic importance in kinship networks and in the maintenance of cultural identity as well as for subsistence (Evans-Pritchard 1974, 1956; Hopen 1970; Lienhardt 1976). Unlike the African pastoralists, who herd on foot and have a symbiotic relationship with their cattle, the American cowboys, mounted, became the dominant masters of the Longhorns—and of the very land itself which sustained them.

The Texas Longhorn shaped the North American cowboy complex, but the wily animals could be herded over such vast distances only on horseback. Therefore the cowboy was of necessity a mounted man, and it was as an equestrian figure that his lifeway and distinct society would develop. Opening up the semi-arid Great Plains for profit required an aggressive strength and vigor, and the success of the cattle industry depended upon tough men as well as tough cattle and horses. All three had to face the primal land itself—the huge and awesome wilderness, beautiful yet terrifying. To meet it, real courage—mental as well as physical—was demanded. For some people found the landscape brooding and solemn, melancholy, and even oppressive; they were affected by the burdensome and depressing quiet, which "bore down upon the mind," sometimes to the point of madness. Often the desolation of unexplored reaches meant loneliness, a sense of isolation. Even the cattle were felt to be susceptible at times to the effects of such an inhospitable wilderness (Freeman 1959:550). It may have been partly responsible for the indefinable mystique of sadness that was thinly masked beneath the jocular surface of cowboy personality.

The impact wielded by the virgin land itself cannot be overemphasized. Nothing in the Eastern or European past of those who first entered it had prepared them for such an experience. The effect on the perceptions was no less marked than the effect on the body. As Frank Waters expressed it:

> Noble nature, uncontaminated by the gross touch of humanity, brought out the best in man. It also brought out the worst. The overwhelming immensity of the land with its limitless plains and huge brooding mountains not only dwarfed man to an infinitesimal speck. Its haunting timelessness overemphasized his own brief and dangerous span. Everywhere he was confronted by the force of alien natural laws inherent in the landscape itself—the ineffable spirit-of-place of a new continent to which he was not yet attuned.
>
> (Milton 1971:28)

Entering this land of sweeping grandeur, the cowboy faced its rigors head-on. Obscuring its magnificence were sudden and frequent storms, with lightning which could cause death to man or beast or start a disastrous prairie fire. Drenching rain brought cold and discomfort, often leaving pneumonia in its wake. Torrential downpours created mud for horses and cattle to trample through, and flooded rivers which animals had to be forced to cross by swimming. No one reading Andy Adams' chronicle (1903) of a trail drive can forget the herder who drowned during such a crossing. Indelible, too, are the accounts by cowboys of "bogged cattle" and the herculean struggles necessary to rescue them (Adams 1903; Siringo 1950). Freezing weather would alternate with blinding blizzards during the long prairie winter. Extreme summer heat, with little available shade, was overwhelming. Drought made thirst the most dreaded of many imminent hazards for men and animals. Thirst-crazed cattle were difficult to manage on a dry drive, and in extreme cases went blind from its effects (Adams 1903:64). Dry weather brought choking dust blowing into the cowboy's nose and mouth. Wild animals could attack men or their herds. Noises or sudden movements caused the herders' most feared and frequent calamity—the stampede. Night guard duty was a measure designed to help prevent stampedes, or at least to warn sleeping cowboys quickly once it did start. Night herdsmen, after a long day in the saddle, were said to have thrown sand in their eyes to keep awake for this vigil. Once cattle had stampeded, it took many hours, even days, of constant riding without stopping for food or rest to regain the herd. Rounding up the maddened animals was a task involving, at best, great exertion, and at worst, serious injury or death by trampling. Prairie dog holes caused horses to fall, often breaking their legs and throwing the rider, with injury or death resulting. Whirlpools and quicksand also took their toll.

The isolation of the country offered the nomads and their herds little protection against human enemies that often laid in wait. Bands of renegade Indians sometimes attacked the trail drivers, threatening to kill them and drive off their stock unless a bargain could be made. Sometimes they charged exorbitant rates for passage through land they claimed to own. Cattle rustlers were a menace, and cases of torturing and killing trail hands to get possession of their cattle were recorded. Other cattlemen using the same trail or range might wrongfully claim animals when two or more herds intermingled. In the early open-range days there were violent disputes over land and water rights, conflicts between cattlemen and homesteaders or small farmers who claimed the same territory or whose interests were opposed, and bloody "wars" were fought between cowboys and sheepmen or between large and small ranches. Wilderness and sparse settlement meant the absence of institutionalized law-enforcement and no time to take claims to authorities. Dubious "frontier justice" was the result, and sudden death could be the fate of the accused, innocent or guilty. Here again, the vastness of the land itself was determinative. Illustrating this is a statement by Granville Stuart, a Montana rancher who had come up through the ranks as a cowboy:

> The civil laws and courts had been tried and found wanting. The Montana cattlemen were as peaceable and law-abiding a body of men as could be found anywhere but they had $35,000,000 worth of property scattered over seventy-five thousand square miles of practically uninhabited country and it must be protected from thieves. The only way to do

it was to make the penalty for stealing so severe that it would lose its attractions.

(1925:196)

Stuart disclosed that at the end of his fall roundup in 1883, tallies showed at least a 3% loss from rustling (1925:195). Being nomadic, the only things a trail herder could use for protection against such extremes were what he carried with him on his horse. Survival meant either quitting or being shaped to fit the rugged land. If he endured, he became what Hough described as the true cowboy, an inextricable part of the West itself, the "product of primitive, chaotic, elemental forces, rough, barbarous, and strong." When we come to see him as he actually was, the writer adds, "then we shall all love him; because at heart each of us is a barbarian, too" (1923:339).

Some cowboys, barbarians though they may have seemed, were literate enough to document the hardships imposed by their hostile environment. The journal of cattle-drover George C. Duffield, written in 1866, for example, is typified by these entries:

> travelled 6 miles rain pouring down in torrents & here we are on the banks of a creek with 10 or 12 ft. water & rising & Ran my horse into a ditch & got my knee badly sprained

> No breakfast pack and off is the order   Rain poured down for 2 hours. Ground in a flood. . . . Gloomey times as I ever saw.

> Hard and long to be remembered day to me   we swam our cattle & Horses I swam it 5 times. Upset our wagon in River & lost many of our cooking utensils again.

> was on my horse all night & it raining hard.

> Swimming cattle is the order   This day will long be remembered by me   There was one of our party Drowned & Several narrow escapes & I among the no.

> am in the Indian country . . . believe they scare the Cattle to get pay to collect them. Many men in trouble   Almost starved not having had a bite to eat for 60 hours.

Indians came to Herd & tried to take some
beeves   Would not let them. Had a big muss
One drew his knife and I my revolver.

We hauled cattle out of the mud with oxen
half the day.

Was in the saddle until daylight   am almost
dead for sleep.

I was sick last night   had a chill & the cholic
this morning   feel badly yet   Everything parching
under the scorching sun.

(Spence 1966:204–210)

While Charlie Siringo (1950) used his natural talent to give his 1885 autobiographical account of trail life a light touch, the reader learns of more calamities than just the ever-present "grey backs" (lice) in the cowboys' clothing. One finds recounted again hunger, snow which covered the buffalo chips so that no campfire could be made in that country where there was no wood, the agony of contracting smallpox along the trail, and a poignant sense of rootlessness. Like those of Siringo, Adams (1903), "Teddy Blue" Abbott (1939), and the compilations of Hunter (1963), all of the cowboys' own records are filled with stampedes, experiences of being thrown or kicked by a horse, or gouged by a rampaging steer. They tell of working eighteen hours a day, seven days a week, and making a journey of some eighteen-hundred miles with no comforts other than a bedroll and campfire.

One might easily ask what there was about cowboy life that drew men to it, a dilemma summed up by James McCauley in his own account of life on the range: "that is real living . . . but 'tis the violant kind and lots of people love it beyond a doubt" (Tinkle 1959:125). The conditions of the environment and the very nature of the cowboys' work served to bind them into a tightly knit and distinctive society. Pride became a vital aspect of cowboy adaptation, pride molded by the successful meeting of the ever-present challenges. Each man had an inordinate sense of satisfaction in being a cowboy, and often expressed it in disdain for all other occupations. Cowboys felt that workers like farmers and tradesmen were stupid drudges to be pitied because they did not know the adventure, the rough and reckless freedom of the nomadic life (Branch 1961:123). As a horseman par excellence, the cowboy obtained feelings of power and exaggerated masculinity from his mounted state which contributed to his haughty self-image. Not only did he triumph over wild nature, but he had control and mastery of domestic animals as well. E.C. Abbott, who experienced the existence first-hand, characterized cowboys as being "wild and brave from the life they lived," adding that "in fact there was only two things the old-time cowpuncher was afraid of, a decent woman and being set afoot" (Abbott & Smith 1939:9). These were the twin threats that could destroy the essence of the wild free life, and avoiding them was an obsession. Cowboys would go out of their way to do any type of work from the back of a horse. Answers to requests that a job be done were in the affirmative, with the specification "if I can do it horseback." A cowboy would gladly ride twenty-four hours without whimpering, but would "hate your guts" if asked to plow ground or do anything afoot (Webb 1936:252). Adams called the cowboy "too proud to cut hay, and not wild enough to eat it" (1969:6). In a more serious vein, because of his great pride in his calling, the most severe punishment on the range was to be "set down" in the presence of a man's fellow riders. This meant surrendering the horse that belonged to one's outfit and hitting the trail on foot—in disgrace (Adams 1969:7).

Because a cowboy who was required to travel even a distance of a few yards always did it on horseback, there was a widely diffused belief that he could not walk and was indeed a kind of hybrid centaur (Freeman 1959:554). Larry McMurtry states that the cowboy was "scarcely competent to move except on horseback," and that "walking for pleasure" was "considered to be due to lunacy or bad upbringing" (1968:152). Indeed the cowboy's symbol of identity, his boots, reflected this. The high heel helped him to dig in when he had to rope from the ground, and also prevented the danger of his foot slipping through the stirrup. But it was also by means of its slanting heel that his foot was made to appear smaller. Cowboys are on record for having gone to much trouble to get tight boots, and usually ordered them a few sizes too small. The tightness and high heels had a crippling effect upon walking and resulted in a toddling gait (Freeman 1959:555). This gave the (desired) impression that such a man was proud of being little accustomed to using his legs. He did not wish to be confused with a big-footed farmer who spent his life walking behind a plow.

The cowboy's trademark is his wide-brimmed hat, an article of clothing that has become legendary through the many uses it served on the range. Like the cowboy himself, of whom it appears as an extension, the hat is an example of adaptation to work in a difficult environment. Providing shade from the sun, and protection from rain, snow, wind, and dust, the Stetson was also a whip to urge a cowboy's mount or drive a lagging steer, and a signal flag to wave at a distant comrade. It could be used to feed or water a horse, gather eggs, fan a campfire, or as a makeshift pillow. Held in the hand for balance, it could help a rider stay on a bucking bronc. Whatever purposes it served, a cowboy's hat was, and still is, worn with great pride, and it is seldom removed throughout the day. When he does take it off, custom (which is still strictly observed) designates that no true cowhand lays his hat rightside up. A hat must rest upside down to protect the crease and to keep the wearer's luck from falling out. Once placed, it should not be handled by another person. As I heard this expressed by one 80-year-old wearer of a Stetson who had cowboyed all his life in Montana: "out here, no one messes with someone's hat!" A warning still repeated in cattle country advises that a cowboy is a special breed of man, so "leave his hat alone and leave his woman be!" The hat may act as a regional badge, for styles differ according to areas, but it is also a very important individual expression. For the cowboy it becomes a part of himself, equally essential to his own well-being as to the performance of the tasks of his daily life.

Probably only out of the American wilderness, where the harsh land tended to make every man an equal, could come a common laborer like the cowhand who would raise his status to that of an aristocrat, becoming what one writer referred to as "the only reigning American royalty" (Cholis 1977:29). According to Abbott, cowpunchers "set themselves way up above other people who the chances are were no more common and uneducated than themselves" (1939:247). Forbis has recounted an incident of the early range when the pride of these New World cavaliers was demonstrated to an English visitor. Asking the ranch foreman "Is your master at home?" elicited the response, "The son of a bitch hasn't been born yet" (1973:29).

If, as has been claimed, the saddle was his throne, it was his horse that kept the cowboy a king. His skill as a mounted man gave him a sense of superiority and imbued him with the attitude of aggressiveness characteristic of history's horsemen, in the tradition of the Mongols under Ghengis Khan, the Bedouins of Arabia, and certain Indians of the North American Plains. Thus, the cowboy's haughtiness is part of a behavior complex which Bennett called one of "mastery and ascendance" (1969:91), and which he, as well as Evans-Pritchard (1974) and Goldschmidt (1965), found to be characteristically associated with the pastoral way of life. Evans-Pritchard has described the Nuer "pastoral mentality," in which the herds-man's outlook upon the world becomes an obsession. The pastoral life, he asserts, "nurtures qualities like courage, love of fighting, and contempt of hardship," in contrast to the settled life that "shapes the industrious character of the peasant" (1974:26).

As a mounted herdsman, the cowboy was superb. Horsemanship was his dominant skill, and as McMurtry (1968) has noted, the cowboy's ego needs were closely bound up with horsemanship. As a Texas native who grew up with cowboys, McMurtry expressed doubt that he had "ever known a cowboy who liked women as well as he liked horses" (1968:148), and has suggested a "sacramental relation-ship between man and horse," a deep bonding he calls "mateship" (1968:27,72). Anthropologist John Bennett (1969), in observing contemporary mounted inheritors of the cowboy tradition in the Great Plains, however, points out that the emphasis is decidedly placed on the rider's skill in making the horse do his bidding, rather than upon the horse or upon a relationship shared between them. My own field observations, especially in the contrasting light of my experience with other types of human-horse relationships, generally support this conclusion.

In the last analysis, one cannot take the romantic view that there was always a real partnership; there was a duality in the relationship of cowboy and mount. The old range adage that the West was hell on horses and women rings true, for if horses were half trusted friend, they were also half servant. Long hours of being ridden, often without adequate food or water, was the horses' lot, as were sadistically cruel bits, heavy saddles, and elaborately pronged spurs. The equipment used on his mount was clearly for the cowboy's convenience. Ornately tooled leather for bridle and saddle and silver design on long-shanked and spaded bits bespoke a cowboy's pride in being a horseman, not his love for his horse. Mastery was often his trademark, the horse its object, and this was reflected in the cowpuncher's frequently heard boast that he "could ride anything that has hair" (Seidman 1973:178).

On the other hand, a cowboy usually took good care of the mount he so completely depended upon, and range ethic demanded that after a day's work he feed and water his horse before himself. Certainly this was common sense, since he believed a man afoot was no man at all, and the preserving of his maleness was a foremost consideration. Some cowboys felt a sense of identification with their horses akin to that which I have suggested for the Plains Indian warrior (Lawrence 1976), and perhaps somewhat comparable to that feeling a Nuer boy has for his "ox of initiation," with which he is to have an intimate association the rest of his life (Evans-Pritchard 1956).

His horse was a cowboy's constant companion. Not only his work and his convenience, but also at times his life, depended upon it. Unlike the cattle he herded, which he viewed collectively and only rarely knew as individuals, his horse was a unique being with a name, whose nature he must understand in order for the two to work together. In his loneliness and isolation, he probably anthropomorphized his horse and no doubt sometimes gave it whatever affection his rough exterior concealed. He usually cared for it more than any other creature in the world, and the hard use he gave it might best be understood in the light of the harshness of his own life. Cowboy writings abound with instances of their deep feelings for horses. Charlie Siringo's devotion to "Whiskey-peet" from whom he "couldn't even bear the thought of parting," is evident to the reader of his autobiography (1950:113). And at the end of the trail, Andy Adams finds the successful conclusion of the drive little compensation for the parting between man and horse which he felt so keenly. "For on the trail," he wrote, "an affection springs up between man and mount which is almost human. And on this drive, covering nearly three-thousand miles, all the ties which can exist between man and beast had . . . become cemented" (1903:382).

I suggest that the cowboy's close and often exclusive contact with animals penetrated into his very being so that he virtually took on their nature, or rather merged it into his own. There may be more than humor to Charlie Russell's story about the Eastern girl who asked "Ma, do cowboys eat grass?" and received the reply "No, dear, they're part human" (1927:1). The rawness of his life and proximity to nature and animals may well have shaped a character who was "more mustang than man." Highest praise for a fellow-worker from Teddy Blue Abbott took the form of "He *was* cow—one of the best cowhands I ever saw" (Abbott & Smith 1939:110). Range experiences like that of crawling inside a freshly killed cow carcass as the only way to survive frigid weather (Rollins 1973:355) or dragging a bloody butchered animal over a prairie fire to extinguish it (Rollins 1973:185) must have had an animalizing effect. The cowhand most valued on the trail or range was the one who possessed a mystique about cattle. Such a man is referred to as one who "knows cow," having an intuitive knowledge of the animals. To "think cow" meant one could predict bovine behavior and thus manage a herd more efficiently. This trait is still admired in ranch country. Like other pastoralists, cowboys believed that all farmers lacked this kind of insight.

In the same way "cow sense," which made for a good herding and roping horse, was the most valued asset for a mount. The way their association with animals influenced the cowboys' toughening process is indicated by Abbott's statement that cowhands "used to brag that they could go any place a cow could go and stand anything a horse could" (Abbott & Smith 1939:8). Siringo, writing of the harshness and deprivation of his early years, told of his animal-like dependence upon "Brownie," the milk cow who "had been a friend in need." He revealed that "often when I would be hungry and afraid to go home for fear of mother and the mush stick, she would let me go up to her on the prairie calf-fashion and get my milk" (1950:19). The fact that the life of a herder can have the effect of making him resemble animals is known also to other pastoral peoples. The sheep-herding Kurds of Afghanistan, for example, have an adage which states that to make a man of your son you should let him become a shepherd, but warns that you must take him away before he becomes an animal (Bois 1966:22–23). And a poet writing of the cowboy expressed the same idea of the brutalizing influence of life with animals:

Of rough rude stock this saddle sprite
Is grosser grown with savage things.
Inured to storms, his fierce delight
Is lawless as the beast he swings
His swift rope over.

(Spence 1966:216)

With conviction, Larry McMurtry reflected that though having spent most of his life with Texas cowhands, he had "never known a cowboy who was truly a gentle man" (1968:168). He points out that the cowboy's working life was spent in one sort of violent activity or another, and it might be expected that violence would be extended from animals to humans. Identifying cowboys with the tools of their trade, he calls them "neither harder nor softer than saddle leather" (1968:169). Violence toward animals was part of virtually every daily range task. At the least, the creatures were swatted, kicked, quirted, bitted, spurred, roped, and driven to the limit of their endurance. The common term "cowpuncher" refers to the practice of using metal-tipped poles to prod cattle into railroad stock cars (Towne 1957:74). Cows' tails were often twisted to make them move— sometimes until the bone snapped—and sand might be rubbed into the eyes of stubborn animals for the same purpose.

Consider branding—burning the hide of cattle and horses with a red hot iron. In the huge open spaces of the West this was (and is) taken for granted as the only way in which valuable live property can be labelled. Animals are first run down, roped, and then, in the case of cattle, tied up. Any degree of empathy would surely be prohibitive to the operation. Here is a brief description of "the strangely crude and confused" spectacle of calf branding:

> The bawling and squirming of the calves and the bellowing of the watching cows was matched by the raucous shouts and the fervid swearing of men running about stripped to the waist and smeared with blood and dust, branding-iron and knife in hand. The calves could hope for no gentle treatment in such a moil. In an excess of temper not a part of his regular character a cowboy hit by a flying hoof might retaliate with a vicious stab from his knife, or sink his spurred heel against the stomach of the offending calf.
>
> (Branch 1961:61)

Woe to the Easterner or dude who dared insinuate that branding was cruel. His perfidy was not tolerated, and such a presumptuous tenderfoot could himself be brutally hazed. Even branding, though, was not considered enough to denote ownership of cattle. At the same time animals were "marked",—meaning that certain folds of skin, usually the dewlaps, were cut or, more commonly, their ears were sliced, notched, or "chipped" (having a piece removed from them), in a characteristic way to further distinguish them. The Jinglebob Ranch was named for its tradition of cutting so far into the calves' ears that only a small portion was left and the rest hung down like a jinglebob (Webb 1936:259). Various state regulations sometimes prohibited the removal of more than half of a calf's ear (Rollins 1973:216). At the same time male animals were (and are) castrated without anesthesia as part of the seasonal routine.

"Bronco-busting," the taming and training of wild horses to be used for riding, was as brutal as any activity involving man and beast; commonly termed "breaking," the aim was to conquer the horse physically and in spirit. Typically, there was no gradual gentling and training with an intent to establish mutual confidence between man and animal. Rather, full-grown horses were abruptly roped, thrown, saddled and bridled, and usually beaten into submission by "rough riders" whose aim was to "break the pony's heart on the first riding" (Rollins 1973:266). The object was to quickly impress upon the bronco the notion of human supremacy, so that it would leave a lasting impression. The absolute right to instill fear and inflict pain in order to establish man's mastery was unquestioned. Such a code,

based on the exigencies of environment and its exploitation, molded a
breed of man to its rigid demands. There was a process of selection, so
that a man whose sensibilities could not accept that code would never
advance past the tenderfoot stage.

Charlie Russell saw the early cowpuncher as "Old Maw Nature's
adopted son" (Adams 1967:49–50). The Cowboy's Prayer designates
him "partner of the wind and sun" (Schatz 1961:92). Such similies
are to some extent true, and cowboys thought of themselves as
working hand in hand with nature. Certainly in every phase of their
life and work they were dependent upon natural forces. In its early
days, cattle herding made use of the land in its natural state, though
of course not in the same balanced way as native animals like the
buffalo.

It is important here to distinguish the concept of "nature" from
that of "the wild." Nature is a more inclusive term, encompassing
the tame, or domesticated, as well as the untamed, or free. Nature,
then, is subject to manipulation by man. But the wild remains
outside the sphere of his influence and/or dominion. "Feral" denotes
those forms that have escaped from domestication and become wild,
but in a strict sense these would not be included in "the wild" because
they have been changed to some degree, at some time, by human
intervention, and are thus not in an original state.

Cowboys were in the forefront of the conquest that would ultimately destroy the primal condition of the Great Plains. Their
livelihood often depended upon the annihilation of competing native
wildlife. Although the cowboy at times saw beauty in nature, he was
usually less in harmony with it than he was lord of it. For he shared
the exploitative philosophy of the American frontier: nature was there
in abundance beyond measure—for any man's taking. Whatever was
destroyed along the way was of little concern. Wild species were
tolerated only so long as they did not potentially hinder the cattle
herder's economic pursuits, and death to all predators was the rule of
the range. "Coyotes, bears, timber-wolves, mountain-lions, and
stray dogs" were among those "marked for slaughter," according to
Rollins, and "every strange and unattended canine found wandering
on the range was prejudged to have had a murderous intent, and was
sentenced and executed at sight" (1973:39). As will be described in
detail in Chapter 9, intensity of hatred for such denizens of the wild
was often out of proportion to whatever harm they were actually
responsible for, an attitude which has carried over to a great extent to
modernday ranching. Cowboys, notwithstanding, liked to think of
farmers as the despoilers, and Charlie Russell expressed the ranch-

man's point of view when he lamented that "history and romance died when the plow turned the country grass upside down" (Adams 1967:46).

There is some resemblance between Plains Indians and early cowboys in their wild nomadic existence and their love of freedom. Regarding Indians, cowboy E.C. Abbott said he was "sure struck on their way of living" (Abbott & Smith 1939:18), and his friend Charlie Russell admitted "we were just white Indians anyway" (Abbott & Smith 1939:19). But beneath the superficial similarity, their ideologies differed. Generally, the Plains Indian was sustained in his world of nature by a belief which envisioned life as a circle encompassing all living creatures on a plane. Most cowboys, under the influence of the traditional Judaeo-Christian ethos, embraced a linear mode of thought, in which the world of living beings was a hierarchy, with man at the top, below God. Though his Bible-reading days may have been confined to childhood, a cowboy was nonetheless indoctrinated with the prevalent religious tenet of man's dominion over the rest of nature, and his daily life confirmed it. Some cowboy spokesmen, like Charlie Russell (1927) and Charles Goodnight (Haley 1936) had the artistic sensitivity to see God in the beauty of nature. The huge scale of the land made some see God in its grandeur. Rollins tells of a cowboy looking into the Grand Canyon of the Yellowstone and saying, "God dug that there hole in anger and painted it in joy" (1973:69). Abbott though, said 90% of his fellow cowpunchers were infidels. He related this to the life they led, coming in contact with nature and realizing that praying for aid did not bring results. "You could pray all you damn pleased, but it wouldn't get you water where there wasn't water" (Abbott & Smith 1939:33).

The cowboy, I suggest, came to find self-identity through being constantly at war with that portion of his universe which can be conceptualized as "the wild." His resultant attitude was that of looking upon it as "the enemy," and this frame of reference has been handed down in large measure to his ranching descendants. Yet the cowboy would not have desired all of the wild realm to vanish, were this possible, because he often praised it. He must have found satisfaction in the act of conquering, and the very process of opposing the wild became a part of his being and his way of life. At the same time, for example, that a cowhand might extoll the life in which the coyote's howl may be heard nightly, he would kill in a moment any coyote in sight. Not only was there the willingness, which could be conceived of as arising out of necessity, to destroy any part of the wild that did not fit his scheme, but beyond this, there came to be an active desire, as a force in itself, to do so. A contrast helps to elucidate the aggressive attitude of the cattle frontier toward the wild. The Sioux Chief Standing Bear expressed the different concept of his Great Plains native people this way:

> We did not think of the great open plains, the beautiful rolling hills, and winding streams with tangled growth, as "wild." Only to the white man was nature a "wilderness" and only to him was the land "infested" with "wild" animals and "savage" people. To us it was tame. Earth was bountiful and we were surrounded with the blessings of the Great Mystery. Not until the Hairy man from the east came and with brutal frenzy heaped injustices upon us and the families we loved was it "wild" for us. When the very animals of the forest began fleeing from his approach, then it was that for us the "Wild West" began.
>
> (1933:xix)

Although the cowboy figure looms large in American consciousness, there is no specific cowboy, historic or legendary, who generally personifies the role. Rather, the image is composite; this may be related to the fact that his environment and the work itself determined him, so that his identity merges into his vocation. It appears to be more the way of life than the man that comprises our concept. Abbott called cowpunchers "the most independent people on earth" (Abbott & Smith 1939:248). Individualism is the one word most closely associated with the cowboy, and, after analysis, I believe that what is usually meant by this term is individualism in relation to the rest of the world. It refers to the idea of his being outside the constraints of the wider, more "conventional" society. This sense of personal freedom, then, is one important factor in explaining the strong and almost universal appeal of the cowboy image. Related internally to his own cowboy group, however, he seems to have been too much in conformity with it to be considered a true individualist.

It is a recurring pattern among pastoralists to experience, at least for certain periods of time, a nomadic life apart from the larger social order, in which they do not conform to its demands, and establish a separate order of their own. In Paul Riesman's ethnography of the pastoral Fulani of Africa, for example, he described an interval characterized by a spirit of reckless joy and freedom for the young male herders (1977:156–160). This occurred when they departed from the pressures of their regular social community for a sojourn with their cattle in a distant pasture. This experience in the "bush" was one of pleasure in the company of their peers and of extreme delight in closeness to their cattle, which "embody the highest values

of Fulani society." During this time of transhumance the herdsmen
live only on milk, which is consumed with an air of revelry, and
drinking-water in which cattle have wallowed, urinated, and defe-
cated. They must keep watch over the animals twenty-four hours a
day, making their own needs secondary, and all their movements
must be determined by the needs of the cattle. Riesman's insight is
that by thus submitting to the cattle, which are outside human
society, the Fulani herdsman thereby liberates himself from the
influence of that society (though, due to the high value his culture
attaches to cattle, he is still well-regarded for his action). The
transhumant interval in the bush, away from women and older
people, has come to stand for a type of freedom, and the opposition
bush/village plays a major role in daily life (Riesman 1977:158). This
is a subject to which I will return in Chapter 9.

American cowboy society was a distinct group to which individuals belonged by virtue of certain prerequisites. Disdainful of routine,
members of this group rebelled against the work pattern of the
civilized, industrialized world they left behind. In wishing to be "no
slave to whistle, clock, or bell" (Schatz 1961:92), they could also free
themselves from the past, for in cowboy society all that mattered was
one's ability to adapt and succeed in the rugged work itself. No other
credentials were required—or asked for. Curiosity about a fellow's
history was taboo; he may have come West because of a ruined
reputation or "because there was a longer distance between sheriffs"
(Adams 1967:15), but that was considered his own business. Even
asking his last name might meet with disapproval and advice from an
old cowhand that the man in question "likely gave a first-class funeral
to the rest of his names, and I wouldn't ask him for no resurrections"
(Rollins 1973:64). Such a man could be a proficient cowpuncher, and
that was the important thing. Wilderness democracy was being
forged through the demands of a harsh environment—suggesting the
terms of Turner's frontier thesis.

One exception to this cowboy nonchalance about a man's past
might be his attitude toward long hair. For a man with a "load of hay
on his skull" could be covering up a past record of horse stealing—a
crime that could not be tolerated on the range. According to one
custom, a horse thief who was not hanged was banished after the
infliction of loss of the upper halves of his ears as a distinguishing
mark. Of course, a long-haired cowpoke could merely be a bluffer
who wanted to be considered "tough and wild" (Rollins 1973:145).

For the typical cowboy, the appeal of nomadic life was strong and
undeniable. He neither knew much about nor desired to follow any

other calling. Andy Adams said "I took to the range as a preacher's son takes to vice," admitting that "the vagabond temperament of the range I easily assimilated" (1903:7). At the age of three Charlie Siringo was already developing his roping skill by lassoing crabs on the Texas shore (1950:8). And E.C. Abbott recalled "I was with Texas cowpunchers from the time I was eleven years old. And then my father expected to make a farmer of me after that! It couldn't be done" (Abbott & Smith 1939:34).

It was a prime requirement that a cowboy must endure the rigors and privations inherent in his occupation without complaint. Once begun, gripes about the ever-present hardships would have been contagious, obsessive, and would have made the work impossible by crippling the social cohesion upon which its success depended. So it was axiomatic that "there ain't much paw and beller to a cowboy" (Adams 1967:5). In order to reinforce this important characteristic of stoicism, cowboys were careful not to express sympathy toward one another. Thus each individual could help preserve the cheerful exterior necessary for a smoothly functioning unit. Typically, a cowhand might say to his fellow who was about to mount a notorious bucking horse: "you want me to throw your overcoat up? It'll be cold up there" (Adams 1961:41).

Cowboying was synonymous with youth, the average hand being in his early twenties. It was a society of white Anglo-Saxon domination, in which Mexican and black cowboys were hired but were often discriminated against, and were not generally promoted to foremen. Indians were employed, but rarely did a trail boss or rancher agree with the frontier cattleman who once told General Brisbin that "Indian herders were the best in the world" (Savage 1975:94). Most cowboys looked upon Indians as part of the wild, and categorized them with elements that must be cleared away in the taming or civilizing process. Plains Indian skills may have originally laid the groundwork for an understanding by early white pioneers on how to survive the harshness of the Great Plains, but the native tribes had been virtually driven from the prairies before the heyday of the cattle range. Ironically, their signals had remained as the most practical means of communication on the trail.

Cowboys were "a bunch of brothers" (Abbott & Smith 1939:249) who generally felt more comfortable with each other than with outsiders. There was fierce loyalty between individuals of a particular outfit, and each made great efforts to regulate his behavior in such a way as to avoid the criticism of his fellow-cowpunchers. This peer pressure resulted in conformity within a hard-working and unified group, whose members would do just about anything to prove their outfit was the best on earth. Their shared labor and the common enemy of a hostile environment bound them together, even to the point that their nursing of each other in illness was "faithful and untiring, . . . for a dangerous life tends to make men womanly, . . . though in no wise ladylike" (Rollins 1973:68). Evidently the men could assume a nurturing role when isolated. Their small society became complete in filling almost every need.

Initiation into the cowboy brotherhood was stringent, however, as testing rites may be in any society. Constant proving and re-proving of one's manhood were required, and if nature and the arduous work did not offer enough tests, the cowhands themselves provided more. A tenderfoot, or "pilgrim," received rough treatment, and had to show that he could take it cheerfully in order to gain group acceptance. Pranks ranged from verbal hazings through being given the wildest bronco to ride or having sand added to one's food, to being sentenced to a beating with a pair of chaps by a kangaroo court. Making a fool of the newcomer was the object. Such customs helped maintain the endurance necessary for a rough life. Thus harshness from within as well as from without eliminated all but the fit, a functional process, since a weakling or coward who could never survive the rigors of a cattle drive or roundup was quickly eliminated. It was common for a cowboy to keep riding with broken ribs or even more severe injuries, or to stay in the saddle all night without complaint; and such feats were tacitly admired. The survival of a way of life depended upon the high value placed on individual toughness.

Cowboy sources (see especially Freeman 1959:549) include in the list of those who were weeded out not only the weakling, but also the visionary, thus underlining an important rule of cowboydom—a man must be a pragmatist. Bookishness, or the hint of it, was deplored. Mock punishments were meted out for a cowhand who used big words. J. Frank Dobie refers to cowboys as "bookless and booted" (Siringo 1950:xxii). Most cowboy writings denigrate formal schooling and credit nature as their teacher. Presentday ranch hands indicated to me that they continue in this tradition, and Bennett's study of cattle ranching in the northern Great Plains (1969) revealed the same ethos. Old-time cowboy E.C. Abbott felt that his education had been an actual disadvantage to cowpunching, and took pride in the fact that he and his fellows "didn't know a thing in the world except cow" (Abbott & Smith 1939:163). Often, when they were not busy telling tall tales or "talking horse," ranch cowboys would recite from memory the contents labels of canned goods. The usual reading matter was mail-order catalogues, though Rollins tells of one cowhand who delved into a bit of Shakespeare and praised it as being "the real stuff," adding "he's the only poet I ever seen what was fed on raw meat" (1973:158). Generally cowboys were involved with concrete matters; they were not prone to be interested in the abstract or philosophical. No doubt this was due to the kind of man attracted to being a cowboy and to the effects of the rough life which demanded practicality for survival. It is probable that the land itself, with its endless and awesome vistas, might have had some influence as well, leading them to turn to nature and not to "culture" (in the sense of aesthetic pursuits).

Men in the cowboy fellowship seem to have been, to an unusual degree, absorbed in their work. It was not merely a "job" but a way of life and they were willing to follow their trail boss or foreman through hell without complaint. The task of guarding their outfit's valuable and mobile property was regarded with such seriousness that a cowhand would give his life for it if necessary. Writing about the frontier in 1883, Colonel R.I. Dodge observed that "for fidelity to duty, for promptness and vigor of action, for resources in difficulty, and unshakable courage in danger, the cowboy has no superior among men." But he goes on to describe the cowboy's propensity for the "most ignoble of all vices": that of becoming "the most reckless of all the reckless desperadoes" whenever he rode into a frontier cowtown such as Abilene (1883:611).

No man became wealthy from his labors as a cowboy, and it was typical to have a live-for-today philosophy. With no family responsibilities to bind them, cowpunchers could be prodigal. When they rode raucously into one of the infamous frontier cowtowns, they let off steam and blew their money. Most would drink, gamble, visit brothels, and dance. All would eat lavishly, hoping for delicacies such as oysters, and many would get outfitted with a fresh set of clothes. A new saddle, costing far more than a horse, might be bought. At a rate of pay ranging from twenty to forty dollars a month, few left town with much money in their pockets. Some might have to ride away fast, if there had been a fight. Gun duels were probably more frequent than fist fights, which Abbott says were considered by cowhands to be "nigger stuff," beneath their dignity (Abbott & Smith 1939:247). Andy Adams has described the loyalty among trailhands whereby a culprit's outfit would rally to support him when he had to flee from the vengeance that might follow a violent episode (1903:344–346). Traditionally cowboys have delighted in mischief and have associated it with masculinity (McMurtry 1968:158).

Strangers meeting an outfit on the trail or range could expect hospitality, as is often the custom in dispersed pastoral societies, where isolation might be dangerous and help freely given could generate future reciprocity. The classic figure of the lone cowboy represents only a portion of the herdsman's total existence, for the very landscape itself led men to rely on one another and fostered periodic cooperation. On the trail, nightly gatherings around the campfire became a community ritual, preserving group solidarity. Talk must have centered not only on their domestic horses and cattle, but on incidents in which there had been confrontations with the wild and the untamed wilderness that was all about them. Extremes of weather like lightning and hail may have been experienced, a pack of wolves or a bear might have been seen or a few stragglers from a remnant bison herd; a trail-hand might have encountered Indians. Tales often dealt with such hazards of wild nature as quicksand or tornadoes, maulings by grizzly bears, narrow escapes from mountain lions, and attacks upon themselves or their stock by wolves or coyotes. Perceptions of these wild elements of the environment were of utmost importance in their daily lives as herdsmen, and their virtually unanimous categorization of them as enemies stimulated them to make these dangers the subjects of many stories involving conflict and the overcoming of fear. Circled close to the fire, within the familiar safety of their group, and with watchful night-herders on duty nearby, it was appropriate to bring out in the open the dangers of their environment which they would veil with braggart humor and tinge with fantasy. For theirs was a capricious land and the cowhands were mindful of the wily predators that lurked somewhere beyond the domesticated realm of which they and their sleeping beasts partook.

Occasionally, tales might center on love, but usually it was a love that had proven untrue or a sweetheart the cowboy had left in order to follow his calling. Women were almost entirely excluded from the world of the cowboy. "Decent" ones, alluded to earlier as comprising one of the cowpuncher's only two fears, were indeed a threat, since marriage inevitably meant leaving the wild free life of a herder to settle down. Believing that "when a man gets into a woman's loop he's as helpless as a dummy with his hands cut off" (Adams 1967:11), eligible women were best avoided. Like all nomads, cowboys looked down on the idea of life in a permanent abode. Women on the trail were considered to be "as useless as a fifth wheel" (Dobie 1969:107).

When Emerson Hough wrote a story of the cattle-driving era, *North of 36*, and included a heroine on the trail, all hell broke loose from cowboy critics. Abbott declared that "the appearance of any such woman in pants would surely have made the cowboys stampede to the bush" (Abbott & Smith 1939:7). So-called "good women" were kept at a distance with the remote respect of exaggerated chivalry and a feeling on the part of cowboys that they were not worthy of associating with such women. The cowhands' preference for the company of men and horses rested on their adaptation to a life of adventure and rough manners which they felt a marriageable girl could not share. In his high evaluation of a life of action, a cowboy relegated the realm of the mind and spirit to the feminine world, and this disparity left little room for common ground between the sexes.

On the frontier women came to be generally regarded as a "taming" or civilizing influence. This concept is familiar as a theme in many "Western" stories and films, and indeed has been important in cattle country from its earliest days. It has retained this prominence down through the present time, as confirmed by data from field work with ranch people. Bennett, also working in the Great Plains, observed as I did, that women in ranch families are likely to obtain more education than their male counterparts, speak and dress at a more sophisticated level, and acquire skills and interests more associated with "town" life. Bennett concluded that women could be "a quiet but important force for social and economic change" in Plains ranch life (1969:188). Indeed this is generally corroborated by historians of the American West, by whom women have been credited with being the innovators, the bringers of "culture" (in the sense of music, literature, and the like), as well as the "civilizers." This is in distinction to European societies, for example, in which men are considered to have been the cultural innovators.

Because women were irrelevant to the cowboys' exclusive domain of their cattle herds, male society was idealized. Masculinity came to be associated with the power and dominance exerted in that sphere. The herders developed their own customs and manners in response to their environment and occupation, and these made them more comfortable with their horses and comrades than with women.

In order to preserve this way of life, sex roles had to be kept separate and strongly opposed, a characteristic of many pastoral societies (Goldschmidt 1965:405). If they ever did love a woman, cowhands agreed it would be one "what's all over goldurned fluffs" (Rollins 1973:67). Upon meeting a "masculine-mannered woman" the cowboy response would be "For God's sake, woman, why can't you let us look up to you?" It was believed that "You can never trust women, fleas, nor tenderfoots. Marriage is as risky as braidin' a mule's tail" (Adams 1967:12). In cowboy autobiographies and in the hundreds of life sketches collected in the *Trail Drivers of Texas* (Hunter 1963), it is evident that most cowpunchers never married. Very few wed before they became ranchers themselves. Even after the trail days, unmarried cowboys were preferred for range employment.

One of the most notable traits of the cowboy was his speech. Distinctive and laconic, it found expression through the terminology of the herders' environment—the animals, the land, and the work. Probably the huge silent expanses in which the cowboy was immersed and his constant association with "critters" to which he often spoke but who could not reply diminished any tendencies toward loquaciousness. His language had another ingredient, as much a part of the cowboy as his big-brimmed hat, and that was humor. No doubt it would have been difficult to have withstood his life of violent action and hardship without this element. Humor became the cowboy's standard reaction to the trials of life. It was the best solution for many trail and range troubles, and "solved more problems than the six-gun" (Adams 1968:70). It could raise morale in the bleakest of situations and interrupt a progression of events which might lead to a fight. As an example, one of the worst vicissitudes for the cowboy was the notorious Great Plains weather. After one bitter winter that gave way to furnace-like heat, a cowhand was observed addressing himself to the sun: "Where the hell were you last January?" (Adams 1968:10).

Time spent alone during his long rides, lack of concern with the details of the civilized world, and membership in a bookless society gave opportunity for his thoughts to crystallize into his own original terse and earthy similes. He might describe someone as "helpless as a frozen snake" (Adams 1968:17), or say an ugly woman "kinda looked like she was weaned on a pickle" (Adams 1968:26). Being "quicker of tongue than of trigger" a cowboy could ward off melancholy with sharp humor. "How deep do you reckon this snow is?" one cowboy asked, and the reply was "What the hell difference does it make? You can't see nothin' but the top of it nohow" (Adams 1968:12). Rather than complain of sickness a stoic cowhand would say: "Pod'ner, I shore got one of them headaches that's built for a hoss and I got a taste in my mouth like I'd had supper with a coyote" (Adams 1968:16). To censure a man directly for cruelty to a horse might mean a fight. But a rider who brutally jerked his horse's mouth until it was bloody reportedly stopped this behavior for good when asked "If you want to split him, why don't you do it with an axe?" (Adams 1968:8). Through jokes, Easterners and outsiders could be belittled, and jargon could be used to "keep tenderfoots guessing." Tensions that were bound to grow up between men so closely confined in constant association could often be eased by laughter.

Humor as a mechanism for diverting aggression and hostility has received attention from anthropologists, particularly functionalists such as Radcliffe-Brown (1965:90–104). Many cultures have special joking relationships with certain classes of people which act as social buffers to compensate for the deference with which other categories of persons must be treated. Jokes are an effective way to keep a person's behavior in order without unduly offending him, as in the above case of the cowboy's cruelty to his horse. Anthropologist E.S. Bowen gives insights from her African experience which might apply to the cowboy: "In an environment in which tragedy is genuine and frequent, laughter is essential to sanity." The people she studied were "weather-beaten by their constant exposure to disease and famine. Unable to escape . . . they admired those who were able to jest under it" (1964:295-296).

In addition to being adept humorists, cowboys were proficient singers. This, too, was related to the needs of their life and work. The main practical use of singing was its effect of quieting the cattle at night; it also helped drown out sounds that could cause a stampede. Two cowboys riding back from a stampede, one on each side of a herd, would often sing so their partner would know their position. If the sound stopped, the other knew something was wrong and would attempt to come to his aid quickly. Many sources attest to the fact that the animals themselves enjoyed the sound of music. For the cowboys, singing provided needed relaxation after their day's work; it also kept them awake when on night herd duty.

Cowboy songs express ideas and thoughts that the men did not openly phrase in speech. Cowpunchers characteristically kept their feelings hidden. In the words of the self-composed or often-repeated songs, however, their mental preoccupations are often revealed. Cowboy ballads (Larkin 1931; Sackett 1967; Thorpe 1966; White 1975), unlike some other types of work songs, are virtually always concerned with the vocation itself, and show the cowboy's absorption with his environment and tasks, as typified by "They feed in the coulies, they water in the draw" (Sackett 1967:41). Some, like "Git Along Little Dogies" (Larkin 1931:96), were sung while on the move and echo the rhythm of a horse's gait. Singing relieved the monotony of the cowhand's work, and must have lessened the loneliness of his long hours of solitude. Singing the lines "The cowboy's life is a dreary, dreary life. He's driven through heat and cold" (Larkin 1931:40–41) gave vent to feelings about the harsh plains better than tabooed complaints about extremes of weather. And good-natured chanting of the words to "The Old Chisholm Trail":

> No chaps, no slicker and it's pouring down rain
> I vow I'll never night-herd again.
>
> Oh, it's bacon and beans most every day
> I'd as soon be eating this prairie hay.
>
> (Sackett 1967:15)

was more acceptable than grumbling about climate and food. In "Git Along Little Dogies", telling the cattle "It's your misfortune and none of my own" (White 1975:16) reveals a cowboy's feeling of superiority over his herd and delineates the significant difference in his way of viewing cows and horses. Even death will not detach him from his horse; in the song "I Ride An Old Paint" he asks that when he dies his comrades

> Tie my bones to his back, and turn our faces west;
> We'll ride the prairies that we love the best.
>
> (Sackett 1967:70)

In "I'm a Poor Lonesome Cowboy" the cowhand gives expression to his plight as an exiled orphan with no true family to give him help and affection, with the somberly repetitive refrains:

> I don't have a father . . .
> I don't have a mother . . .
> I don't have a sweetheart . . .
>
> I'm a poor lonesome cowboy
> And a long way from home.
>
> (Sackett 1967:46)

Fear of death, the wild, and longing for the old familiar circle of domesticity that he has rejected, come across in the rhythm and words of his favorite musical lament, "The Dying Cowboy":

> Bury me not on the lone prairie
> Where the coyotes howl and wind blows free.

rather,

> I wish to be laid where my mother's tears
> And my sister's too can mingle there.
>
> (Sackett 1967:48–49)

Seldom did the subject turn from the male world of comrades, dogies, and ponies to that of sweethearts, but when it did, such ballads usually told of leaving them. In "The Colorado Trail" the woman described is on a pedestal, unavailable to the sad cowpoke who remembers her

> Eyes like the morning star,
> Cheek like a rose,

and he asks the forces of nature in which he has immersed himself to mourn his loss:

> Weep, all ye little rains,
> Wail, winds, wail.

(Sackett 1967:62)

"The Trail to Mexico" tells of the sadness of a cowboy who lost his love to another when he left her to "follow my herd to Mexico"; of his dismay he sings:

> Oh, curse your gold and your silver too,
> And curse the girl who can't prove true.

(Sackett 1967:74)

"The Cowboy's Heaven" depicts human after-life in terms of a Great Roundup (Larkin 1931:100–102). In the familiar idiom of dogies, mavericks, and stampedes, the song says that a cowboy will go to heaven if he behaves well. If not, he'll be "cut in with the rusties"— the cattle that are not good for anything but to be shot for their hides.

In the classic "Goodbye, Old Paint," the cowboy is leaving Cheyenne, Wyoming, and must part with his best friend, a paint horse who is too old to go with him. The cowboy is also saying farewell to his sweetheart, Polly, who asks him to sit with her while his horse eats some hay. But he answers

> My horses aren't hungry, they won't eat your hay;
> My wagon is loaded and rolling away.

> My foot's in the stirrup, my bridle's in my hand;
> So fare thee well, Polly, my horses won't stand.

(Sackett 1967:70)

His final expression of regret

> Goodbye, Old Paint, I'm off for Montan'

is reserved for the animal, implying that he feels more sadness at leaving his horse than his sweetheart. This song was often sung after the last dance, on the rare occasions when cowboys attended such an event, so that it echoed after them as they rode away to their ranch or trail camp. It set the tone, perhaps, for their return to the open spaces and the work they were adapted to—the raw, rough, nomadic life of action, of male camaraderie and mounted mastery, and of freedom from domesticity.

Being remote from towns for the greater share of their working lives, cowboys relied upon the materials at hand—the elements of their work and environment—for their diversions. And, as Rollins points out, these men, "from their virile life, liked virile playthings" (1973:155). For amusement, two unbroken broncos, two steers, or a bronco and a cow might be harnessed to a wagon in which the carousing cowboys attempted to ride. Though in quieter moments they liked to play cards and gamble, betting was more lively when it involved a mortal combat between two captive tarantulas or a match between a king snake and their hated common enemy, the rattler. The cowboys' most popular recreations always involved living creatures, wild or tame, and the element of contest. On ranches they would often "wrastle down" calves or colts for fun. They disliked any form of running games, preferring to stay mounted for recreation as they did for work. Sometimes they simply raced their horses for sport, or rode out on the plains to rope antelope, jack rabbits, or, indeed, any type of animal, for it was a truism of range life that a cowboy would use his lariat on "anything that moved." If a bear could be roped and dragged alive back to camp, the creature might be pitted against a bull in a fierce battle to provide amusement. Such events were probably not held frequently on the Plains, since bears are indigenous to higher country, but they did occur when one could be caught. On ranches located in California, however, where the California grizzly bear (now extinct) was once common, cowboys made great sport of such bull and bear contests. Eventually these matches became spectacles involving pageantry, and were held in amphitheaters (Haynes & Haynes 1967:75–87).

Such diversions reflected the cowboy's way of life, and helped to express the attitudes and feelings that gave him a place in his particular sphere. For his work always put him in certain relationships to living things—domestic creatures, as well as the undomesticated, the land, and those portions of nature that fell within his realm as the tame, and outside of his realm as the wild. His livelihood depended upon a universe ordered in this way, and his conceptual world was shaped by it.

After the trail-driving era had been supplanted by the open range cattle industry in the West, a new and highly significant phenomenon, necessitated by the unfenced range, was developed by the cattle industry. This was a seasonal occurrence known as the roundup, which was to become not only the culminating economic process of ranching, but also, for a time, the central social event of cattle country as well.

The roundup entailed a massive gathering up and sorting out of cattle within a certain specified region of the range, so that each man could make legal claim to his mobile property. Its primary purpose was not only to allow each cattleman to establish or reestablish ownership of his animals, but also to determine their exact numbers and condition so that he could reckon up his financial gains or losses. The roundup grew out of the earlier custom of neighboring stockmen getting together informally to look over each other's herds for strays. From such beginnings it developed into a highly organized, thorough, and systematic affair, a cooperative enterprise with the official sanction of the cattle-ranching community.

At roundup time, cowboys rode over huge sections of rangeland in ever-narrowing circles, searching for cattle and driving them to a central area where they were identified and claimed. Those bearing no marks of ownership were then publicly branded according to rigid specifications designed to avoid mistakes and prevent dishonesty. Ordinarily there were two roundups each year: one in the spring for the branding of the new calf crop; and one in the fall for the purpose of gathering beef cattle for shipment to market and for the branding of late or previously overlooked calves. At either time animals might be "cut out" (separated from the herd) for sale. Any medical procedures which were carried out were done at roundup time, as was the castration surgery already referred to. Presentday ranchers have told me that after the testicles are removed from the cattle, they often spear them with a wire, roast them in the branding fire, and eat them on the spot. The alternative is to gather up the day's harvest and take it back to town, where someone puts on a community dinner comprised of these freshly cut sexual organs which have been fried in deep fat. They are known as "calf fries," and are commonly served in Western restaurants under the name of "mountain oysters."

The roundup was a system instituted for mutual protective action, planned and regulated by set rules. All ranchers with an interest in the particular region participated, and were represented by officials who presided to insure order and fairness, and "tally" men who kept records. Though it is claimed that branding was a necessary procedure on the unfenced cattle range, it is noteworthy that the practice was continued after the West was fenced, and into the present day. In the early days in Texas brands covered the entire side of the cow. This practice was altered only because of the complaints of leather manufacturers, who did not want the hides damaged to that extent (Rollins 1973:218). But the brands were made smaller, not discontinued. Brands have been called "the heraldry of the range," thereby likened to the adoption of a coat-of-arms, family crest, or totem (Boorstin 1974:22), and ranches are often named for the particular configurations that distinguish their stock. Brands serve to establish ownership, but, beyond this, such marking and mutilation represent what may be an almost universal association between the establishment of mastery and the infliction of pain upon the conquered. In a herder's world, sharp differentiation of the tame from the wild is a prime concern; those of the domesticated realm must be set apart. The patterns seared and cut into their flesh signify human control and domination, and clearly demonstrate that the marked animals have undergone the nature-to-culture transformation.

Just as the nightly campfire gatherings of the trail drives had offered an opportunity for common forms of expression and sociability, so now the range roundup became a kind of ritual—the harvest festival for cattlemen. It was not only the time and place for hard work, but also for reunion with friends and associates, and a time for exchanging news and stories. Thus it served to solidify the larger community by means of shared interests, attitudes, and customs. It was the occasion for members of particular outfits to assert their individual rights, and yet at the same time reaffirm their sense of being a part of the cattle kingdom. The skills of the cowboys, of course, made the mechanics of the roundup possible, and so it was natural that these should be prominently demonstrated at such times. With a spirit of competition and a flair for display, cowboys would race their horses, and, after taking wagers, stage contests to settle the question as to which one of them could ride the meanest bronc for the longest time or rope a calf or steer the fastest. Sometimes they had held such informal tests at home; when riders on one ranch heard there was a bronc at a neighboring outfit that "couldn't be rode" they would make the trip over to try to prove that it could be done. At the roundup, though, there was a greater opportunity for these trials, and more people to watch and encourage them.

One of the earliest accounts of cowboy sports at a roundup comes from a letter written by an observer who noted that

Early cowboy contests involving a "bronc that couldn't be rode" evolved into the saddle bronc event of modern rodeo.   (*Robert Ridley Photo*)

> This round-up time is a great time for the cowhands, a Donneybrook fair
> it is, indeed. They contest with each other for the best roping and
> throwing and there are horse races and whiskey and wines. At night in
> the clear moonlight there is much dancing in the streets.
>
> (Westermeier 1955:344)

It was in this way that cowboy roping and riding matches developed
and became popular—the utilitarian skills of the roundup becoming
intensified as the sport of cattle country. The contests later became
known as "rodeo," from the Spanish word "rodear," which means "to
encircle or surround," and had come to denote a roundup. After the
open range cattle industry gave way to fenced ranching, the cowboy
skills of the roundup came to be practiced—and exhibited—for their
own sake.

Local roping and riding matches developed out of a spirit of
competition between cowboys of one outfit or between those of rival
outfits. Onlookers cheered for their favorites, and were likely to back
their preferences with bets. Soon these small range contests grew to
regional proportions, attracted spectators, and were moved to towns,
central locations where more people could gather from the outlying
areas. The enthusiasm they inspired was a natural outgrowth of the
fact that in that day "men of the range talked, thought, and dreamed
cattle and horses" (Westermeier 1947:33) with the same obsessive-
ness that is observable in ranch country of the present time.

Several locales claim the honor of having staged the first rodeo.
One of the earliest to attract attention was a bronc-riding contest that
grew out of rivalry between neighboring outfits and which was held
at Deer Trail, Colorado, in 1869 (Vernam 1972:396). In 1872
Cheyenne, Wyoming, one of the most important centers for the
cattle industry, was the scene of an exhibition of Texas steer riding
and later bronc riding. And in the early 1880's several of the region's
ranches held a steer-roping contest on the main street of Pecos, Texas,
with the courthouse yard being used as a corral (Westermeier
1947:34–35). Even though admission charge, prizes, entry fees,
grandstands, and arenas were still in the future, tradition holds that
this was the first official rodeo. Prescott, Arizona, was the location of
a more highly organized contest in 1888, in which prizes were
awarded and admission charged. That city's claim that its show is the
"Grand-daddy of 'em All" rests on the fact that it is the oldest
continual annual rodeo in America, and awarded the earliest known
rodeo trophy. Montana was not far behind, with a cowboy competition for trophies and money held at the cattle town of Miles City in

1891, as an entertainment for the Montana Stock Growers' Association (Westermeier 1947:35).

By this time, rodeos were becoming public events, as each Western town tried to outdo the other by holding a bigger and better exhibition to dramatize the skills of its cowboys. From such beginnings rodeo grew steadily into a spectator sport, and was taken over by cities like Cheyenne, whose "Daddy of 'em All" Frontier Days was first held in 1897, and has continued as one of the country's largest and most impressive rodeos and as a festival of Western traditions. The other two of the sport's most prestigious shows started a short time later—the Pendleton Roundup in Oregon in 1911, and the Calgary Stampede in Alberta, Canada, in 1912. With the development and expansion of such large-scale celebrations, rodeo became a big business as well as a sport. In 1929 the managements of several leading rodeos formed the Rodeo Association of America (Robertson 1974:88). Official organization for contestants came in 1936, when a group of professional rodeo participants banded together to protect their interests. They called their first organization the Cowboys' Turtle Association, "because we were slow as turtles doin' somethin' like this" (P.R.C.A. Press Release 1978). The efforts of these men resulted in the formation of a governing body—renamed the Rodeo Cowboys Association in 1945 and the Professional Rodeo Cowboys Association in 1975—composed of contestants and former contestants, to regulate all aspects of the sport.

The origins of rodeo can be traced to the Wild West Show and to the special skills of the American cowboy. In describing the working cowboy I have emphasized some of the ways in which, as a unique type of pastoralist, his life and society were influenced by conditions on the Great Plains. Particular attention has been given to the cowboy's relationships to the domestic animals with which his life as a herder was so intimately involved, since it is from these associations that the spirit and action of rodeo are derived. In addition, the cowboy's attitude toward, and interaction with, the realm of the wild are especially important to the elucidation of concepts of the tame versus the wild, which, I suggest, are at the heart of rodeo.

This study of the cowboy, as a background for the analysis of rodeo, serves to make clear the complex of traits—toughness, endurance, individuality, masculinity, and the mastery of nature—that has been passed down to modernday ranchers of the Great Plains. It is essential to understand the character of the American cowboy and something of the cattle ranching life which forms his contemporary setting, in order to gain valid insight into rodeo—the inheritor of cowboy tradition and the sport of the ranching society. The next chapter, centering on rodeo and its way of life, emphasizes the parallels between rodeo participants and their counterparts, the working cowboys of trail and range.

4

RODEO AS THE INHERITOR OF COWBOY TRADITION AND ITS ASSOCIATION WITH RANCHING

> *In purely pastoral societies, where no crops at all are raised, and where society is wholly or partly nomadic, a number of traits have been identified as especially typical: emphasis on masculinity among the men, and a general cultural stress on the male role; a marked pattern of hospitality; ritual content suggesting the importance of mastery over animal species.*
>
> (Bennett 1969:333)

As THE PERPETUATOR of the contests which grew out of life on the cattle trail and range and received particular emphasis at the seasonal roundup, rodeo is also the direct inheritor of cowboy tradition and ethos. This remains true even though an increasing number of today's rodeo contestants are "athletes" who came to the sport from a rodeo school rather than from a ranching background. For they are the often-publicized exceptions, and in field studies I found that they conform to the rodeo group almost indistinguishably. Writing on this very subject, the editor of professional rodeo's official journal draws attention to the new young "city kids" who are becoming expert rodeo contenders; he believes "It's a healthy sign because those kids have adopted the Western tradition and attitude" (Searle 1976:3). The important thing I wish to stress is that overall there is an inextricable connection between the sport of rodeo and the cattle ranching industry.

Modernday ranching, as well as rodeo, reflects to a great degree its heritage from the beginnings of the range cattle industry—the era of the cowboy. It is essential to understand that generally throughout the West, and particularly in the Great Plains areas where my field work was carried out, the sport of rodeo is an integral part of the ranching way of life. The cattle ranching society considers itself the most essentially "Western" of any group, with the most direct historical roots traceable to the American frontier. The ranchers' intimate association with, and complete support of, the sport of rodeo is considered by them to be an expression not only of their central concerns with horses and cattle, but also of their regionalism and their devotion to the colorful pioneer past whose spirit they wish to preserve. Thus the rodeo, in its broadest sense, serves to "Keep the West Western" (a slogan used on rodeo posters), and in its more specific focus it provides continuity for, and revitalization of, the whole complex of ranch traits.

Without exception, all ranch informants revealed that rodeo is an important, even essential, part of the cattle industry. One man, when asked if all the ranchers in his area of Montana supported rodeo, said "Yes, of course, all real ranch people do"; he added, "though we may have a few phonies in this business, too." Ranchers' connections with rodeo ranged all the way from very direct and intense down to more tenuous, but they were always in some way evident. For example, many ranchers were, or had been in their youth, rodeo contestants. Almost all of them had at one time tried their luck in the sport. Some ranchers were also involved with the Cowboy Hall of Fame (which refers to rodeo, not working, cowboys) and were members of the Rodeo Historical Society, so that their viewpoints were composite, drawn from both spheres. Many ranch informants had sons or sons-in-law who were rodeo participants, and others were members of rodeo committees. Several were rodeo stock contractors as well as being in the ranching business. At the very least, they were spectators. Some ranchers indicated that lack of time prevented them from going to more than five or six rodeos a year, or from being an official for more than one annual local show. There were no ranch people who did not indicate their support for rodeo in some way, even if it was just to follow the news about the winners or to voice general enthusiasm for the sport. Conversely, the vast majority of rodeo participants were either ranchers themselves or came from ranching families. If they were not, they had usually worked on a ranch, or had some other livestock association—an uncle who raised horses, for example. Contestants who came from a city or other non-ranch background invariably said they would like to be ranchers or hoped to be in the future. In short, I never found a Great Plains rancher who had no interest in rodeo, or a rodeo participant who had no interest in ranching. The interconnection between the two was firmly established. And it is demonstrable in other ways as well. For example, "Hoof and Horn," the official publication of the P.R.C.A., calls itself "the Magazine of Ranch and Rodeo since 1931." Though the rest of its pages are ordinarily centered on the world of rodeo, the editorial page, "Hoofbeats," often contains discussions of the concerns and problems of the cattle industry, such as the price of beef, ranchers' profits, and the like. And the various cattlemen's journals generally include rodeo news.

Drawn as it is from the festive spirit of the trail cowtown and cattle range roundup, it is not surprising that rodeo has retained an atmosphere of celebration. With the larger shows usually set within a giant midway, often the central attraction of a state fair, rodeo is a carnival either literally or in atmosphere. And, though rodeo contestants always take their participation seriously, there is still time for sociability—for the reunions reminiscent of the roundup. Motor homes and trailers have replaced the cowboys' bedrolls and the trailside campfire, but modern rodeo nomads still gather together to hold song fests and various other meetings which serve to promote solidarity. These may be benefit picnics, association-sanctioned auctions, or church services sponsored by the Cowboy Chapter of the Fellowship of Christian Athletes. A city like Cheyenne during Frontier Days becomes the scene of general revelry and hell raising which recall the era of the "wild, wicked and woolly" cowtowns—Dodge City or Abilene. As though to express a general feeling of nostalgia for the lost frontier, there are gatherings in bars with much drinking and carousing; cowboy singers croon rodeo ballads, and patrons become embroiled in Western-style fist fights. At the Hitching Post in 1978, the star country-western singer, also a leading rodeo contestant, stopped briefly in the middle of his song to voice his regret at "a brawl going on down there that I'm not a part of." Downtown, a rodeo cowboy whooping it up might steal a pickup horse and ride it into a barroom.

Like that of the cattle herders from which its patterns were adopted, rodeo society is nomadic. Though no longer herders in the same sense, the contestants still follow where the stock goes, on a long trail that leads from show to show. The vast distances that serious contenders must travel mean that they are constantly enroute to their next booking. Their phrase for rodeoing, "going down the road," gives central emphasis to their nomadism. Family ties are loosened and marriages often strained to the breaking point by frequent and lengthy separations.

Each rodeo contestant, though, by virtue of the sport's absolutely fixed tradition, pays homage to the place he has declared to be his "hometown," though he may not have been there for years. This place of origin becomes very important in the structure of rodeo; without fail, whenever a contestant enters the arena it is announced in connection with his name. The announcer's procedure is to say, for example, "here is Donnie Smith, a cowboy from Billings, Montana, riding the bronc named Spaceship," or, "next comes the Sheridan, Wyoming cowboy, Billie Daniels, on the good bull, Cyanide." Reflecting upon this practice, I suggest that it serves as a mechanism for symbolically relating each contestant to the land, as the cowboy had been physically related to it. It seems especially appropriate that land, as the essential aspect of the cattle industry, and indeed the central element of the Western experience itself, be represented in the context of the sport which mirrors that experience. Thus each performance, even in a city arena, revitalizes the connecting link between man and land. In this way the cowboy still possesses his homeland, and is possessed by it.

Being a wanderer, the rodeo cowboy is yet tied to the land by the bond between his name and that of his hometown. Wherever he travels, this gives an individual stability to each member of a mobile group. In addition, I found that each can be cheered as a "hometown hero," remembered by his place of origin and representative of that place as he moves around the country. Thus, not only does he gain a sense of identity through his attachment to his area, but he also engenders a feeling of solidarity among those who share it. Pride in, and loyalty to, the various regions of the West are demonstrated, for example, in the opening ritual of many rodeo performances, in which several contestants ride around the arena behind the flag of their home state. As each state's contingency is announced, special attention is drawn to it, as "Here are the fine cowboys from New Mexico, Land of Enchantment," or "Here are our own riders from the great state of Montana, the Treasure State." At a specified time during each performance of Cheyenne Frontier Days the announcer mentions every state and the number of license plates from that state which have been counted in the parking lot. As this is done, people in the audience seem to experience a sense of identification with their state, and there is a great deal of shouting and cheering.

The rugged Western landscape which the states embody has always been linked with the hardihood it breeds in men. As the editor of "Hoof and Horn" phrased this:

> It's a fact that rodeo has always belonged to those of Western heritage and ranch toughness, born and bred on ranches and in rodeo arenas. Sort of

like the Nordic ski traditions which made those countries invincible for
so long.

(Searle 1976:3)

Undeniably, at the very heart of rodeo lies that spirit of toughness and
endurance that was forged in the cowboy by the harsh conditions of
the Great Plains. As the advertisement for a recent rodeo book claims
"there has never been a ritual celebration of man's courage, will, and
unconquerable spirit to match the American rodeo" (Hall 1976:back
cover). It continues to emphasize and reaffirm the physical and
mental courage which were demanded on the cattle trail and range,
qualities which remain highly valued in the ethos of today's ranching
population.

Hall states that

> from Charlie Siringo to Larry Mahan and the younger men on the circuit,
> the ingredients for a cowboy have remained the same. Rodeo has
> inherited all that the Old West had to offer—the hardship, the exaggera-
> tion. What was once a tough life is even tougher today. The cowboy is no
> ordinary man, he never was. And, true to that tradition, rodeo is no
> ordinary sport

(1976:11)

The extremely demanding nature of the contests, with the associated
risks of injury and death, attracts men who must be strong and
anxious to prove their physical prowess. Stoicism is a prime requisite,
and like the cowboys of old, rodeo participants avoid complaining. It
is not an infrequent occurence for one of them to break an ankle in the
chute and go on to finish his ride. Many compete with broken limbs
in casts or their entire chests taped because of fractured ribs. One
particularly hardy stock contractor with typical rodeo nonchalance
had to leave the arena early in one show because of a broken leg. He
was taken to the hospital where the leg was set, then returned to
reenter the arena, riding his horse with the leg in a cast. He was
greatly admired for this, and at subsequent rodeos announcers often
drew attention to the incident. A few months later I saw him riding
in the arena again, this time with his entire arm in a cast. At one
rodeo I was close enough to hear the impact of a flying hoof striking a
pickup man's head. He was knocked unconscious, yet returned to
ride a few minutes later. His associates joked with him about it
during the rest of the day.

When a contestant is hurt, he tries to walk out of the arena by
himself, and usually waves away any offered assistance. "I have a
dread of being packed out of there," many told me. Contestants often
raise objections to being put into the ambulance, and some refuse to

let doctors examine them when they are taken to the hospital. When the injury is severe and a man is placed on a stretcher in the ambulance, it is as though when the sound of the siren dies away the world closes in on him. For, though his comrades will later be solicitous, no further mention of him is made during the performance. In contrast, at a horse show, as in some other sports, a public announcement concerning the extent of a rider's injuries is made as soon as such news is available. Nor was there any publicity given to the death of a bareback bronc rider which occurred in the arena at Cheyenne in 1978. Occasionally a moment of silence will be set aside at a rodeo in memory of the contestants who died during the previous year; this is followed by a recital of the Cowboy's Prayer.

Ranch children are socialized into the tradition of toughness at an early age by parents and relatives who exalt its value and give them little sympathy. In one instance, for example, a small boy on a ride was kicked in the leg by the horse next to him. His older sister reacted immediately by hollering to him that it was his own fault. His mother rode over and said to the other rider "Never mind, he'll live through it; no problem," and told the rider not to worry about it and not to punish his horse. No one stopped to examine the child's leg until about an hour later when an older boy removed the young fellow's boot, revealing a large gash. This boy, a former rodeo contestant, told him that as long as he could wriggle his toes it wasn't broken, and related his own experience of once making an eight-second ride with a broken ankle.

Such attitudes are reinforced by a child's peers, who put a boy under constant threat of betraying weakness or fear. I observed a ten-year-old ranch boy who was hit by his father—unintentionally on this occasion. The father was astounded when the boy cried, and told him "I've seen times that you've been hit a lot harder than that by your friends without crying."

Following rigid custom, children on the youth rodeo circuit get their own riggings ready, and parents are taboo in the chute or contestants' area. When a child bucks off and appears to be hurt, the announcer tells the audience "He'll live; it's a long way from his heart," and repeats his comment "These kids are tough." Moving through the various divisions of rodeo which correlate increasing age with more difficult events, the young contestants learn from each other the complex of "toughness" traits associated with rodeo. They wire on their own spurs before they ride, chew and spit tobacco, and try to suffer pain and discomfort without complaint. By about eight years of age they are using their participation in a man's sport to

Youngsters learn to ride rough stock by beginning on steers or cows before progressing to tougher events on bulls and broncs.

(JJJ Photo)

90

RODEO

separate themselves physically and emotionally from the company of women and girls.

In addition to emphasizing cowboy toughness, rodeo embodies the element of risk which is an inherent part of the cattle-raising lifestyle. Here I am referring not just to the many dangers and the frequent injuries that are sustained by the participants, but to the fact that the sport itself is structured to include a gamble. The "luck of the draw" as mentioned previously, is central to virtually every contest in rodeo. Not even the most skilled contestant can hope to win without a good draw, and luck must be with a winner all the way. Many contestants try to court good fortune by means of wearing a certain color outfit, sticking a lucky feather in their hat brim, or fastening a piece of their bronc's mane to their belt loop. In the rodeo song "Daddy's Biggest Dream," a bronc rider wants to make his crippled father's dream come true by making a championship ride, and says

> He gave me the hatband from the tail of that old
>   bronc that broke him up
> And said that if I'd wear it every time I rode
>   that it would bring me luck;
> His superstition must be comin' true 'cause I
>   drew the rankest horse that's in the string,
> And here in Okie City with some luck I'll fill
>   my Daddys biggest dreams.

(Pack & Pack)

Putting one's hat on a bed is considered by cowboys to bring serious bad luck, and rodeo folks have adopted their belief in this act as an evil omen. Even those who said they were not really superstitious told me about terrible things that had happened to them and their families when they broke this taboo. A rodeo bullfighter at Cheyenne related that he once put his hat on the bed in the morning, and that same afternoon the bull hit and crippled him. Later in his career this man was injured on three or four occasions when his son went to the rodeo with him. The next time the boy said "you are going to get hurt if I go with you." He took him anyway, and the bullfighter got his head split open. He told me that the thing the boy remembers best about that day was the excitement of a ride in the brand new Cadillac that took his father to the hospital. Eating peanuts before one's ride is also said to bring bad luck; and the belief that a yellow shirt forebodes disaster for the wearer is so strong that I never saw one worn in any rodeo.

The paradox of the cowboy's attitude toward risk has been expressed this way:

He craved a special freedom; and once he had gained that freedom he was proud enough and jealous enough of it to guard it with his life one moment and reckless enough to turn right around and risk it in the most foolish way the next moment.

(Hall 1976:10)

The current saddle bronc champion says entering a rodeo is like "gambling on myself, by putting up my entry fee." Generally the pastoral way of life is noteworthy for its association with risk, and in his monograph on the Tibetan nomads, Robert Eckvall points out how uncertainty affects these herdsmen:

With acceptance of risk as the basic factor, the subsistence routine becomes a successive taking of chances, and when risk taking becomes a habit, the habit may well leave its mark on personality, thus giving to the nomadic pastoralist something of the character and outlook of the gambler. This may partially explain . . . his arrogant assurance in situations of disaster, for chance, that has gone against him, may well be with him next time.

(1968:91)

Risks of all types, as previously described, were part of a cowboy's daily life on the American Great Plains, and are also characteristic of ranching there today. In contemporary times, natural hazards in raising cattle are compounded by the capricious forces of supply and demand which influence the beef market and thus control the modern cowpuncher's livelihood. I heard a cattle-broker express the trickiness of today's livestock business by saying that he always felt "the next phone call may bring the golden pot at the end of the rainbow."

Rodeo folk, like the cowboys before them, are tightly knit into a distinctive society often called a "breed apart." Like their cowboy antecedents they comprise a group of generally young male associates who understand each other through a shared way of life and common values, attitudes, and aspirations. In the standard rodeos of the Great Plains area they are predominantly of white Anglo-Saxon descent, and their officially sanctioned religion is a form of born-again Christianity. This is a belief system which interprets the Bible literally and consequently grants to mankind undisputed dominion over the earth and its creatures. In discussing the religion of the contestants, a bareback bronc rider told me "If you're going to rodeo, you have to believe in God. You are taking risks, facing death every day, and you need to believe in God. If a man had a business job in a city, I could see where he might get away from it; then you could forget about it until your time comes."

Admittance to rodeo society demands that newcomers prove themselves worthy to be members by demonstrating toughness. Before being fully accepted they may expect to be initiated by hazing and rough pranks, and must show that they can "take it" good-naturedly. Rodeo men resemble working cowboy herders in sharing an inordinate pride in their calling and a disdain for all other occupations. Tee-shirts and signs displayed at rodeos proclaim "if you ain't a cowboy, you ain't worth shit," and the pervasive arrogance of the contestants, a common trait among pastoralists, confirms this attitude. A large share of their self-satisfaction is said to come from meeting the challenges provided by such a rough sport. In small ways, also, they remind themselves that they are specially set apart—"only cowboys are tough enough to dip snuff." They love the life of violence, action, adventure, and uncertainty, and look forward to the acclaim of the crowd if they perform well. They refer to rodeo as a way of life, "certainly no way to make a living!" As though of one accord, contestants told me "going to rodeos is in my blood; I'm hooked on it," and roping event participants declared "I'm a rope-a-holic." Their addiction may have started in childhood. Entering a youth rodeo is virtually a rite of passage for a ranch youngster. Little Britches contestants show great enthusiasm for the sport, and parents support them in it. Their children "rode before they could walk," parents told me, "and they are constantly roping; they rope anything that moves." As several mothers expressed it, "my kids eat, breathe, and sleep rodeo."

Echoing their counterparts, the cowboys who "didn't want to be caught on the blister end of a shovel" (Adams 1967:27), rodeo people value a way of life they perceive of as free, and share a dread of routine clock-oriented labor. Frequently a contestant would tell me he rodeoed because he was "too lazy to work and afraid to steal." McMurtry, in his highly critical essay on the sport, says cattlemen really believe "rodeo hands are lazy fuckups, men, essentially, who fear danger less than they hate work" (1974:17). He contrasts this view with that of rodeo's apologists who claim that contestants are "men of such largeness of spirit that death beneath the horns of a bull would be preferable to the loss of their freedom." Indeed freedom was mentioned often by participants as an attraction of rodeo life. A leading steer wrestler who had left government employment to go down the road expressed this feeling of independence: "When you rodeo you've got pretty much of a free rein on life and you're your own boss."

Their rodeo membership makes them part of a society with

considerable inward conformity. To a large extent rodeo folk talk, think, and act alike. Their lingo is distinct and not readily understood by outsiders. Many speak with a kind of standardized accent, a drawl influenced more than a little by Texas, where, after all, the American cattle industry began. Rodeo clothing standards call for longsleeved shirts, and they are now the accepted style in Western stores. Short-sleeved Western shirts are just not available except as an oddity for "dudes." A rancher told me "If you see a man wearing a short-sleeved shirt, you know he's not a real cowboy." The importance and degree of uniformity of Western dress in the ranching and rodeo society cannot be overemphasized. Fortunately, very early in my field work in both rodeo and ranching I realized wearing it was essential for acceptance. I have since learned that others have had similar experiences. A wildlife management official admitted he could accomplish nothing with the ranchers without wearing cowboy clothing. He also told me of a minister called to a church in range country who could win no influence with, or respect from, his congregation until he adopted Western dress and hauled a horse trailer behind a pickup. Professional rodeos require that even men and women representing the media wear long-sleeved shirts, boots, and a Western hat to the shows. Many of them consider this a hardship in the summer heat, burdened as they are with cameras and headsets. At the Calgary Stampede even the spectators were urged to conform. When I walked through the carnival to reach the rodeo grounds on a specific day, I was presented with a prize by an official who said "thank you for dressing Western." It is traditional that during the "Heldorado Days" rodeo in Las Vegas, Nevada, visitors who are not in cowboy garb are seized by city officials and placed in "jails" resembling circus wagons until they pay a fine for their release.

Most, though not all, regular rodeo contestants have close-cropped hair, and ranchers are noted for conformity in this. A few years back, during the heyday of the hippie, cattlemen were known to beat up any long-haired males they found, or drive them far from town and abandon them. Rodeo people generally place great stress on this "square" or old-time American image, and there is a rodeo song lamenting the loss of the "clean-cut denim style" and the fact that some contestants now "cover their ears with hair," and "even have a moustache or goatee." The chorus reflects

> This new breed look of theirs don't
> Make 'em look nothing like a man.
> Don't tell me the old cowboy look is

Gonna die out for good.
I wish I knew what we could do
To get 'em lookin' back like they should.

(LeDoux)

One of rodeo's superstars tells the story of what happened to him when he first began to let his hair grow longer. One night he was grabbed in his hotel room by two strong-armed rodeo men, while a third, a champion bull rider, came at him with a knife. Fearing the worst, he was relieved to hear their explanation that if he was going to grow long hair he would have to wear short pants to go with it. With that, they proceeded to cut off his Levis at the knee! Today informants still insist that he would not get away with his hippie tendencies were it not for his remarkable skill in the sport. A Professional Rodeo Cowboys Association official recently told me that longer haired contestants still do not gain acceptance "unless it's one of our own." By this he meant one from the inner circle of current top professional competitors who was cooperative with the association.

Male-bonded rodeo society has its own private jokes and traditions, and participants often speak of "one of ours" in referring to members. When asked about the arena death of a bronc rider at Cheyenne, a Professional Rodeo Cowboys Association official said "Yes, we lost one," and even though he had not been personally acquainted with the man, he choked up so that he was unable to talk further about it. The poster announcing the rodeo cowboy benefit picnic and auction held during the Calgary Stampede urged the men to "come and support your own." At this affair there was food, drink, and a general spirit of camaraderie. All seemed to be united in the common cause of raising money to help their fellow participants. Recipients were men with injuries who needed funds for medical purposes, or who were "down on their luck." A hat was passed for contributions to help in replacing some valuable barrel racers' horses which had been destroyed in a fire. Donated items were auctioned and re-auctioned, bringing amounts far exceeding their actual value, so great was the feeling of solidarity and the generosity prompted by it.

The loyalty which rodeo contestants show within their group is exemplified by the practice of helping each other in spite of the fact that they are seriously contending rivals for prize money and championship titles. In the chutes they adjust one another's riggings, saddles, and ropes, and provide advice and encouragement. Tradition dictates that contestants divulge honest knowledge from their own past experiences about the stock another man will ride, and this information often means the difference between winning and losing.

It is customary that, while rodeo folks may fight between themselves, they will defend each other fiercely against outsiders.

The apparent paradox of rodeo—cooperation within a competitive structure—can be regarded as a reflection of ranch life, in which experience has shown that

> Handling cattle on a large scale is of necessity a cooperative enterprise, in which over-achievers, more often than not, only get in the way. Individual brilliance is considered immodest and in most cases offensive, and the constant emphasis on ranches is on group work, not specialized show-offy expertise.
>
> (McMurtry 1968:14)

This tendency toward subordination of the individual may explain the custom followed by standard professional rodeos, which do not provide a special time of recognition for winners. There is no ceremony like the one in a horse show, for example, in which the top four or six exhibitors re-enter the ring and receive awards and acclaim. The rodeo audience may be unaware of who the winners are unless they keep their own record of scores, and typically no special mention is made of them during the show. Behind the chutes at Cheyenne, I saw the bull-riding champion who had just received his prestigious buckle-trophy, as well as a bronze figure of a bull rider, walk away with them, alone. I relate this custom not only to the nature of ranch work, but also to the fact that, as previously mentioned, there are no individual outstanding cowboys that history remembers and celebrates. Rather, the cowboy figure is a composite, apparently submerged into a group identity, and embodied by the work itself.

While rodeo society possesses strict inward uniformity, it stands very much apart from the greater community, in the same way that the cowboy herders were set apart from the conventional world at large. The rodeo group seems to have taken on a permanent aspect of being liberated from the constraints of the regular social order. It remains in a state of rebellion against "civilized" and industrialized existence. The men like to think of themselves as wild barbarians. They wish to preserve their reckless, careless society in which they feel impervious to the constraints of the workaday world, and they retain an attitude of "cowboy nonchalance" toward values which are important to that alien world.

With this separation, however, comes the inevitable sadness born of the nomad's restlessness, the feeling of a loner who not only will not, but cannot, relate to the rest of society. He takes on the image of the archetypal Lone Cowboy, who must always ride off into the sunset—an exile who can never be one with the settlers, or even with his own family. Priding themselves on being footloose, rodeo contestants nevertheless tend to be taciturn and often appear lonely and sad, except when they gather together, joking and fooling in tight little circles. They have a distinctive halting, almost dragging, gait, often with a limp, which is emphasized by their tight boots and their spurs which clank with each step. When rough stock riders arrive at the chute area, they invariably carry their rigging, saddle, or bull rope with bells in one arm, always with some part of it dragging behind them making a scraping sound in the dirt as they walk. Their gesture seems to indicate a reluctance, as though they were impelled, against their will, to come to this place and accept a new challenge. In their other hand they carry a satchel, usually donated and endorsed by Winston, and significantly dubbed their "war bag," containing all other necessary equipment and clothing. Like wandering cowboys with horses and bedrolls, they appear to have all their earthly possessions on their bodies at that moment. They seem entities unto themselves, separated from the outer world, locked into the challenge of a particular place and a moment in time by an obsession to conquer.

Like the herders in whose wake they follow, the professional rodeo contestants are utterly absorbed in their pursuit. Their fun is their work—an attitude shared by the cowboys before them, who turned for recreation to their own working skills. The world of rodeo men is, by choice, not a broad one. As a group they conform to the bookless and booted image, and, though some have been to college and received their start in intercollegiate rodeo, education is deemed by most to be irrelevant to their universe. They openly profess their lack of sophistication, their endorsement of rural values, and a strong identification with country versus city in the country/city dichotomy, a concept that will be discussed further. Though many of them dream of settling down on a ranch someday, they tend to have the nomad's live-for-today outlook. Even top winners say they have little money left at the end of a year, so great are their expenditures as they go down the road.

Rodeo contestants have taken on the cowboy tradition of meeting all circumstances with humor, rarely acknowledging the serious side of life. They display the same stoicism and have the same taboo against complaining. Their frequent injuries, their losses, their endless travels, and their loneliness are handled with humor. They develop an enviable talent for jokes as a diversionary mechanism. I

have seem them keep up sharp and witty banter, evoking hilarity for
hours, even days, at a time.

The poetic or lyric quality often associated with pastoralism is
manifest in rodeo by a tradition of music and ballad-making. Long
hours of boredom while traveling and waiting, solitary one-night
stands and lonely evenings far from home lead inevitably to singing.
Accompaniment is provided by strumming a guitar or playing an
harmonica, jew's harp, or other easily portable instrument. A new
musical genre of rodeo songs has come into being, with lyrics which
express the ethos of the sport and its way of life. As with the cowboys,
a society whose members tend to keep thoughts and emotions to
themselves finds an outlet in song.

Country-western music has a close association with rodeo, and
several prominent contestants double as entertainers. One champion
bareback bronc rider has gained popularity by writing and singing
songs which reflect his own rodeo experiences, and a top contender in
the sport has earned a reputation as a singing star which rivals his
all-around cowboy title in rodeodom. Many of the lesser known
contestants also have a flair for singing. The highlight of the Casper,
Wyoming, four-day rodeo in 1978 was the acclaimed "Champ versus
Champ" in which the 1977 world's champions in the three standard
bucking events challenged the three top animals in those divisions.
Before they made their rides, the men were asked to perform in front
of the chutes. Two of them, the bull rider and the saddle bronc man,
sang to the accompaniment of their own guitar-strumming. The
bareback riding champion, however, told the audience "I'll just do
the job I came here for," and declined. In trying to get at the roots of
the association between rodeo and country music, the saddle bronc
champion offered me the explanation "I guess we're all hams at heart,
anyway." A woman who was a barrel racer, wife of a saddle bronc
rider, daughter of a rancher, and former "Miss Country-Western
California," discussed the subject with me. Her perceptions were that
this type of music was associated with rodeo because it deals with
"everyday life and everyday living." In discussing its unmistakable
strain of sadness, she said, "life is sad."

Just as the cowboy's lyrics dealt mostly with his life as a herder, so
the rodeo songs focus on a contestant's concerns—the animals, the
danger and pain, the clowns who save his life, lost loves, and loneliness. They express much that cannot be said openly and sometimes
ideas that lie deeper in his mind than he cares to probe consciously.
One of the most frequently sung ballads at rodeos is "The Dalharted

Cowboy" (McGinnis). The lyrics tell about the plea of a rodeo cowboy that when he dies his comrades make a saddle out of his hide, for a lady to ride, so that he may spend eternity "between the two things I loved the best—my good horse and a beautiful lady" (in that order). Another song cautions

> I'm a wild raging stallion,
> In a race with the wind— . . .
> Don't rein me too tight.

(McGinnis)

Throughout Frontier Days, contestants express their special feeling for Cheyenne by refrains that describe that town as the closest place to heaven that they have ever been or expect to be.

One of the most revealing songs gives the advice

> Mammas don't let your babies grow up to be cowboys,
> Don't let 'em pick guitars and drive their old trucks;
> Make 'em be doctors and lawyers and such;
> Mammas don't let your babies grow up to be cowboys
> 'Cause they'll never stay home and they're always alone,
> Even with someone they love.

and offers the explanation that

> Them that know him won't like him and them that do
> Sometimes won't know how to take him;
> He's not wrong, he's just different, and his pride
>   won't let him
> Do things to make you think he's right.

(Ed and Patsy Bruce
"Mammas Don't Let Your Babies Grow Up to Be Cowboys,"
©1975 Tree Publishing Company, Inc.,
and Sugarplum Music Company.)

In July 1978 at Calgary I heard a bronc rider sing, only hours after he had been hung up in his bareback rigging and dragged several times around the arena. Obviously in great pain, he mounted the platform and joked about singing a song on the subject of "hanging up and dragging." But he chose instead lyrics which said

> I grew up a-dreaming of being a cowboy,
> Loving the cowboy ways.
> Pursuing the life of my high ridin' heroes,
> I burned up my childhood days.
>
> I learned all the rules of the modern-day drifter,
> Don't you hold on to nothin' too long.

Just take what you need from the ladies then leave them
With the words of a sad country song.

Cowboys are special with their own brand of misery
From being alone too long.
You could die from the cold in the arms of a nightmare,
Knowing well your best days are gone.

Pickin' up hookers instead of my pen,
I let the words of my youth fade away.
Old worn out saddles and old worn out memories
With no one and no place to stay.

My heroes have always been cowboys,
And they still are, it seems.
Sadly in search of and one step in back of
Themselves and their slow-movin' dreams.

Women are the subject of many rodeo songs. An interesting
association between sexual attraction and bronc riding is revealed in
the words

'Cause tight levis and yellow ribbons will make a
    cowboy swim a river
That before he jumps, he knows is way too wide,
And they'll make him throw a saddle on a bronc
    he's never seen,
One he knows he'll never break to ride.

A fickle woman and the irresistible appeal of a rodeo man are featured
in

I was a hell of a man till she became a rodeo fan;
It must have been the smell of the cows that turned her on
To them calloused hands;
    . . . Lost that woman to one of them Wyoming bull fighters.

And the "bad woman" image receives attention:

> He was all-around cowboy back in '49;
> From the top it's been a long way down,
> Since the whiskey and the women started winnin' his time,
> They rode him high and hard to the ground.

(Routh and Pollard)

"Rodeo Rose" starts out like a different kind of love song:

> When I first saw you I didn't think you were too purty;
> Kind of dumb lookin' and tell you the truth really ugly.
> But I wanted and needed what you had to offer,
> So I swallowed my pride and together
> we hit the road.

But the hearer gets a surprise, for Rose is not a woman:

> Rodeo Rose, I'm mighty glad that you're mine,
> You're the best thing this cowboy could find.
> You've been with me mile after mile and never complained;
> And it wouldn't surprise me if you're the first truck
> in the Cowboy Hall of Fame.

(LeDoux)

Woman as domesticator, and the opposition between the lives and aspirations of men and women are themes in "Up Jumped the Devil," a ballad of Billie and his young wife Linda. Billie has a chance to win at a big rodeo the next day, but

> Third place won't pay for a motel,
> Their bed's a dusty old car;
> Their money's all gone.
>
> Billie—he's dreamin' of "Up Jumped the Devil,"
> A black bull that's never been rode.
> Linda—she's dreamin' of a little white house—
> Billie promised she'd soon call it home.

While Billie sleeps

> Linda was cryin',
> Inside she was tryin'
> To find words to tell him about his child.

(Pinkard and Dain)

Elements of rodeo are subjects of descriptive songs, like the one about the clown:

With greasepaint and rednose and baggy old clothes,
His track shoes, barrel and broom,
He earned his keep fighting the bulls
And savin' us hard riding fools.

(Robertson & McMahan)

The ever-present appeal of chewing tobacco is celebrated in music:

Copenhagen makes me feel so good
Copenhagen the way it should.
I put a little chew in my mouth, so spittin'
And slobberin' all around the house
That Copenhagen makes me feel so good.

It's a cure-all too . . .
It cures fits, warts, freckles, coughs, colds, runny nose.
Guaranteed not to rip, run or snag.
Makes conception a wonder and childbirth a pleasure.
That's Copenhagen.

(LeDoux)

Many of the songs are thinly disguised apologies for the actions of the
men and expressions of the paradox that, while the rodeo supposedly
gives them a life of freedom, they are bound to it in such a way that
they are not at liberty to leave it. For example:

You set out on the road to seek your boyhood dreams
To satisfy that hunger in your soul.
You wouldn't turn back now even if you could;
You were born to follow rodeo.

(LeDoux)

***

Lord, I ain't really a bum—I was once a clean cut
Mother's son—and you know down deep inside I still am.
But this rodeo life's got its hold on me
And there ain't no way it'll set me free.
You know I've got to be—a rodeo man.

(LeDoux)

***

My manners are not refined or even polished
And my speech may be crude to most, you see.
I guess that I was just born a dreamer,
But in my life I relish pride and being free.

(LeDoux)

***

Rodeo—you've cast a spell
I see the farmers plowing and I see
The cattle feeding on the hill,
As I ponder on the question
Will I settle down—I guess I never will.

(LeDoux)

***

Rodeo, I'm tied to you,
Your call has won my heart and soul.
You're a woman and you've cast
A spell upon this man—you've got me, rodeo.

(LeDoux)

Loneliness finds expression, as it did for the cowboy:

Sometimes this old road gets so lonesome
Away from home,
And there ain't no way in sight
To get on back.

And nobody knows the way it feels
To suffer through this livin' hell,
Unless you've been on down that road yourself.

(LeDoux)

It is when they deal with animals—the other half of the contest—
that rodeo songs are at their most witty and original. The man-horse
contest is well represented by "The Yellow Stud," a portion of which
relates that

The yellow stud with wild eyes, the feared hated man
Finally stand face to face in the hot dusty sand;
The battle starts and rages on, beneath the burning sun,
The cowboy tried but couldn't ride this yellow outlaw stud.

He sold him to a rodeo, it spread throughout the land,
The legend of this yellow stud, the baddest of the bad.
Then one day at Cheyenne we knew it had to come
The best of all bronc riders, he drew the yellow stud.

The wooden gate flew open, the stud bailed out high
The explosion of yellow hair seemed to fill the sky.
The stud kept getting stronger and thrashing up the earth;
The cowboy blew a stirrup and crashed into the dirt.

(LeDoux)

Several songs deal with the theme of man versus bull, one of the best being "Bad Brahma Bull." Here are a few stanzas:

> While they're puttin' the bull in the chute
> I'm a-strippin' my spurs to the heels of my boots;
> I looks that bull over and to my surprise
> It's a foot and a half in between his two eyes.
>
> On top of his shoulders he's got a big hump,
> I cinches my riggin' just back of that lump;
> I lights in his middle and lets out a scream
> He comes out with a beller and the rest is a dream.
>
> At sunnin' his belly he couldn't be beat,
> He's showin' the buzzards the soles of his feet;
> He's dippin' so low that my boots fill with dirt,
> He's makin' a whip o' the tail of my shirt.
>
> He's a snappin' the buttons right off a my clothes,
> He's buckin', he's bawlin' and blowin' his nose.
> The crowd was a cheering both me and the bull—
> He needed no help while I had my hands full.

(Fletcher)

In 1967 at the National Finals, bull riding history was made, and a song commemorates this event. At this championship rodeo

> The cowboys are the toughest,
> The stock's the best there is.
>
> There in the chutes is
> A cowboy we all know—
> He's a young man now, he's forty-six,
> And he's made him a mighty draw;
> Yes, Freckles Brown has drawn a bull
> No one has ever rode,
> And tonight bull riding history's made,
> And a cowboy's gained a crown
> His bull was called Tornado,—
> And the cowboy, Freckles Brown.
>
> Now while we're giving credit,—
> Friends we know the credit's due,—
> Freckles is a hero,
> But you know Tornado gets some too;
> 'Cause without that bull to show him off,

No cowboy's got a call,
'Cause the only time he'll ever win
Is to get lucky on the draw.

So if bulls have got a heaven,
And somehow we're sure they do,
Why let's hope Tornado's up there,
And that the Lord has let him through;
I hope his pasture is the greenest,
And his stock tank's never dry,
I hope there ain't a single spur
To gouge his ugly hide.

And I hope them cowboys up there
Keep him fat and treat him kind,
And I hope he lives forever
On bunch grass belly-high.

                                                    (Steagall)

The most stirring rodeo song, to me, and at the same time the most revealing, asks the basic question

Why does he ride for his money,
Why does he rope for short pay?
He ain't gettin' nowhere
And he's losin' his share—
He must've gone crazy out there.

In this verse, interestingly, a process has taken place which has blended the rodeo contestant with the cowboy—for "out there" seems to imply more than out in the arena, or out in the West; it can be taken to mean "out there with nature." The next lines make this evident. The answer to the question asked in the stanza above is that if people don't understand why:

Then they never seen the Northern Lights,
They never seen the hawk on the wing,
They never seen the spring hit the Great Divide.

Thus through a relationship established with nature and the wild "out there" there has been a transformation of the rodeo contestant into the archetypal cowboy facing the elements of raw nature. In my belief, it is through such a sense of involvement with the force of the wild as it is opposed to the tame that the compelling essence and mystique of rodeo can best be understood, and I will be returning to this subject for detailed analysis.

It is the quality of individualism for which the rodeo contestant is best known by others and which he feels is an essential part of his own identity. This is a trait closely associated with the American frontier, and something dear to the hearts of cattlemen, past and present. Modernday ranchers have as their greatest fear any loss of their own autonomy, and uniformly preach against the evils of government intervention in their lives and work. With the ardor of stump revivalists, they expound about federal "parasites" who must be supported by people like hard-working ranchers. In contrast to themselves as earning a living by their own efforts, they look upon these agents as shirkers who do no useful work in the world. Such men, they say, spend their days thinking up ways to deprive stockmen of essential grazing land. In addition, the ranchmen believe that these government men mismanage game and wildlife which would be better handled by themselves, on a local basis, and maintain that they put the wilderness to no useful purpose. Cattlemen view official restrictions on the free enterprise upon which they feel the cattle industry depends as deplorable examples of bureaucratic crippling of the spirit of independence that made America great.

The rodeo world reflects the characteristic of individualism in its very structure. For, as announcers and sports writers often point out, a rodeo contestant still manages to retain his individualism in a day when this is rare. He is not a member of a team. (There have been some efforts to make rodeo a team sport, and a few instances of it having been done, as televised on a 1979 Merv Griffin Show. But the Professional Rodeo Cowboys Association is completely antagonistic to the idea, and all informants, both contestants and officials, were decidedly against it.) At standard rodeos a contestant has no coach and no sponsor, and enters rodeos wherever and whenever he wishes. He pays his own entry fees, travel expenses, and insurance premiums, and the only money he receives is what he wins for himself. This is believed to make him the last vestige of a dying breed, the true representative of the American pioneer spirit. The rodeo man has taken over the image of the lone cowboy riding over the vast unfenced range, who calls no man his master and has no ties to the settled life. Rodeo, within its structure, seems to express the opposition of the individual to society and highlights the varying relations between these two elements as they are reflected in the context of cattle range traditions. The one large-scale cooperative enterprise of the open

range cattle industry was the roundup, which, as noted earlier,
developed into rodeo. Thus it might be said that the rodeo contestant
plays out his own celebration of individualism against a backdrop of
the ritual that formerly supported the cattlemen's collectivity. It is
relevant to note that Goldschmidt in his work on the characteristics
of pastoralists concluded that in their societies

> ritual life will tend toward greater emphasis upon rites of passage which
> focus on the individual and his status, rather than rites of intensification,
> which reinforce group solidarity and, in so doing, tend to submerge the
> individual within the community.

(1965:405)

Rodeo, like the American cattle-herding experience that gave rise
to it, is a masculine sphere. The sport is considered by the large
majority of informants—participants (except for the few women
contestants), officials, spectators, and those connected in any way
with standard rodeo—to be a man's game, suitable only for males.
"Greater physical strength," and "the way they're built," were often
cited as reasons behind this exclusivity. Even an anthropologist has
made the assumption (which seems to be generally accepted) about
pastoral life that

> Stock must be cared for by the men; it can be no cultural accident that
> this is universally true of large-stock pastoralists. While the onerous
> work of hoe farming may be done by a pregnant woman, the handling of
> stock requires *the masculine freedom from child-bearing* [italics mine], and
> probably also the masculine kind of musculature. The male control of
> animals creates a predilection for patri-orientation . . . and tends to
> reduce the social role of women.

(Goldschmidt 1965:404)

Following the pastoral model, masculinity is exalted within rodeo
life. Performing riding and roping skills well, mastering the stock,
conquering fear and pain, and consequently being accepted by
rodeo's fraternity assures a participant of his manhood and continually reaffirms it. (The concept of child-bearing as antagonistic to
stock-tending will receive attention presently).

Along with its spirit of machismo, the North American horse-
cattle-cowboy complex as inherited by rodeo, has drawn from the
Spanish many items which stand as symbols of its emphasis on
masculinity. These serve to proclaim explicitly the conquering force
of male domination. A cowboy's ever-present spurs, the long shanks
on his horse's bit, and the horn of his saddle on which his rope is
dallied, are familiar as phallic symbols and denote male power.

Rodeo stock contractors typically carry a stick, whip, or goad. Electric prods, used in rodeos to give stimulating shocks to animals, particularly bulls, are much in evidence protuding from stockmen's back pockets, symbolizing male control. (It is significant that the P.R.C.A. rules for bull and bronc riders state that a contestant may determine not to have his animal touched with a "hot shot." However, if the rider denies use of the hot shot and his animal does not buck, the man is penalized by not being granted a re-ride.) The booted foot, often considered a blatant sexual representation, is of course inseparable from the image of the cowboy, who traditionally wears the type with sharply pointed toes. Foot authority William Rossi claims that "the machismo shoe" or boot is

> one of the most savagely sex-ridden of all male footwear styles—
> chauvinistic, aggressive, sadistic. For macho shoe-wearers it isn't
> enough to be or appear masculine. They must stomp this impression into
> the minds of others, especially females.

Such boots, he goes on to say,

> reflect a kind of swashbuckling personality, hostile and ruthless and
> challenging. The cowboy boot has its own machismo character, the
> cowboy and his boots representing an image of aggressive male thrust, of
> hardy toughness.
>
> (1976:114)

Significantly, my experience included a conversation with a stock contractor and rancher whose opinion was that the only way to deal with a person who insults you is "to give them a Tony Lama Facial." Tony Lama is a popular brand of Western boots; he was talking about kicking someone in the face. A rival boot manufacturer, the Justin Company, attempts to draw the attention of rugged males to its footwear by use of the sexually suggestive slogan "Have we got a pair for you!" in conjunction with a picture of a woman in a tight fitting shirt.

His broad-brimmed hat, usually the most expensive item he owns, is as important to the rodeo participant as to the cowboy on the range. Strict rules, enforced by fines, dictate that he, as well as all officials, must wear his hat at all times in the arena. Within this required tradition of conformity, however, the style he chooses, its manner of being creased along the crown, and its band or other decoration bears the rider's own individual stamp. The big hat, with its phallic shape emphasized by the crease in the crown, and the width provided by the brim, gives powerful expression to the aggressive sexuality of the rodeo man, creating as it does an image of him as a larger, taller, and more impressive figure. It is remarkable how much younger and more handsome most rodeo contestants appear with their hats on, and indeed many are almost unrecognizable without them. The fact that they often conceal the beginnings of baldness is only one of a multitude of reasons contestants are scarcely ever seen without their hats. Cowgirls' hats, it should be noted, are quite different, with the sides of the brim ordinarily rolled up, making the whole hat narrower. Their usual bright or pastel colors, too, make them appear less substantial than the cowboys' hats of white, tan, black, or brown.

The significance of a rodeo man's hat, I learned, is structured into the very performance of the sport itself. For, particularly in the case of rough stock riders, contestants' hats almost invariably fly off their heads during the action of their events. Generally each man, after being bucked off or finishing his ride, walks slowly (and often dejectedly, if he has done poorly or has been hurt) over to the spot where his hat had landed in the dirt, picks it up, shakes or brushes it, and puts it on. Thus appearing as a lone figure, he is provided with a few moments in the arena in which to compose himself. This allows for an easing of tension before the next rider enters, and seems to let the man "wind down" from his few seconds of almost unbearable anxiety. Upon completion of a particularly good ride, a rodeo contestant will throw his hat up in the air when his score is announced in a gesture of victory. A low marking, on the other hand, may make him throw it down forcefully in disgust.

Another significant element in rodeo is the invariable tradition of awarding trophy buckles. As mentioned earlier, these coveted items are outsized and ostentatious belt-fasteners worn in proximity to, and serving to emphasize, the genital area. If the cowboy is a type of knight, as has been suggested, then it might be said that this metal adornment is a vestige of his armor—perhaps the modernday analogue of a "cod-piece." This was a decoration that, according to a study of male symbols, "cannot have had any practical significance, but was meant as a phallic exhibition, a demonstration of power, a threat signal of the same nature as the helmets hammered into the shape of lion masks" (Vanggaard 1972:165). Close observation reveals that some bronc riders perform a type of pre-ride ritual which fits such a male emphasizing pattern. During this repetitive procedure a man holds his two clenched fists, one in front of the other, extending outward from his genitals, while he rhythmically flexes and unflexes his arm muscles, grimacing and quivering from the exertion.

These forms of behavior suggest the use of maleness as an aggressive force, not necessarily as an erotic element, just as it is said that for the Greeks "the phallus symbolized the full force of manliness, not just procreative power" (Vanggaard 1972:21). Other peoples, the same study points out, have "equated phallic power with the power of the spear, the sword and the axe" (1972:102). Accordingly, I am convinced that the cowboy's male symbols relate principally to his role in conquering—the land, the animals, nature, the wild, as well as himself and his own fears. Conquest of women, of course, is part of this. But rodeo men, like cowboys, often seem more concerned with showing off the might and power of masculinity than in attracting the opposite sex. For it has been said that "love in the cowcountry was a brusque thing, an incident and not the aim of life in this woman-starved country with its iron traditions of clanship between men" (Branch 1961:201).

In the West, riding in a saddle is perceived of as basically a masculine pursuit. A sign often seen at rodeos, and which I observed glued to a bronc rider's saddle on several occasions, reads "put something exciting between your legs." There is more than an attempt at humor or "punography" here. For indeed, rodeo people, like cattlemen, very often categorize women with horses. Both, they say, "need to know who's boss"; both are unpredictable, wild until a man tames them, good for only one purpose, and so forth. The slogan frequently seen on rodeo participants' trucks—"Cowgirls like to horse around"—expresses this likeness. One bronc rider, associated with rodeo all his life, believes that "horses and women are the same: they don't know if you treat them good or bad. If you treat them bad they don't know it, and if you treat them good they might divorce you. If you treat a horse good, it might kick you in the leg and break it. Women are like horses—you can't depend on them. You treat a woman nice and she might be running around. You treat a horse good, turn it out to pasture, and it may run away on you." What he was getting at here is a concept which I could identify as a common thread running through many similar conversations, and a theme uppermost in the thinking of informants. This is the notion of *predictability*, an attribute which they tend to see existing in varying degrees as a characteristic of forms of life which occur at intervals along a continuum with wild and tame at opposite poles. It became clear that I was finding evidence of a constant, almost unconscious measurement exhibited by these people, a sizing up, as it were, of each element or phenomenon of their universe. Predictability was associated with tameness, with being conquerable; unpredictability was associated with wildness, with being less easily conquered, and was generally viewed with antagonism.

It was relatively common to find rodeo men grouping horses with women, but their concepts regarding bulls seem to include another aspect. Frequently a bull rider would tell me that after being repeatedly injured in this event his wife or sweetheart would demand that he "choose between me and the bulls." An incident related to this happened in the context of a rodeo at Lame Deer, Montana. There, the audience's attention was drawn to a special bull named "Black Joe," which the stockman was particularly proud to own. Just before the bull was released from the chute, the announcer proclaimed "Our stock contractor today says he thinks more of this bull than his wife!" Since bulls stand as male symbols in rodeo, it appears that the men perceive them, and the event which involves them, as part of the masculine camaraderie complex, a bonding which excludes the female element, and indeed is in opposition to it.

Rodeo signs and stickers provide insight into the ways in which women are associated with animals. Such slogans as these are examples of a type of doubletalk that reveals underlying meaning:

> Ropers handle anything horny.
> Bareback riders do it on their backs.
> Bull riders ride the wild humpers.
> Team ropers change positions.
> Steer wrestlers get it on the side.
> Keep on buckin'.
> I'm a liar, a drinker, and a wild filly rider.
> Cowboys stay on longer.
> Calf ropers get it in the box.
> Bull handlers have better shots.
> Bronc riders do it with rhythm.
> Bull riders can't afford hookers.
> I'm a lover, a fighter, and a wild bull rider.

Here it is evident that women and livestock have not only become interchangeable entities meriting similar conceptualization and stimulating similar responses, but they have come to be identified as one.

As noted earlier, women's participation in standard rodeo is strictly limited to barrel racing. When included, this event stands in sharp contrast to the others because it entails no human-animal agonistic elements. Also barrel racing competition is structured so that it exhibits no ranch connection—that is, nothing which appears purposeful is accomplished. The girls are expert riders, but they generally wear pale-colored or gaudy outfits that make them look unfit for the range and about as useless as that "fifth wheel" mentioned previously. Men in rodeo either condescendingly tolerate this event or oppose it entirely, and sometimes manage to eliminate it from the regular program. Girls Rodeo Association shows do include rough stock events and timed events like calf roping as well, but male rodeo informants do not acknowledge them as a serious reality. If asked, the men say with disgust that they have never been to a girls' rodeo, and do not intend to go. They invariably add that women are just not strong enough to participate in this sport.

Such an attitude starts early in the lives of rodeo males. A young bull rider who qualified for the Little Britches finals at North Platte, Nebraska, referred to the fact that "the dingy girls' events are held in the track rather than the arena, to get more of them over faster." Regarding girls who ride bulls (not allowed at Little Britches rodeos), he told me "I don't know any boy who doesn't wish they'd get their heads stepped on. They have no business riding bulls. It's bad enough for a boy to get his head stepped on, never mind a girl." He had never watched the girls ride, he said, but he had seen pictures of them, and added: "They don't get on anything really rank anyway."

A girl at the same show told me that she was there for the barrel racing since her sister was competing in it, but that she really wants to ride rough stock and doesn't care what the boys think. "They have their fun and should let us have ours, if we're dumb enough to do it." Her father, she said, is against her riding bulls or broncs, and thinks she should do something ladylike such as barrel racing. Her mother is in favor of it, though, and would do it herself if she were younger.

An interview with a champion steer wrestler at Sheridan, Wyoming, was particularly revealing of a typical male opinion of women in rodeo (and other issues). This young man, six feet six inches tall and weighing two-hundred and forty-five pounds, had been formerly employed by the Federal Bureau of Investigation, but had left to go on the rodeo circuit. He told me he was very resentful of "athletes taking over from ranch cowboys" and said "this is hurting rodeo." He claimed that the influx of people from the East, causing the West to be "built up" is also a factor damaging to rodeo. Explaining his event, he said "you have to overpower the animal in steer wrestling, although, like Judo, it also takes balance. It's still a physical feat." He indicated that he feels "something must give up life so that life can go on. If not, if you are too liberal, you end up eating vegetables. Competition is necessary: you die if you can't make it; everything must give way to something else." He believes "women should not rodeo any more than men can have babies. Women were put on earth to reproduce, and are close to animals. Women's liberation is on an equal to gay liberation—they are both ridiculous."

Almost every male informant was against female participation in rough stock events, believing that "women don't have the build for it." One stock contractor, who runs a rodeo school and sometimes has girls apply for admission, believes that "women are not structured right to take bumps and knocks." A bull rider asserted that all females lack the coordination that it takes to rodeo. Two young contestants were convinced that "men's bodies are stronger and able to take more pain. This is due to the fact that men are known to secrete more adrenaline than women." It is the factor that makes a man under stress "suddenly able to pick up a refrigerator." Studies they had "read in veterinary science prove this," they said. Many men seem to have a preoccupation with keeping the female body intact. One father at the Little Britches rodeo articulated this concern: bronc and bull riding is "too masculine for a girl; it prevents her from being completely feminine. She may get scarred up or get a broken nose." He said his daughter "only rides in barrel racing, but even so she can't keep her fingernails, and it is bad enough that she cuts her legs up doing that, without competing in the rough stock!" Several informants were concerned that "women have more tender parts to injure."

Uniformly in such discussions men alluded to women's sexual and/or child-bearing functions. The manager of the weekly rodeo in a small Montana town, who is also a rancher, told me he does not want to see girls ride bulls. "When they buck you off," he said, "half of the bulls will come looking for you. They will hook you, or step on you. If a girl is stepped on in the right spot, it will end her family-making days." He indicated that it would be all right to ride horses, he could see that. In this he echoed a dichotomy of attitude that I would frequently find expressed by rodeo people—horses might be acceptable for either sex, but bulls are decidedly the province of males.

The editor of a rodeo magazine, also a contestant himself, told me "I'll be damned if I can see a woman bull rider; it's a tradition, women are supposed to be feminine, and a bull rider is not. It's rough, dangerous, gut-tearing, and jaw-breaking." He "could conceive of a female saddle bronc rider, because in her duties on a ranch, a woman might be riding across the prairie and have her horse blow up.

She would have to be able to handle that." But he "can't relate at all to the idea of a woman bareback bronc rider or a bull rider." He "wouldn't ask a woman bull rider out for a date." When looking for a wife, he had "wanted a womanly person, not a hired man." His wife sings country-western music, and does some barrel racing. He admitted, "This barrel racing is okay, if it's her thing," but "I don't encourage it."

Another steer wrestler told me that his event was the one thing women in rodeo could never do. He explained the reason for this was that chest injuries were so common in this event, and women would surely injure themselves in a delicate area—their breasts—leading to cancer and necessitating surgery to remove them. Female breasts were also the subject of attention at the all-girls rodeo in Billings, Montana. There the (male) announcer, quipping with the (male) clown asked "what did you say?—Oh, did I hear about the new piece of equipment the girls are using at this rodeo?—Oh, a rawhide bra you girls have to have!—I guess many of you girls need them."

Clown acts clearly reveal rodeo ethos, and one of the most explicit was performed at Red Lodge, Montana. I saw this sequence repeated several times, and it was always received with great enthusiasm by the crowd. Members of the audience made comments like "watch this, this is a really good act," and it was followed by much laughter and applause. The announcer asked the clown in the arena "What are you going to do?—You say you are going to get yourself a good-looking girl?" The clown then went into the chute area and came out carrying a shapely woman over his shoulder, her body limp and her blonde hair dangling. The clown, with the woman in this position, walked across the arena, and the announcer questioned him again: "What are you going to do?" Then he repeated the clown's answer for the audience—"Oh, you're gonna take all the padding and makeup off and see what you've got." The clown then disappeared with the woman into a chute, where they remained hidden for a few minutes. Various articles of women's clothing were then tossed out of the chute for the spectators to see—jeans, shirt, then underwear, and at the end two large round pink baloons with nipple-like projections. Next the clown emerged from the chute, this time with a young girl about three or four years old, with long blonde hair and wearing a sunsuit, having replaced the woman carried over his shoulder. The announcer then said "So this is what is left when the makeup and padding is taken off!" Thus the message is conveyed: a woman is just a big child underneath her sexy exterior. And by this, of course, she is rendered unfit for any of the serious duties, or sports, that "he-men" undertake. Woman as a brainless sex-object, and made closer to elemental nature by being characterized as a child, is a frequently repeated theme in rodeo. It leads quite logically to the notion that women, since they are juvenile, should and indeed must, be dominated by men, along with the rest of nature.

The process of conquering a woman has its metaphoric counterpart in the male conquering of the West itself. The cowboy then becomes the archetypal representation of the male element in the conquest of virgin land. Henry Nash Smith in his study of the American West as symbol suggests by a question, but does not discuss further, a concept of the West as female:

> Is it wholly meaningless, for example, that the West, the region close to nature, is feminine, while the East, with its remoteness from nature and its propensity for aping Europe, is neuter?

(1971:255)

It seems that the American cowboy has come to be generally conceptualized as the central instrument in "taming the raw land." Stating this in terms of the nature/culture dichotomy, I suggest that in this conquest the cowboy stands for "culture" in the form of an aggressive and controlling force being exerted over "nature" as represented by previously untouched land—the frontier wilderness. Within this context, nature is the feminine element and culture is the masculine.

In another sense, though, it is noteworthy that as part of the same process of domination, the cowboy eventually came to identify himself with the land—the wilderness beyond the frontier that was being acquired by the westward movement. By becoming one with it, he then would have conceived of himself as belonging to the "nature" rather than the "culture" polarity of nature versus culture. Here I am using "culture" to mean tamed, domesticated, or associated with town or city, sophisticated, and "nature" to denote wild, free, associated with rural areas, simple and artless. Rodeo has picked up many of these sometimes conflicting themes relating the cowboy to nature and culture, and structured them into a sport composed of contests and performances which serve to express them symbolically.

The opposition of country/city is frequently represented in rodeo. Like cowboys, rodeo people want to be categorized as simple country folk with unrefined minds and manners and possessed of little formal education or appreciation for intellectual skills and pursuits. They actively seek to be identified with country music, country dancing, blue denims and red bandanas. The rodeo song "I'm Country" expresses this feeling:

There's a little word and it fits me to a T.
I don't know how to spell it, but it's country
and that's me.

I chew tobaccer and I spit it on the ground.
I talk to the cows when no one ain't around.
I've trapped on the mountain when the snow's
Fallin' down. Yessir boys, I'm country.

I'm as country as a bronc on the western plain.
Just as wild and harder to tame.

City folks think I'm crude I guess,
You can tell I'm a hick by the way I dress.
But that don't matter, I'm happy as can be,
and proud as heck, I'm country.

(LeDoux)

Rodeo people extoll the advantages of a life as far from town as possible. They relate this distance from town to freedom itself, an association made clear by William Crawford when he wrote of his fellow rodeo contestants as "untamed men" who "came to disdain town men, seeing in them the same look of astonished despair seen in bull calves' eyes at branding time; yoked, roped and held, dehorned, branded and earmarked, and their manhood knifed out" (1965:63). Here men of the town are not only viewed as defeated and powerless, but castrated as well, so that they become symbolically neuter. In contrast, the rodeo contestants are masculine and unrestrained, identified with the wild country, and are themselves the conquerors.

One informant, in giving me his ideas about women in rodeo, revealed perceptions which relate significantly to these oppositions of feminine/masculine and city/country. This man was a cattle rancher, a former participant who "rodeoed all my life," and father of a barrel racer. Regarding girls who run barrels, he said "Ordinarily they throw their hat in the corner of the camper as soon as they get to a rodeo, and go out and chase boys." But in contrast he felt that "a girl who would ride rough stock would be a different breed of girl; she is rougher, more masculine. You would seldom see her on dates. You see her with her father, and out with the stock all the time. She stays in the country, you don't see her in the city." In this case it is evident that there was a clear and definite association of feminine with city and masculine with country.

Many informants conceived of rodeo as necessarily a rural affair, entirely out of place in a city. At the rodeo held in Rhode Island as a novelty in connection with a town's centennial observance, a sophisticated city dweller gave me his perception: "urbanites do not really appreciate rodeo." One stock contractor was convinced that even the best rodeos could not be successful in cities without accompanying livestock shows and exhibits to "make them go" with the people. The same rodeo that would fail in a city, according to his thinking, could be a huge success if held out in the country. I found also that to ranchers, cities are places where women go, mostly to shop; they hold little interest for menfolk except perhaps once a year for a cattle auction or horse sale. I have already referred to evidence from Bennett's study (1969) that ranch wives and daughters were much more apt to be associated with city or town life than their husbands or fathers. In this sense, as in the foregoing example of the female rough stock rider being seen in the country, "city" has a feminine connotation and "country" a masculine one. This, as I have pointed out, is a reversal of the concept of country identified as a wild and feminine element conquered by male force. The mystique of domination remains an integral part of the cowboy image. It is my belief, however, that the cowboy, as the prototype of the rodeo man, despite his role in conquering the rest of his universe, wished, and still wishes, to keep himself outside the bounds of the conquered spheres and in the realm of the wild. I suggest that through a sense of identification with the undomesticated land—the country—he is able to conceptualize himself as he wants to be—untamed and free.

The cowboy syndrome dictates that feminine elements are to be brought under domination, but it also considers women to have dangerous potential as tamers of men. For this reason rodeo men, like the cowboys, stress the avoidance of the "good woman." Women are sharply categorized, and the "bad" ones, like the camp followers or carnival pickups, are the women to whom the rodeo man feels he can relate, just as the trail hand in the cattle town believed he could best be understood by the prostitute. In each case the "bad" woman will know that the man must move on, and will not try to interfere with his nomadic life. The roughness and mobility of rodeo living and its male-camaraderie complex leave little place for a "good" woman. In addition, the pervasive loner image of the cowboy makes love relationships difficult. In one of the best known rodeo movies, "J.W. Coop," for example, the hero is referred to as "the original loner."

The girl who loves him must make all the advances, for he is not much interested in sex. In one scene he puts her off saying "later; I want to see my friends now."

Rodeo songs make explicit the idea that a wife or sweetheart will inevitably be hurt by the rodeo man's wandering lifestyle, and ballads tell of fleeting loves that could not last. The classic story of rodeo life, *The Bronc Rider* (Crawford 1965), written by a participant and endorsed by the professional rodeo association, contains no references to loving or bonded relationships between rodeo contestants and women. The female character who receives the most attention in the book is a "dirty bitch" who marries a rodeo man for her own convenience, is not only unfaithful to him but also responsible for his death, and schemes to get his money. "When y'all gonna get married?" is used in the book as a sarcastic insult from an enemy, and is answered by "Screw you!" (Crawford 1965:19). The author makes explicit reference to the belief in sex as a male weakener (1965:75). It cannot be coincidence that the hero makes a mistake which causes him to be severely injured immediately following a sexual experience. Later, when he suffers from what he calls a "yellow fear spot," his cowardice is accompanied by impotence; fear, he says, "took his balls away" (Crawford 1965:177–178).

A negative view of marriage is often expressed in rodeo. When a horse leaves the arena slowly, for example, the announcer is sure to remark "that's a married horse," and when a bull balks at the exit gate, there is the assurance "he's a married bull—he don't want to go home!" An outstanding example of the way in which performance may express a particular ethos is a specialty act reflecting the ranch/rodeo attitude toward marriage. This act was recently presented at all performances of the International Rodeo Association Finals. The cowboy star of this popular routine rides into the arena on a flashy paint horse and demonstrates his highly perfected skill in the art of roping. Accompanying him are his wife and small daughter, who are dressed in outfits matching his, but who appear on foot rather than horseback. They perform a bit of very minor and inept roping on the sidelines, while he occupies "center stage" with his spectacular feats of lassoing and rope spinning. As the highlight of his act he spins a large coil of rope around himself and his horse, excluding his family who stand a short distance away. The announcer draws attention to the special skill demonstrated in this performance and to its title— "The Cowboy's Wedding Ring." Here the cowboy has symbolically articulated the view that his wife and child are basically irrelevant to his universe. Mounted, in a position of dominance, he towers above them as subordinate figures whose status and skills are demonstrably inferior to his own. As females, his bonding is not to them; they are but reflections of his sexuality. His image as a cowboy with its traditional life of freedom from domesticity and his close relationship with his horse are shown to be the essence of his world, as they are set apart by the encircling loop of rope that is the herder's stock in trade.

Once again relating the rodeo contestant to the cowboy, and placing them both in a larger frame of reference, Barker-Benfield's (1976) study of male attitudes toward women in the nineteenth century indicates that men of the frontier were conscious of the challenges involved in taming the vast American wilderness. They generally considered women a threat or a distraction which could prevent them from accomplishing their mission. The author suggests it may be for this reason that Americans have traditionally roman-ticized men working alone—the cowboy or the solitary woodsman —rather than pioneer couples. For example, Barker-Benfield cites the case of "the lone hunter of Cooper's *Leatherstocking Tales*, Natty Bumppo," who "realized the promise of total mobility because he was free of women" (1976:8).

Keeping women remote—and therefore powerless to provide a challenge—by categorizing them as delicate and treating them with an attitude of exaggerated respect is a cowboy tradition which has extended to rodeo. A leading bareback bronc rider told me that the reason officials generally prohibit the presence of women behind the chutes is that the men may swear or use bad language, or contestants may be caught "putting our tail-piece in our pants" (a cushion used to shield a rider's spine). When a rodeo official tried to get permission from a particularly unwilling stock contractor for me to go behind the chutes, the answer was "Well, okay, I guess so, if she is good looking and can put up with my swearing." I often noted that foul language, as well as other rough practices considered to be the province of males, was used as a mechanism to put distance between the sexes. Even in their own association rodeos, girls are fined ten dollars for swearing or using bad language. The (male) helpers of the rodeo manager "would turn us in if they were out to impress somebody," the contestants told me. One girl was severely reprimanded by a rodeo worker for saying "shit" when her leg was being "mashed" by the bull in the chute before her ride. A world's champion professional bull rider told me recently that he does not approve at all of women rodeo contestants whom he characterized as "chewing Copenhagen and talking dirty." A stock contractor and rancher told me "women shouldn't compete in rodeo any more than I'd expect them to pack a rifle and go off to war. Some girls in our country go to rodeos and even chew tobacco; they're not the least bit feminine."

Rodeo serves to keep sex roles sharply distinct as they were in the cowboy herding tradition. Most female rodeo contestants themselves agree with men who say that women cannot possibly compete with men in the sport because they do not possess as much physical strength. At the annual Girls Rodeo Association Finals in Texas, one of the top women rough stock riders, who had been champion all-around cowgirl for several years, told me that women do not ever intend to compete with men, and that there would be no competition anyway because of the disparity in strength. She said the men in rodeo "don't resent us as much now that they know that." She accepted this even though she was a very tiny woman who, by means of greater skill, almost always won over bigger and stronger women. Most other female contestants also agreed that "girls are not built for it" to the extent they would have a chance to beat males in competition. At the end of some rodeo seasons there is a program on national television entitled "Battle of the Sexes" featuring the reigning woman bareback riding champ pitted against a current male champion bronc rider; the man ordinarily wins by a small margin.

At all-girl rodeos the male announcer continually urges the contestants to "Hurry up and keep the show moving," and hollers "Let's go, girls!"—a practice never observed in standard rodeo. At a girls' rodeo in Montana the announcer told the audience, "These are not full-time rodeo riders, they are housewives and secretaries"—a comparable announcement of which would never be tolerated in men's rodeo. It was especially noteworthy that throughout every ride in the 1978 Girls Rodeo Association Finals, the announcer urged the contestant on with "ride him, Joanne, come on, concentrate, think about it all the way, stay with him!" which would be unthinkable in the course of regular male rodeo. At another girls' rodeo, a contestant was hurt, and while she was being put into the ambulance the announcer told the crowd that she had just asked someone nearby "will you check and see if my makeup is smeared?"

Even though some girls have rebelled against tradition and male disapproval to become rough stock riders, it is significant that the Girls Rodeo Association itself does not stress these events or even seem particularly proud of them. Their official logo depicts a barrel racer, and this symbol appears on all jewelry, stationery, and other association-sanctioned items. Their monthly publication features barrel racing and gives little attention to bronc and bull events, with scarcely any photographs of them. Girls' rodeos do not have a saddle bronc event; contestants say that is because the equipment is too expensive or they fear being hung up in the stirrups. When I asked the (male) stock contractor for the girls' finals why this event was lacking, he told me that "saddle bronc riding takes finesse, it requires balance and coordination; it is where the real art of rodeo is." He said "it takes a lot of practice and girls don't practice enough." Whatever reasons are given by informants out of their own perceptions, it must be remembered in analysis that this event is considered to be the sport's classic event, the one that relates to cowboy skills and ranching—the cornerstone of rodeo.

In many rodeos where girls compete, such as youth or Little Britches affairs, it seems as though their events are staged to reflect incompetency. For example, "break-away roping" is set up to allow the calf, the main object of pursuit in ranch work, to escape from the roper. And in many girls' events small goats are used—poor substitutes for calves in ranchers' eyes. Often the act of tying an animal with a ribbon, or even taking one off as in "steer undecorating," takes the place of the real ranch skill of roping. In these ways useful range work is made into a mockery for a girl. At the women's finals, though, there was authentic calf roping and the female ropers showed great skill. The high scores in the team roping event there demonstrated that two girls are fully capable of success in roping a steer. When asked if a representative from the Professional Rodeo Cowboys Association would be in attendance for the first annual girls' finals (as there had been for the first annual Northeast circuit finals in New Jersey that same year), the women officials said "No, that's a sore subject."

In spite of the detail with which I have described girls' rodeos, it must be stressed that they are rather infrequent occurrences and that they have a negligible place within the sport as a whole. Looking at standard rodeo in general, still almost entirely male-dominated, it is evident that the cowboy sport has retained the pastoralist tradition of separating women from large livestock. During my initial struggles with rodeo personnel to gain admission to the chute area, I learned how strongly ingrained this tradition is. I was told such things as, "most stock contractors don't allow any women behind the chutes. Women have no business being there. It's for your own safety; women don't know how to handle themselves around the stock and might get hurt." There was little logic to the prohibition, for it did not seem to matter what training or experience with livestock a woman had. Sometimes no reasons were given; an official simply said "some of them [stock contractors] are still chauvinists, I'm afraid." After finally obtaining permission and spending a great deal of time behind the chutes observing and talking to the men, I concluded that they were largely motivated by a strong feeling about what they conceived of as the feminine nature. It just seemed to be a part of the order of their world that, as Evans-Pritchard phrased it, "where the women are the cattle are not" (1973:38).

Several complex factors are no doubt involved in this time-honored and emphatic tradition. One element that comes through clearly, however, is the idea that the role of childbearing and the occupation of herding large livestock are mutually exclusive. This concept was frequently implied and expressed by ranch and rodeo people, and several examples of their thinking have been indicated in the foregoing discussions. It appears as though cattle-tending—and the whole cattle obsession which has been described as a characteristic of certain pastoralists—may be in some way a male compensatory mechanism, a masculine analogue, as it were, for women's role in reproduction. Functioning in such a way, it might account for the marked male protectiveness and jealous guarding of the realm of cattle as men's exclusive domain. Riesman's analyses of his data on Fulani pastoral life are relevant to this idea. He felt that as a male grows older there is a greater "liberation from nature's hold over him through his biological processes." Women, on the other hand, "when they are most fully feminine, are at the mercy of nature," and are therefore "at the mercy of men" (1977:86).

This has important bearing on the proprietorship of cattle. For, Riesman explains, to the Fulani, nature

> is a force truly other than and independent from man as an intelligent being. That is why women can experience the feeling of freedom without having to own cows, since, as we have shown, the physiological and social functions of the female body mean, in the Fulani mind, that women already participate in nature to a higher degree than men. Thus an intriguing parallel begins to form in which the woman's relationship with her nature would be represented by the mother-child couple, while the man's relationship with his would have the image of the man-cow couple.
>
> (1977:257)

Indeed many of my own experiences in the realm of livestock would support this line of reasoning. I have observed that whenever a choice as to the handling of animals is in order, men (or boys) generally assume as a natural given that theirs is the province of the large stock, and thus they relegate the small or "pet" animals to women. A feeling that women are essentially "maternal" comes in to play here, and is often implied or directly expressed. One cannot interpret this animal allocation according to sex as due only to the dictates of logic, since male stock-tenders or veterinarians ordinarily cannot overpower and restrain a large farm animal singlehandedly. They, like women, need the help of a strong assistant. And the separation of women from large stock appears to me to lie deeper than merely representing a symbolic recapitulation of human sexual dimorphism in size and strength, although this type of association may be a surface explanation. It is true also that in most livestock people's perceptions there is a trait of "roughness" associated with the handling of large animals which cultural conditioning has dictated should be absent in a woman. Many times I have heard the opinion expressed that it is all right for a woman veterinarian to treat "pet" horses, but certainly not those in the categories of, say, race or draft horses. Similarly I remember an exceptionally gentle dairy farmer, who, unlike many in his occupation, treated his cows like "ladies," and always called for my services when they were sick in preference to those of a male doctor.

Ordinarily, cattle breeders, stockmen, and ranchers perceive their occupation and everything connected with it as a male concern. What seems to me significant is my observation that it is especially in situations when reproduction is the issue involved that these men become most defensive about their exclusive claim to livestock interests, and women are taboo. At calving and foaling time, for example, women on many farms have in the past been kept away from barns and stables. As a veterinary student I was told by several upperclassmen who had been raised on cattle farms "I certainly wouldn't want to have my wife beside me when I was delivering a calf." On an official veterinary school field trip to the Hanover Shoe Farm, famed for raising fine trotting horses, the women in the class were prohibited from entering the breeding barns. Our exclusion from this part of the tour was explained as an old tradition which (at that time) had never been broken in the history of this prestigious farm.

It is common practice on Western ranches for women to separate themselves from the livestock sphere, not just in the everyday world of work but in interest as well. Often I observed ranch wives absorbed with their children or grandchildren while the men "talked horse and cow" during their leisure time. There seemed to be a reciprocal relationship in these realms, consistently demonstrated by the lives of men and women. Ranchers' wives of all ages, ranging from their twenties to their sixties, told me that their husbands had generally viewed their children as belonging to the women. Offspring were considered strictly a feminine responsibility, and the men assumed little part in their care. Thus it would appear that the mother-child couple was regarded as an entity, as in Riesman's description of the Fulani. However complex its underlying causes, the pastoral tradition of separating men from women and women from livestock was exemplified by the American cowboy, whose life was so intimately bound up with cattle and who was generally disdainful of the company of women. The same tradition is part of the rodeo man's outlook.

The idea of women as subject to the authority of men is prevalent in the ranch/rodeo ethos, and is supported by the rodeo-endorsed Cowboys for Christ religion. At a meeting of the Cowgirls Chapter of this organization the (male) guest speaker acknowledged the "help of you girls," by granting that "behind every good Christian man there is a good Christian woman somewhere" (but there was no indication she might stand as an equal with him). The born-again Christian women gave testimonies regarding their conversions and subsequent happy lives, often referring to their relationships with their children and the influence of these upon their religious experiences. At a luncheon following this meeting several women told me that "it says in the Bible women are subordinate to men. I let my husband be the boss and make the decisions."

With the cowboy, who dreaded only two things in this world, the rodeo man shares not only the old fear of a decent woman who might domesticate him, but also the fear of being set afoot. He finds much of the satisfaction in his way of life as a mounted stockman through his association with the rodeo animals. Though people who view animals in a different way from his may find it difficult to understand, the rodeo participant feels a genuine need to be around them. He enjoys the sight, smell, and sound of the beasts which continually surround him in his sport and which become so much a part of his nomadic existence. Most contestants say that they consider the rodeo livestock to be athletes in their own right, and highly respect them for doing their jobs well. Special admiration is shown by rough stock riders for the "really rank animals," for it is only in drawing one of them that a contestant has a chance to make a winning ride. The bucking horse or bull of the year in each event is chosen by vote of the professional rodeo cowboys, and this award is greatly coveted by stock contractors. Rodeo people develop deep feeling for spirited bucking animals on which high scores can be made, and those which are considered unridable—or nearly so. At one Montana rodeo the announcer told the audience: "the four-footed athlete, 'War Paint,' owned by the stock contractor, just died at thirty-eight years of age and will be put in a museum in Pendleton so people can see this famous rodeo horse." He classed the bronc with the outlaw horse, "Midnight," one of the greatest of all time, whose headstone over his grave (which was moved in 1966 to the grounds of the Cowboy Hall of Fame in Oklahoma) bears the inscription:

> Under this sod lies a great bucking horse;
> There never lived a cowboy he couldn't toss.
> His name was Midnight, his coat was black as coal,
> If there is a hoss-heaven, please God, rest his soul.
>
> -By a cowboy.
> (Hanesworth 1967:120)

Probably the most celebrated bucking horse in rodeo was "Five Minutes to Midnight," an almost unconquerable animal who had been ridden less than a score of times in a thousand appearances. And rodeo lore keeps alive the memory of "Tornado," the bull who was finally "conquered" by the beloved middle-aged cowboy, Freckles Brown, after successfully bucking off all aspiring contestants in the animal's 400 previous go-rounds. The rodeo song "Mighty Lucky Man" reveals a contestant's feeling for the rough stock that make his happy life possible. Though he is thankful for a bit of money, a housetrailer, and his wife and son, he emphasizes

> But the one thing that I'm most thankful for
> I guess it was a stroke of good luck
> Is when the Lord looked down on this big old world
> And made those horses that buck.
>
> I wonder what my life would be like today
> If it weren't for them buckin' old broncs.
> I'd probably be tied to a desk and phone
> Or slavin' at some greasy gas pump.
>
> (LeDoux)

Rodeo people are extremely defensive about the issue of treatment of rodeo stock, and totally exasperated with humane organizations and animal control associations, which, they say, have made relentless attacks on them without legitimate provocation. Informants invariably brought up the subject themselves in conversation, telling me "you would be amazed to know how many people have taken a pot shot at rodeo." Their suspicions that this will happen again have made it very difficult for a stranger to get close enough to the sport to study it from the inside. Outside observers often perceive it as cruel, and many times some of those who are alien to its spirit and values have initiated movements to prohibit it. Participants uniformly evidence a dread of any such threat which might result in "setting them afoot," and ranch/rodeo people continually assert there is nothing cruel about rodeo. The animals, they argue, are well-fed, made to work only for very short intervals, and, in the case of the rough stock, would "long ago have been made into glue or meat," if it were not for their role in the sport. Good treatment is always perceived by them in a comparative, rather than an absolute sense, and they point out that animals on ranches are subject to much harsher treatment than those in rodeo. A ranch horse, for example, is commonly worked for many hours a day, and might still be ridden even though it was lame. They quote the large sums of money which are represented by each rodeo animal, and assert that stock contractors would never want to do anything to damage such investments. And anyway, participants feel that "a dog cooped up in a city apartment suffers more than a rodeo animal," as does "an American Saddlebred show horse with its long hooves and tail-set." If a person thinks rodeo is cruel, they say, he or she "doesn't understand the sport, and must be an Easterner or a little old lady with tennis sneakers."

Rodeo people call attention to the fact that the contestants get hurt far more frequently than the animals. One official told me that "during the ninety-day period of the heavy summer season in professional rodeo there are about three-hundred and sixty cowboys injured to every one head of stock. A working ranch hurts more stock in a week than rodeos do in a year. Injuries usually involve bulldogging cattle and roping calves. Rodeo animals rarely die as a result of their use in the sport, and when they do, it is of a heart attack." The same man, though, told me after Frontier Days was over that twenty-seven animals had been lost during the nine-day rodeo. Nine steers had been destroyed as a result of steer roping, and one on the last day had suffered a broken neck. Four or five cows had been killed by being caught in the loading ramp. One of the horses in the chuckwagon race had gone down in harness on the track and had to be destroyed.

Many contestants expressed the opinion that "animal-control people, or those who think rodeo is cruel to the stock should have to ride a bull and see who it is that gets hurt." All informants compared animals with contestants using this frame of reference. The fact that the animals did not choose this dangerous occupation as did the men was not mentioned. A champion bull rider, also a partner in a Texas rodeo school and rodeo company which owns its own stock, summed up the opinion of many contestants: he said that "if there were reincarnation, I wouldn't mind coming back as a rodeo bull or bronc. They have the best life imaginable, working about eight seconds a week, and having the rest of their time to loaf, screw, and eat."

Like the cowboy, the rodeo participant is utterly absorbed in his way of life, and accepts its ethos as unquestioned. His attitudes are supported by his associates, most of whom hold similar views, and in many cases by a religious belief that reinforces this outlook. The high percentage of men in rodeo who have ranching backgrounds, and adoption of its characteristic traits by the others, insures that contestants for the most part share ranch-oriented values. As with the cowboy, it is probably also true that the rodeo man's peculiar emphasis on toughness and his own harsh demands upon himself are factors in his perception of what constitutes cruelty toward livestock. It seems as though the elements of his outlook which were derived from the cowboy pastoral model had combined to commit him to an established mode of relating to animals which would fit the new context of the world of rodeo.

Without exception, ranch and rodeo informants say they believe animals were put on earth for the express purpose of man's use. Ranchers take for granted an image of themselves as masters of the land with innate rights to manipulate it and their livestock to meet their own needs. Rodeo people, too, say they feel certain that animals exist for human use. An official of the P.R.C.A., also a saddle bronc contestant, typified the views of many when he told me "horses are meant to be used; if there were no use for horses—in rodeo, race, show, or pleasure riding—the cost of keeping them would be prohibitive; they would end up in a killer-plant, an abattoir." He said "my wife has a dog, a pet, and it is not good for anything else," adding "but you like a good bucking horse because you win money on him."

Professional rodeo's officially endorsed religion, Cowboys for Christ, is a born-again phenomenon increasingly embraced by greater numbers of the sport's participants. As mentioned previously in connection with the subordination of women, it is a fundamentalist dogma in which Biblical authority is supreme. One of its most prominent and active leaders, a former rancher and professional rodeo contestant who says he had a specific call from Christ to undertake his mission among rodeo people, spends full time on the circuit going down the road with them. He believes that to minister to them, "you have to be one with them, smell like them; they wouldn't accept you unless you were one of them." The animals, he says, "though they are an integral part of a cowboy's life, don't have souls. The Lord gave animals to people to use them. An animal has no spirit; man has both a spirit and a body." His job is to help the rodeo people to see that "the Lord will take care of them on the road, and heal their horses as well as help their marriages."

Speakers I heard at rodeo services often assured the congregation that the Lord would take care of the cowboy's horse for him so that he could go on with his career. One pointed out that "years ago cowboys made fun of church, but now they tell each other 'I'll pray for you,' and they give testimonies about times when the Lord saved their horse's life or momentarily filled the animal with power so they could win." Another rodeo grandstand preacher described a miracle he had witnessed. The night before a contestant was to appear in the Cheyenne roping finals for which he had qualified, his horse came down with colic. The owner "gathered a group of faithful Christian cowboys, they annointed the horse, and all of them prayed in association for help. The animal was cured by the Lord, and the next day the rider won $5,800 on this horse. If God won't take care of a man's horse, He won't do anything. The Lord showed he would do this, and He will take care of you." Following the service, I discussed this episode further with the preacher. "A miracle like this," he told me, "came about because of the faith of the men who had been saved and the intervention of their prayers to the Lord." It had no relation, he made clear, to any association between the Lord and the animal world. The beneficence resulted purely from the Lord answering a personal prayer for a specific event, through human faith on the part of those who had been born again.

The framework of this religion is expressed through rodeo idiom and related to the life and value system of the sport. Christ is considered to have been the one original rodeo cowboy, when he rode into Jerusalem mounted on "an unbroken colt." Jesus is believed to have been the first bareback rider, for, as described in the Bible, he rode that colt without a saddle. The life of the Lord in his three-year ministry, during which he was constantly on the road, is said to illustrate a similarity to the rodeo cowboys' lives of continual travelling. The preacher points out that "Jesus was a simple man, and his gospel is simple; the people who followed him were down-to-earth men, like rodeo cowboys are today. Jesus gave examples using the things rodeo people use in everyday life—livestock: sheep, cattle, and horses. These people understand such things, so the parables become clearer. In rodeo and in the cattle business we do separating of cattle, sheep, and horses; we do this when everything is bunched together. Jesus spoke of 'separating the sheep from the goats,' and cowboys have worked this way in rodeo or on the ranch, where they have culled sheep. This is the way Christ is going to separate us—the believers will enter heaven, while others will not. The Bible says Christ will be revealed to us sitting on a white horse—like a grand finale for a cowboy. It does not say it will happen sitting in a million dollar synagogue with an organ, or in a big building covering a city block. It says we will see him on a horse. It is so much like rodeo cowboys it isn't funny."

Another religious speaker compared "the Bible, the rule book for life," to the Professional Cowboys Association Rule Book, "whose regulations have to be obeyed in the arena." Several pointed out that "Christ's birth in a stable makes it easy to relate to Him." "Through Christ you are on the winning team." Though the preachers believed that there was no possibility of animals being included in an afterlife, and many contestants agreed, some said they "hope the animals could go to heaven," when asked about it. A great number told me they "hadn't thought about it." Some rodeo people, though, were sure that animals could share in immortality, but in all cases they related this to very special animals who had made distinguished records in the sport. One former contestant, now an official, was "convinced such bucking animals as 'Old Wrangler' and 'Tornado,' who were conquered only once or twice out of 300 to 500 attempts, have souls." He said "I hope they will be in heaven and will be treated as good as we are. Without them, we would have nothing to do; we would have to switch to football or mowing the lawn."

Important though animals may be in daily life, the Cowboys for Christ religion disclaims an animal ancestry for man. Evolution is specifically rejected and all creatures are believed to have been created separately and in their present form. One of the most eloquent and influential preachers on the circuit is a former contestant who is now a popular rodeo clown. Wearing his makeup and dressed in harlequin garb, he spoke emphatically to a gathering of five-hundred people assembled in the Cheyenne grandstand on the last Sunday of Frontier Days on this subject. "Before anything else, Christ was with God. He created everything. Recently there has been good news, and the darkness shall not dull it: twenty-five percent of scientists now believe in the creation. Now they have shot holes in all that monkey bit. God is the first born of any creature, and all things were created by Him and through Him. Wait till you see Jesus and see what he says."

In summary, there is a very close connection between ranching and
the sport of rodeo in the Great Plains. Rodeo is the inheritor of the
American cowboy tradition, with the characteristics and lifestyle of
the rodeo contestant revealing a striking parallel to those of the
working cowboy. Rodeo society resembles the cowboy society from
which it is derived and reflects today's ranching ethos and values.
These include the qualities of a modified "nomadism"; a dread of
ordinary labor or a regimented existence; and a stress on personal
freedom, independence, and individualism. At the heart of rodeo
there is the same emphasis on physical toughness, endurance, stoicism, and risk-taking which characterizes the cowboy/ranching ideal.
There is in general the same devaluation of intellectual and aesthetic
pursuits. Rodeo men, like cowboys, stress joking and humor, which
they perceive as an antidote to the hardship in their lives. They also
find expression for their feelings in their own type of music, whose
lyrics center on the special concerns of their world—horses, bulls,
clowns, loneliness, the luck of the draw, and fickle women. Rodeo
cowboys enjoy the tightly knit male-bonded society reminiscent of
their predecessors, within which there is strong loyalty and conformity. They have the same sense of being "a breed apart" from the
more conventional world beyond their own, whose values they do not
share.

Rodeo, like cowboy/ranch society, perpetuates the pastoral tradition of considering large livestock to be an exclusively masculine
domain. The sport's emphasis on maleness as an aggressive force has
earned a "macho" image. Sex roles are sharply separated, and women
are considered subordinate to men. "Good" women are kept remote
by exaggerated respect and the assumption that the tough world of
rodeo, like that of ranching, is entirely unsuited to the feminine
nature. This idea is structured into the sport by confining women's
participation in standard rodeo to the barrel race, which involves no
human-versus-animal contest and which is felt to have no real ranch
connection. Rough stock riders in Girls Rodeo Association events are
considered unfeminine by their male counterparts and earn strong
disapproval and virtual social ostracism from men in standard rodeo.

Though some rodeos are held in cities, the sport is viewed by
informants as a rural phenomenon, incompatible with urban life and
"civilized" values. Contestants, like cowboys and ranchmen, always
identify themselves as "country people." Thus, although the ranch/
rodeo complex generally represents the force of culture extended over
raw nature, there is this apparently contradictory strain in their
identification with the undomesticated land of the country (nature) as

opposed to the tamed or "civilized" sphere of the city (culture). This ambivalence I relate to the ranch/rodeo view of the country as wild and free, qualities they themselves wish to possess, and also to the potential that the untamed land offers as a continuing challenge to their drive for mastery.

Overall, the cowboy, and the rodeo man who partakes of his mystique, may be seen as exemplifying culture, exerting a controlling force over nature, which includes animals, women, the land, and whatever wild elements can be brought under his power. The prevalent religious ideology of rodeo supports the syndrome of man's rightful dominion over the earth and all its creatures, and rodeo participants share with cowboys and ranchers the view of livestock as having been put on earth specifically for human use. People in rodeo perceive of the rodeo stock as well-treated, and always compare them to other animals which do not have as good a life. There is frequent mention of the fact that broncs would be "turned into glue or dog food" were it not for their participation in rodeo.

In the chapters which follow, the various man-animal relationships in rodeo are closely examined and compared, especially in the light of the wild/tame dichotomy which may be conceptualized in terms of the nature/culture opposition. The many complex relationships between man and horse within the context of the sport are considered first.

5

MAN-HORSE RELATIONSHIPS IN RODEO

The hero is a man with a horse and the horse is his direct tie to the freedom of the wilderness, for it embodies his ability to move freely across it and to dominate and control its spirit. Through the intensity of his relationship to his horse, the cowboy excites that human fantasy of unity with natural creatures the same fantasy seen in such figures as the centaurs of Greek mythology.

(Cawelti n.d.:57)

IN CONTRAST to many pastoralists, the cowboy was not just a cattle-tender, but a mounted herder. This gave him another considera-tion—his horse—his partner and essential helper in the task of herding cattle. This animal became the focus in his way of life, and often his greatest concern. Without the horse, his particular form of work and his unique adaptation to it would not have evolved. Indeed it can be said that in pioneer times the prairies of the West had literally belonged to the horseman, for his horse was the essential element by which penetration into the wilderness and settlement there were made possible. The frontiersman's livelihood, as well as his life and safety, depended upon his mount.

It was the herder's relationship to the horse that determined many of the traits of the cowboy mystique. These included his contempt for ordinary labor; the possession of confidence, sometimes extending to aggressiveness, which shaped his self-image as a conqueror; and probably also the chivalric code that tends to be characteristic of a mounted people. Included with these was a quality I would describe as a closeness to animality, a strange merging of his own nature with that of the beasts which so intimately shared his life and work.

Like his counterpart, of whom it has been said "unhorse a cowboy and you unman him" (Westermeier 1976:89), the rodeo contestant

131

finds his identity through association with the livestock, which are still essential to his way of life. Among these, horses are foremost, and they are involved in virtually all standard professional events except bull riding. Horses are the rodeo participants' antagonists in bronc riding and his helpers in the timed events in which cattle are his quarry.

At the very heart of rodeo is the bucking horse, central symbol of its spirit, which has come to stand for the West itself. Born out of the needs of ranching, and exaggerated for the sport of rodeo, the contest of riding a bucking horse, in my view, serves to express man's basic concern with the phenomenon of subduing that which is free, taming that which is wild, and measuring his own part in it. Rodeo people say of their classic saddle bronc event that it "shows the process of making a bronc into a partner."

I think that of all animals the horse is uniquely suited to represent, and demonstrate through constant recapitulation, the conquest of the wild—the extension of culture into nature. For the horse embodies, and is able to demonstrate, the polarities of wild/tame, and within one species it encompasses the varying degrees between them. The equine animal in America includes many gradations along a continuum which I see as existing between wild and tame. Near the wild pole are the feral animals descended from the original Spanish mustangs, a few of which still remain in the West, and which presumably have never been handled by man. Next in progression are broncs, which can usually be handled to some degree, and may be halter broken, but cannot easily be ridden. Near the tame pole in this conceptual scheme are the trained saddle horses—dependable, safe, and obedient to the rider. Then there are the horses that go further, to learn the skills of calf roping and steer tripping, which require still more cooperation between mount and man. Advancing beyond this even closer to tame, and in the direction away from nature toward culture, are the highly trained animals, such as dressage horses who perform intricate feats for their riders. In rodeo, novelty acts involving clowns and their trained horses are often in this category. Still further along in this direction are various high-schooled horses which can perform tricks and sequences under the tutelage of a trainer without a rider on their backs. Some of the maneuvers of calf roping are in this category, since the horse must carry them out after the rider has dismounted.

Thus I would like to assert that the horse, with its many forms running from wild to tame, serves as a symbolic bridge between nature and culture. Since the species partakes of both realms, an individual horse has within it the potentialities for many of the stages in domestication which the species may exemplify. One who deals with horses becomes aware of the ease of transformation which they frequently make evident. My own mare, who is well-trained and quite obedient during a ride, when turned out into pasture afterwards may kick and buck wildly, momentarily resembling an untamed range bronc. She will swerve sharply at such a time and gallop away at a pace little resembling the modulated canter that she had just performed under saddle. If I tried to catch her at that moment it would be impossible, yet a short time later she will come to the gate as docile as a pet. The facility with which the spheres of wild and tame are apparently entered and reentered by the equine spirit seems to be a remarkable quality of this animal.

It was this very quality of horses that a former saddle bronc champion who is now a rodeo manager and director of a rodeo bronc breeding farm recognized when we talked about preserving wilderness. Elucidating the saddle horse's affinity for the wild, which paradoxically exists simultaneously with its tameness, he said "my idea is to keep cars and motor bikes out of a wild area. But a horse is different; a horse is almost a wild animal, and one should be able to ride him into it."

This dual nature, I think, has particularly fascinated people, and accounts for the very special position of the horse in traversing the pathways between the wild and the tame. Other animals, of course, possess this quality to some degree, but the horse, through its various well-defined roles within the fabric of human society, particularly in the West, exemplifies it to a much greater extent and displays it more obviously.

In the case of horses, they are seen as possessing great beauty and power, but to make them useful for human ends they have to be first subdued and then trained to do man's bidding. In this process they must leave the realm of the wild and enter the sphere of the domesticated. Generally, the tradition in the East is to train a horse very gradually, starting even from the day of its birth, when it is first handled by people. Thus it grows up familiar with human contact, is halter-broken at a few months of age, often trained to commands on a lunge line when a yearling, and perhaps broken to harness by two years. When such a colt is old enough to bear the weight of a rider, the animal is already accustomed to the idea of human control, though it can still be fractious.

On the Western range, by contrast, a colt may come to his first day of training with very little, if any, past experience with people and no concept of being subject to their will. Thus an entirely different situation is structured, in which there is an immediate and intense human-animal contest. This is often interpreted as a "battle of wills" in which a person opposes the brute strength of the horse with his own type weapons—whip, spur, and bit, the instruments of culture —because he is inferior to the animal in muscular strength and power. There results a dramatic process, characteristically abrupt and violent, which has become universally symbolic for the act of conquering itself, the process of extending culture over nature.

Cowboys were by necessity intimately concerned with this process because the maintenance of their way of life depended upon the possession of riding mounts trained for obedience. Most cowboys probably broke their own, as part of their job, though there were on the early range "bronco-busters," men whose special business it was to travel around and perform this service for a fee. A usable "broke" horse was then, as it is now, not just a dependable work partner but also a source of great pride to a cowboy, ranchman, or rodeo hand, for a rider tends to feel the power of a horse as his own. The strength and swiftness which he harnesses with his mastery of his horse a man adds to his own self-image. There seems to be a process of identification by the horseman, and this is part of what makes him yearn to own the strongest, ride the wildest, and race the fastest.

I suggest the horse as an archetypal symbol of man's conquering force. The conquest of the animal itself represents the conquest of nature, and it is not difficult to understand why the figure of a man on a horse has throughout history been a sign of conquest. Power and aggressive force have long been associated with the mounted man, from the overbearing hordes of Genghis Khan to the feared Commanche raiders of the American Plains. For implicit in the horse-rider relationship is the fact that the rider has already mastered the horse, and his dominance over the animal may be seen as setting the stage for further conquest.

Indeed the American westward expansive experience was one of conquering—overcoming all types of hardships and obstacles: the harsh and unpredictable Great Plains climate, fierce Indians, vast distances, and awesome alien creatures of the wild. In the process of penetrating this realm, nature itself was forced to yield, as the wilderness was transformed into "civilization" by the imposition of man's will. This may be conceptualized in terms of the nature/culture dichotomy, and expressed by the opposition wild/tame. "Taming the raw land" is the phrase used to describe the winning of the West, and it can be aptly expressed through the transformation of the horse, a creature which is resistant to taming. In his unrestrained running form there resides the essence of wildness and intractability. At the other extreme, in his most subjugated and servile role, as in pulling a plow, he is totally devoid of autonomy. The capacity of the species to embody varying degrees of wild and tame is represented by the many different categories of horses which occupy particular roles in rodeo.

WILD HORSES

From the earliest days on the American frontier, wild horses have held a fascination for travelers who were fortunate enough to see them, and the transformations of the taming process often arrested the attention of perceptive chroniclers. Washington Irving, for example, in making a record of his 1832 excursion into the southern Great Plains, wrote of a mustang just captured:

> I could not but look with compassion upon this fine young animal, whose whole course of existence had been so suddenly reversed. From being a denizen of these vast pastures, ranging at will from plain to plain and mead to mead, cropping of every herb and flower, and drinking of every stream, he was suddenly reduced to perpetual and painful servitude, to pass his life under the harness and the curb, amid, perhaps, the din and dust and drudgery of cities. The transition in his lot was such as sometimes takes place in human affairs, and the fortunes of towering individuals;—one day, a prince of the prairies—the next day, a pack horse!
>
> (1971:122)

Here Irving, through a sense of his own identification with the horse, epitomizes the wild/tame duality by his empathetic perceptions. The freedom-to-slavery transition is made more emphatic by the description of the mustang as a privileged dweller in the Western wilds, untainted by the ills of civilization. Thus wild/tame and freedom/captivity come to be parallel to the opposition country/city or West/East, to fit the romantic concept of the American West as a primeval paradise.

Similarly, Josiah Gregg, in his 1844 journal of frontier experiences, documented the effect of the transition from wild to tame, noting that

> The wild horses are generally well formed, with trim and clean limbs; still their elegance has been much exaggerated by travellers, because they have seen them at large, abandoned to their wild and natural gaiety.

> Then, it is true, they appear superb indeed; but when caught and tamed,
> they generally dwindle down to ordinary ponies.
>
> (1966:208)

Significantly, the same author goes on to describe the reverse
process—that is, the change from tame back to wild:

> It is a singular fact, that the gentlest wagon horse (even though quite
> fagged with travel), once among a drove of mustangs, will often acquire
> in a few hours all the intractable wildness of his untamed companions.

There is, then, nothing stable about the taming phenomenon, and
various stages of tameness can be reached in both directions. Pertinent here is the statement of Anthony Amaral in his description of the
natural history of the wild stallion that "animals capable of domestication are known to be wilder . . . when they have gone wild." He
quotes a stockman as saying that "in a roundup the hardest one to 'cut
out,' the leader of them all in a mad race across the prairie, is the old,
gentle, well-broken saddle or work horse, once he gets a taste of
freedom" (1969:38).

Another writer expresses the same thought, adding the man-horse
identification motif to his comment on the range-born mustang who
reverts to the wild after a period of captivity:

> You can talk about your Patrick Henrys and your George Washingtons;
> you can warble about your country ' 'tis of thee,' the Star Spangled
> Banner and our own red, white and blue; but the upright tail of a
> mustang that wore cinches for years and then got back to the great
> unfenced will continue to fan the atmosphere as the true banner of
> freedom that never does come down.
>
> (Steele 1941:188)

Accordingly, it seems that a feral animal, the mustang, serves as a
more precise symbol of freedom than a native wild animal (using wild
here to mean not belonging to a domesticable species). For a previously tame horse can become the wildest of all when it throws off its
bonds. And conversely when a man looks at a wild horse that has
never been vanquished, it is with the knowledge that the animal
bears within it the inherent capacity of its species for both extremes in
the wild/tame duality.

This explains the apparent paradox that, though they are members
of the animal species most often in bondage to man, the one thing
that wild mustangs seem to stand for in the human imagination is
freedom. Hope Ryden, one of the foremost authorities on the New
World Mustang, emphasized this when she summed up its history:

The wild horse in America has a romantic history that dates back nearly four centuries. His domestic ancestors carried the Conquistadors through the unexplored territory, transformed the Indians' style of life, and gave inspiration to such artists as Remington and Russell. The age of exploration might better have been called the Age of the Spanish Horse, for without this particular type of horse, the New World would have been almost impenetrable. But the most interesting thing this horse ever did in America he did for himself when he took his freedom.

(Serven 1972:17)

In the conquering of the mustang, the frontiersmen found expression for the same sense of mastery which was paramount in the conquest of the West. But there was (and often still is) a contradiction, for at the same time that men wished to conquer the mustang, they also admired its wildness and indomitability. People no doubt envied, and identified with, the wild horse for his freedom and untamed spirit, but at the same time they wished to deprive him of these qualities. In this they showed a feeling of ambivalence, and it is this element that I see strongly emphasized as a theme in rodeo. Ranch/rodeo people express the need to recapitulate the taming of the wild in a ritual glorification of the process which they have structured into a sport. They long to be the conqueror, the winner, the one who can ride the unridable, who can defeat the rankest animal. They say there is no feeling on earth so good as the satisfaction that comes from knowing you have done it, you have made a good ride. Yet at the same time they want the wildness of the animal preserved, so that they may continue to pit themselves against it. It is of great significance that the broncs are never demonstrably changed by the events of modern rodeo; they are not "broken" in the arena, and still appear wild when they leave it after each performance. (In very early rodeo, horse and rider were turned loose and the contest was continued until the horse stopped bucking or the rider was thrown off). Today, the eight-second buzzer abruptly halts the contest, and the broncs are not literally "conquered" (though the word is used) by the contestants in the same sense that, say, the bull in a Spanish bull fight is ultimately vanquished by the matador. It is indeed remarkable the way that this contradiction has been made a basic element of rodeo. For in the scoring, as I have pointed out, the marking for the horse—based on its "wildness," those qualities which have made it the most difficult to ride—counts just as much toward the contestant's final score as the rider's demonstration of skill and control. This preordained and structured counterbalance between the forces of man and animal, tame and wild, dominance and resistance, is, I think, the

Above: The essence of rodeo is a counterbalance between the forces of man and animal, tame and wild, dominance and resistance.　　*(JJJ Photo)*

Below: As a much-anticipated grand finale on the rodeo program, the wild horse race reenacts old-time "bronco busting" on the plains. *(JJJ Photo)*

essence of the sport. The spirit of these oppositions is reflected by the oft-repeated rodeo verse

There isn't a bronc
That can't be rode;
There isn't a cowboy
That can't be throwed.

In a larger sense, this is a reflection of a similar duality of feeling held by the pioneers about westward expansion. For people were attracted to the new land's untamed beauty and vastness and its potential for providing them with room for individualistic self-expression and independence—in short, its challenge. Yet at the same time its isolation and the wildness of its limitless expanses frightened and repelled them. They wanted to settle it, tame it, civilize it, and they relentlessly set about the task of transforming it. They strove to create out of it a domesticated sphere, a manicured garden that would come to resemble the homeland they had left behind. There was the paradox that part of what was destroyed in the process were the very qualities which had drawn them to the new land. The exhilaration born of the gigantic struggle between man and nature on the frontier would come to an end, and they would mourn its loss. Nostalgia would make them look backward to the challenge. Cattlemen from the beginning have glorified the early days of their historic struggle. The attitude of constantly looking toward the past, to a vanishing way of life, remains typical of today's rancher and cowboy. They continually dwell on the advantages of the old days, and, consciously and unconsciously, try to recreate it in their work. Ranchers participate in wagon train expeditions (not to be confused with those staged for tourists), hold roundups which are no longer entirely ranch necessities, and still place horses at the center of their world. It is with great interest that I note a comparison between this behavior and that of the formerly pastoral Lapps (Pelto 1973:162). For when the snowmobile began to make drastic changes in the reindeer herders' lives, men still continued to attend roundups even when these were no longer vitally related to their own subsistence economy. As in the case of the cattlemen, these seasonal events were closely interwoven into their pastoral traditions and values and continued to hold deep meaning for them in a social context.

Their habitual attitude of looking to the past is, I think, part of the pervasive strain of sadness which one always senses about the present-day cattlemen and cowboys. They reveal in their conversations, the editorials in their journals, and in their personal lives a desire that conditions should be, indeed must be, restored to their former and more satisfying state. Unable to completely accept the fact that things cannot be as they once were, nonetheless they cling to old values and an ethos that may not always fit the context of modern life. They isolate themselves in a world of their own in which they perceive existence as being at least partly ordered as though the old life of the cattle frontier still existed. Rodeo is, of course, a major factor in the perpetuation of this cattle-complex mystique, and it serves to dramatize the basic frontier dilemma of man's being simultaneously attracted and repelled by the force of wildness. This ambivalence is articulated through the spectrum of wild to tame exhibited within the sport.

THE MUSTANGS

At the wildest end of the spectrum are the few remaining mustang herds which still run free in certain areas of Western rangeland. They are feral animals, presumed to be descendants of the domesticated Spanish horses that were brought to the New World and have reverted to a wild state. Their continued existence is precarious because of dwindling land and the controversy which rages about their status and value. Those who want the mustangs destroyed say that they compete with cattle and domestic horses for grass, and that they use land which should be reserved for game animals. Since mustangs are feral and not native wild animals, their detractors claim that they upset the natural balance of the ecosystem. Defenders look upon the wild horses as living symbols of the historic and pioneer spirit of the West. They also point out that even though native wild horses became extinct in North America due to some undetermined cause operating just after the last Ice Age, they had previously evolved as a species on the plains of this continent and therefore would still be compatible with prairie ecology.

Even when their own ranches are located far from the regions where feral equines could be a threat, cattlemen as a whole show much preoccupation with the subject of mustangs. The editor of the ranch-rodeo magazine "Hoof and Horn" describes the difficulties which beset the cattle industry. He complains that "In some areas, because of a foolish law, half-starved and worthless wild horses and burros roam the lands the ranchers pay to lease, competing for the sparse grass with the cattle. The rancher already supports much of the nation's wild game" (Searle 1977:3). Evident here is a motivating factor with which I shall deal in more detail in Chapter 9. This is the tendency for stockmen to emphasize the role of "the wild" (in this case the feral) in opposing their interests, and to view it as "the enemy." I am not minimizing the importance of the practical level of the ranchers' problems with mustangs nor the stockmen's necessary concerns with protecting their property, but rather I am looking beneath the surface. For the number of people whose operations are actually hindered by wild horses is small in comparison to the number who condemn the animals, and the ranchers' almost unanimous and vehement reaction against them has significance beyond the economic realm.

Ranchers speak with disdain of the mustangs, asserting that "they take too much room, too much grass. They serve no useful purpose. This country isn't rich enough to afford the land to keep them. People's needs should come first." Rodeo participants often hold a slightly different view, showing some ambivalence toward what to them represents the wild realm. A champion saddle bronc rider who is one of the few without a ranch background thought "we should keep some wild horses; after all, they've been there from the year One." The manager of one very large rodeo, a rancher and former saddle bronc champion, believed that wild horses "should get some protection, but it should be limited"—an attitude that sums up the majority of rodeo participants' opinions. Most felt that to set aside "large areas" is impractical because of the increasing human population in the country. One man, a rodeo manager and rodeo school operator with long experience in the sport, gave me particularly interesting insights. Regarding the issue of saving the wild horses, he said "I would hate to see them all gone, but I sympathize with the people who are bothered by them. I have been too busy making a living to get into it, but I would hate for my grandkids not to see them like I have. But then, these kids will be able to go to another planet and see it there, which I can never do. So it's what's important while you're here."

A saddle bronc rider with a ranch background, who was also an official of the Professional Rodeo Cowboys Association, had evidently given much thought to the issue. In discussing the subject of wild horses he indicated perceptions which are especially pertinent. "Wild horses are not good for anything. If you catch them, their mentality is so low you couldn't ride them. They are just scrub animals. There is no use for them and we should get rid of them. They are inbred, unintelligent, and their body conformation is not good. Inbreeding has a lot to do with it; some breeds are less intelligent, harder to train." Another rodeo man said "as they multiply the wild horses get smaller and weaker." In these attitudes I see a prime example of the use of the nature/culture opposition: they were expressing the belief that without the influence of man—that is, of culture—exerted upon it the wild horse became totally useless. Left to itself—that is, purely to nature—the animal degenerated physically and mentally. The whole complex of domestication comes into play here—the intervention of man through selective breeding to "improve" livestock, to alter its characteristics in order to make it more useful for human needs. In these informants' views, the imposition of culture over the natural animal not only molds the species to human need, but as a concomitant of the process leads to increased intelligence and vigor. According to biologists, however, this is not necessarily true; a wild species can possess more intelligence and vigor than its domesticated counterpart, and often does. But the reason I find these rodeo men's perceptions so significant is their assertion of the idea that what is domesticated through the imposition of the will of man is in so many ways improved. They were the reflection of an ethos which generally places man, and all that results from human manipulatory power, on a level of greater value than that of what is natural, or wild.

THE WILD HORSE RACE OF RODEO

The wild horse race of rodeo is an event which attempts to reenact the process which would occur when wild horses were broken. When this performance is included, it is always the last feature of the program, and is referred to as "the grand finale." The horses used for it are supposed to be animals which have been handled little, if at all, and are not halter-broken. Everything is done to make them appear wilder—particularly shouting and gunfire. To a sensitive observer the horses seem to be a study in fear; every motion of their bodies expresses terror at the unnatural situation into which they have been so abruptly thrust. The announcer at Cheyenne Frontier Days, though, where the event is an old tradition, drew the spectators' attention to "the stored-up cussedness of these wild, vicious, and defiant mustangs." I found it a violent and confused panorama consisting of a melee of plunging hooves and rearing bodies, dust, and the sound of shouts and whinnying. Groups of men pulling and straining on ropes attached to the horses' halters appeared to oppose the balking animals with brute force. Yet they were waiting to subdue the beasts with the accouterments of culture, for they must be saddled and ridden. The event, described as "a rodeo unto itself"—a meaningful title since it represents the spirit of the sport and its origin—has great audience appeal, and ranchers especially enjoy it. One older Montana rancher said "I won the wild horse race at Whitehall in 1938. I liked doing it; it was no different than what I had done all my life. We rode horses that way all our lives. At that time, the country was black with horses. I still train my own horses and wouldn't let nobody break a horse for me yet. Maybe I will at seventy. We break 'em as three or four year olds, and they're wild till that time. We don't raise 'em like in the East, around a barn and in a small pasture. It's a different life for a horse."

Anticipation of the wild horse race builds up throughout a rodeo performance, and announcers take advantage of this to stress the coming excitement. Periodically throughout two rodeos I attended in the rain, announcers made such remarks about the contestants as "Sealey says he's worried about holding these horses; their ears are getting wet," and there was continual banter about the practice of "earing a bronc"—grabbing and biting the horse's ear. Spectators commented long in advance of the event, "the wild horse race will really be something in this mud."

The ear-biting was uppermost in the minds of both audience and participants, and though some of its appeal is no doubt due to sensationalism, I feel there are other factors involved. The mouth contact suggests a kind of close intimacy between man and animal, a feeling that they are in one moment simultaneously conjoined in wildness and bestiality. In the human biting of the animal I see a combination of revulsion and attraction—a ritual in which one is impelled to bite, hurt the animal, yet by doing so, identify with it, become one with it. By inflicting pain in such an elemental way—without whip or spur or prod as extensions of culture, but rather with a part of their own body, as nature—I saw suggested a welding of the two in wildness, a merging of the two in nature. Though informants said of the tradition of "earing" that "it's the best way to hold a bronc," there are undoubtedly other ways of doing it. At Cheyenne, for example, the ear-biting was not allowed due to a local ruling, and the ear was only twisted or pinched, yet the event proceeded similarly in other respects.

THE BRONCS OF RODEO

Rodeo broncs are different from wild horses. As one informant aptly phrased it "they have the wild edge taken off them." They can be handled to some degree, are accustomed to human contact, and are usually halter-broken. It is mainly when one attempts to ride them that they demonstrate the qualities that designate them as rodeo rough stock. Real wild horses, I was told, like the mustangs, do not make good bucking horses; "they are too scared. They would fall down, run into fences with you and break their necks; they wouldn't buck too much. Wild horses try to get away, but bucking horses aren't afraid of anything, they just concentrate on bucking you off." It is clear, then, that in the transition from wild horse to bucking bronc, there has been an intrusion of a certain amount of culture. Broncs can be handled enough to allow their feet to be trimmed, for example, and are routinely shipped by truck. With their status a balance is struck between the extremes of a feral horse at one pole and the "broke" or trained horse at the other. In the case of the broncs, a small amount of human input, or culture, has moved them farther along the continuum away from pure "nature." This balance is the thing that, I believe, makes the bronc the essence of rodeo and the foremost symbol of what it is that the sport, at its deepest level, is expressing.

Rodeo, in its structuring and ordering of events, manipulates the amount of culture exerted upon the broncs in various significant ways. The bareback bronc, for instance, wears no halter or rein, and its free head gives it more control over the rider, while affording the rider less control over the horse. One bareback contestant expressed this by saying the "rider must show controlled wildness." By this he was also referring to the required spurring action of the event. The bareback rigging consists of only the barest essentials—a leather strap with a handhold—allowing the rider to be in direct contact with the horse's back. Interestingly, the leather glove and the leather hand-hold into which the hand is inserted are viewed by the bareback rider as extensions of his body, and many rituals are attached to these items. For endless hours during his apprenticeship and between rodeos, the contestant works on his glove and his grip, until he comes to feel more natural with his gloved hand in the handhold than in its normal state, and feels "it's just like a part of my body." Artificial aids such as stirrups are of course lacking to the bareback rider, so that he is more confined to nature during his event than is the saddle bronc contestant, and exerts less control. It is rodeo tradition that the bareback event occurs first on the program, the saddle bronc some-where near the middle, and the bull riding at the end. When a wild horse race is included, it is always last on the program. This suggests to me that the rodeo begins and ends with the "wildest" events— those in which the human control element is minimized. Thus I view the program as neatly framed by a keynote and a finale in which there is comparatively more of nature and less of culture than is true of intervening events. These wilder events encompass and contain the other events in which the balance of control swings more in the direction of the human element. These are the timed events and the classic saddle bronc event. Superficially, of course, the saddle bronc event is much like the bareback. But in a symbolic way it is quite different. Here the horse wears a halter and the attached rein gives the rider some control of his mount's head. A saddle with stirrups provides more apparatus to signify control, and the event becomes more highly suggestive of the overcoming of the wild through the imposition of these objects representing culture. The close contact between the man's and the horse's body has been eliminated in the saddle bronc event, and the total effect of all the regulations is to swing the balance more heavily in favor of the culture end of the scale. It is significant that points are deducted for losing one's stirrups— signifying failure to maintain control—as well as for touching the animal or equipment with the free hand—indicating too much control. Thus the rider is judged on the amount of force exerted over the animal, and the horse is evaluated on the degree of wildness exhibited in opposing the contestant. Degrees of human control (culture) versus varying amounts of resistance (nature) allowed to the horse are being regulated in order to produce the differently balanced contests that make up the sport of rodeo.

PERCEPTIONS OF BRONCS

Since informants' perceptions of broncs is a topic central to my study, I spent a great deal of time eliciting these from many different rodeo and ranch people under various conditions. One word was most closely associated with broncs in all minds and that was "outlaw." Officials, contestants, spectators, ranchers, and anyone speaking of rodeo categorized the bronc, as the Lame Deer, Montana, rodeo announcer did, as "mavericks and outlaws who delight in tossing the cowboy to the ground." As one rodeo man summed it up, "broncs are crazy, they need some outlaw in them; the best ones have meanness, toughness, and buck bred into them." A saddle bronc rider gave the illuminating insight that "bucking horses are outlaws; they are not really wild, but they don't want to cooperate with society. You couldn't use them on a ranch for nothing, they would keep bucking." One stock contractor likened them to "families of people who rebel against society." A rodeo manager called them "unbroke stock horses." He said "some were, or are, broke, but they don't want anybody to ride them." A saddle bronc rider, also a rancher, said "horses are just like people" (it is significant that many prefaced their remarks with this statement), "some are okay. But these rodeo broncs are outlaws, criminals." Another belief was "it's got to be in him to buck; only about one out of a thousand that are tried will keep it up. 'Midnight' was gentle in other ways, but great for bucking. Broncs are ornery in general, and they've got to have a fighting heart. They are like a prize fighter. You couldn't make these guys [the rodeo contestants] into prize fighters, because they haven't got what it takes. All horses will buck once or twice when they are wild, but then they quit. These broncs, the buckers, will keep it up." Another summed up the essence of a bronc this way: "the horse who will buck is like a barroom brawler. When you walk into a bar there is one man who will brawl. He is like the rodeo horse—his point of resistance is close to the top. If you back him into a corner, the barroom brawler comes out fast. But the passive person, like the horse who doesn't buck, will stay there [in the corner] all day." Another way of putting this was "a good bucker will resist you, and that resistance will come out in the form of a pure honest buck. This is the bronc's way of saying 'I will not be pushed.' " It was frequently stated, "the bronc has an inbred resentment for man." An information sheet given out for publicity purposes by the International Rodeo Association calls attention to the fact that "power, violence, and rebellion" are "terms of pride" when applied to bucking horses, and stresses that violence and rebellion are "natural traits of that one-in-a-hundred horse."

A rodeo manager and former contestant assured me "if a horse wants to buck, there is no way to stop him unless you kill him." Similarly, "there is no way to make him buck if he doesn't want to. A bronc is a horse you are never able to trust or put someone on. He is like a man who was sent to jail for killing three or four people, and they say later he is rehabilitated. But you can never trust him in your heart again, at least I wouldn't." Broncs are often perceived as "bad," as when an announcer at a collegiate rodeo in Nebraska explained "that's how the game of rodeo began—with cowboys getting together to ride bad horses."

Broncs are viewed as rebels against society, who cannot be relied upon for the useful jobs that are meant to be done by horses. Their image is essentially one of unpredictability, a quality generally stressed. Announcers frequently remind the audience that "there is no such thing as a trained bucking horse; you never know what they will do next." Or "bucking broncs are not trained, just mean, and you

The best broncs are considered "outlaws." Power, violence, and rebellion
are terms of pride when applied to such animals.

(Photo by Randy Huffman)

never can tell what one will do." Rodeo people asserted "broncs can change their minds just like humans; they are unpredictable." They want it to be known that "it is not possible to teach a horse the bucking motion; there is no way to train and cue a bucking horse."

It is interesting that a few rodeo people imputed a conscious thought process to the broncs. Illustrating this, one said that "when a bareback bronc finds he cannot buck off his rider [due to a new and tighter handhold] the horse suffers from brain damage [frustration]. They become discouraged this way, and are damaged for a long time." The announcer at Lincoln, Nebraska, attributed premeditated cunning to the equine animal, explaining that "the horse lays a trap for you; he goes easy at first, and waits 'til the cowboy's guard is down, and then lays it onto him." Here, the bronc is imbued with a sense of the purposeful malice and enmity of nature as it opposes man.

With few exceptions, I found that whatever factors informants felt to be responsible for making a good bucking horse, they were considered to be inherent, innate in that particular animal. This is an extremely important point, for it makes clear that in their minds it is always nature, not culture, that produces the buck. The contest could then be considered an uncomplicated example of culture (human) versus nature (animal). (The process of making the bronc wild by means of spurs, prodding, noise, and a flank strap did not enter into these concepts; as I have said, the horses do stop bucking when the flank strap is released in the arena, though they may still remain "wild," in the sense of unmanageable).

The widespread belief that broncs are wild solely because of innate predisposition has practical implications for the sport. For now that good broncs are much in demand because of the increasing popularity of rodeo, attempts are being made to produce them on special farms where they are selectively bred for the characteristic of bucking. The most notable example of this is the Calgary Stampede Ranch, where geneticists and veterinarians under the leadership of the Stampede manager are working with a large herd of horses to produce stock for this gigantic rodeo. The director told me of the plan to use embryo transplants in order to produce the greatest number of the best bucking stock possible. A fascinating point that I would like to emphasize here is that in essence such efforts are an attempt to reverse the techniques which have over centuries been directed toward breeding the buck out of a horse. Historically, through the ages, mankind's progress has been associated with the production of a tame horse, obedient to the rider's will. Now, in order to insure the continuance of rodeo and to preserve the spirit of the frontier past

which the sport exemplifies, people are conversely trying to breed the
buck back into the horse. The hopeful director of one such project
says "so long as we produce horses with the will to resist by bucking,
we'll continue to have rodeo." The efforts being made are, I think,
remarkable testament to the strength of the frontier ethos, and the
importance that is attached to keeping it alive in the minds of the
ranch/rodeo people to whose world it continues to give order and
meaning.

Stressing the inborn nature of broncs, one rodeo official and saddle
bronc rider told me "a bronc has a personality like people do. Every
individual has a different personality. For example, out of a family of
kids, two may turn out to be professional people—a doctor or lawyer,
some white collar and some blue collar workers, and a couple will be
completely outlaws. What is the thing that makes them go in
different directions? A lot of it is in the genes, and this can be related
to bucking horse breeding programs." The degree to which rodeo
people attribute the trait of bucking to genetics is especially significant when one considers the prevalence today of the opposite
notion that environmental conditions are in large measure responsible for behavior. No informant ever attributed the outlaw quality of a
bronc to a condition of its early life, in the way, for example, one
hears that a dog bites someone because it was beaten as a puppy, or a
man embezzles money because of the trauma of a deprived childhood.
As a genetic trait, then, bronc resistance and "orneryness" are viewed
as inextricably a part of nature.

In the outlaw imagery so consistently used by rodeo informants, I
saw that though the contestants think of themselves as conquerors,
they also have a contradictory sense of identification with the creatures they consider outside the bounds of conventional "society."
They express this by their pride in their own lack of conformity to the
code of the greater population. They reveal it in song, where lyrics
place cowboys at the farthest pole from "doctors and lawyers and
such"—symbols of society's acceptance. Once, when I was introduced to a bronc rider described as "flaked out," the informant who
wanted me to meet this contestant did not criticize the rider's bizarre
actions. Rather he indicated his own feelings about nonconformity:
"That guy is the most free you can be, doing his own thing. They tell
him what to do, where to hold the rein, but he does it his own way.
Nobody can be totally free, but he is near it."

Over and over again rodeo people stressed that the greatest percentage of bucking horses are "spoiled saddle horses," or "kids' horses or
riding mounts that go sour." Such animals are believed to be the

commonest sources of broncs, since breeding farms as suppliers are still in the future. It is said that a riding horse "goes bad" or "turns sour," starts bucking riders off, learns he can do it, and is henceforth unsafe to ride. No special event or cause brings this about, the bucking trait is just "in" this particular animal, and presumably has been previously held in check. The dichotomy of wild/tame is exemplified here, as it exists in the horse's dual nature. Thus the animal has the capacity to be in either realm; it can shuck off the restraints of culture that have been imposed on it by man's training, and revert to the wild—its true nature in the case of the bronc. The belief that "the best broncs" are obtained in this way is indicative of the concept that a former state of domesticity means an increased degree of wildness in an animal. Relevant to this is the story a saddle bronc rider told me about a pack horse in Glacier National Park who started bucking off his packs. The animal was of course sold, and eventually became one of rodeo's star broncs. Known as "Descent," he won the bucking horse of the year award six or seven times.

Rodeo stories support the notion, frequently encountered in frontier reminiscences, that horses can go in either direction between wild and tame. A Montana rancher told me "I once got a horse from a bucking string and it was one of the best saddle horses I ever had. I had to educate it a bit. It didn't buck very often; it only piled me a couple of times. After I treated him gentle, he quit this. He was always a one-man horse, though; I was the only one who could ride him. A stranger might make him buck." Thus he indicated that a conversion between wild and tame was made, but it was a fragile and quickly reversible one, and did not essentially change the horse; the animal was only transformed in relation to a particular person. This data again demonstrates the basic duality of the horse which enables it to act as a symbolic intermediary between man and nature, in both directions.

With one accord rodeo people indicate that the flank strap does not make the horse buck. They are adamant on this point, and enraged at the myths commonly promulgated among Easterners and humane societies that the strap is lined with tacks and burrs, or that it is applied to a stallion's genitals to cause pain. Ranch/rodeo people do conceive of the sport as violent and dangerous but not deliberately cruel. An articulate informant, who managed a rodeo school, said the flank strap "only changes the style of bucking on a horse that will do it anyway. Without it he would rear up in front rather than in the rear. Horses bucked differently in the old days when the cinch was the only foreign object that touched the horse's body." Others agreed that the strap "increases bucking potential," and some admitted "it annoys them, as the flank is a sensitive spot." All opinions thus confirmed the notion that it is not something attributable to culture that causes bucking, but an element intrinsic to the animal.

One Wyoming collegiate rodeo contender, who "would rather go down the road than go to college, because it's the most romantic of all sports," said he felt horses "enjoyed bucking." There seemed to be a sense of identification on his part. The idea of play is important to rodeo people, but it merges with work, for their play *is* their work, and they seldom, if ever, turn elsewhere for recreation. Another interesting notion I (rarely) encountered is that bucking is atavistic, representing the old pattern of the equine reaction to attack by a predator. Rodeo's concern with bucking might be theoretically related in this way to the rancher's hatred of predator species and a possible feeling of unity with horses against a common enemy.

In summary the bronc, central symbol of rodeo, seems to represent an outlaw, a force of resistance to conventional society. Rodeo people believe that its rebelliousness is genetic and cannot be taught. Something within a particular animal causes this behavior, and makes it incorrigible, even though the horse may appear docile at times and go through stages of its life when it appears to have been tamed. On the one hand there may be a sense of human identification with the bronc because it is looked upon as free of the constraints of society, but on the other hand there is the predominating idea that the bronc is a wild element that must be conquered. The unpredictability of a bronc is a key quality, and one which expresses the essence of rodeo itself. For, as announcers for the sport often repeat, "anything can happen in a rodeo, and usually does," and "no two performances are ever the same." The bronc's trait of unpredictability fits in with its basic designation as a part of nature over which the more stable force of culture should and must prevail.

HORSES OF THE TIMED EVENTS OF RODEO

In contrast to the bronc, who occupies a position near the wild extreme of the wild/tame dichotomy, is the timed event horse, who appears far along toward the sphere of the tame. Unlike the bronc, the enemy of society whom men admire yet strive to defeat, the roping or steer wrestler's horse is the counterpart of the cowboy's mount, his indispensable servant and companion. If, as a newspaper reporter was told at Cheyenne Frontier Days, the rough stock events comprise the "macho" part of the rodeo and the timed events the "muscle" portion, then muscle power must include that of the horse as the contestant's helper.

THE CALF ROPER'S HORSE

Within the context of the standard rodeo program (exclusive of novelty acts), I view the calf roper's horse as the nearest to the tame polarity. It is interesting to observe how this concept is structured into the sport. If a rodeo logo or motif includes a second equine figure, it is always that of a calf roping horse, his motionless, subdued, and controlled pose contrasting sharply to the leaping, kicking, bucking bronco.

Calf roping is called by rodeo officials "the horseman's sport," the clearest example of cooperation between horse and man. They point out that a large share of the success in this event depends upon the horse. Ropers told me that not every horse has the potential to become a calf-horse. "If the horse doesn't fit you, you get rid of it." A champion calf roper gave insights about this event when he told me "you can't baby a calf-horse; he must listen and respond like a child. They have to fear you a little. You can't make a calf roper out of a horse if it is against their nature to do it. You have to stop then, and get another horse to try it with. You go through dozens and ruin them. You ruin several before you know how to do it." Here, as with the broncs, it is noteworthy that, in spite of the great amount of training given to a calf-horse, there is still something innate within the individual, a capacity or potential, which is a prime requisite. With the calf-horse this is its ability to accept—not resist as the bronc did—the superimposition of culture (in the form of training) over its animal instincts (nature).

All contestants in this event agreed with the champion roper at Big Timber, Montana, who claimed "there is more to calf roping and training a calf-horse than is true of any other rodeo event." He went on to identify the characteristics of the horse's training. "The things they do are against nature. They have to move backwards, pull back against the rope, and they have to stand. What the calf roping horse does is completely against nature. The rider is not on him; he has to do it on his own." There was a preoccupation in the roper's mind with the horse moving backwards. (In horse shows, I remember, a rider is always asked to make his mount take a few steps backwards to test its training). The calf roper stressed this point: "Did you ever see a horse grazing backwards in a pasture? It never happens, and yet the calf roping horse has to go backwards. This is not natural for a horse and it takes a lot to train him for it." So it seemed that the role of culture in subduing nature was again the uppermost concept in the contestant's mind, and moving backwards represented for him the force of schooling that can, with difficulty, overcome natural instincts.

Calf roping horses stand at the epitome among rodeo animals for doing the bidding of man, and perhaps best represent the fulfillment of what society views as the proper role of a horse. Interestingly, ropers' horses were not usually categorized with women as were the broncs. Perhaps this is because the closeness to nature, the unpredictability, and the exciting and sexually suggestive elements which rodeo attributes to bucking horses are lacking. Calf-horses, in contrast, were more likely to be classed with one's children. Ropers felt that their horses must behave toward them like obedient children. A rodeo official, taking every opportunity to emphasize the good care given to rodeo stock, framed his expression in these terms: "The roper's horse gets better care than his children; it's his bread and butter." Within this context, the horse is an underling, a dependent subject to "parental" authority.

Such categorizations are not definitive, and the roper's horse moves back and forth between the "child" classification and that of a partner. Calf roping has also been called "the marriage of horse and man." The partner image is stressed by announcers and described in rodeo programs. As the event is in progress comments are made: "In this contest a lot depends upon the horse," or "Horses deserve a lot of credit in this event." Mounts are described as "usually Quarter Horses, with the speed plus the knowhow to get back off the rope. It's up to the horse to hold the calf on the ground by backing up on the rope." The image of the calf-horse as a working animal committed to its task is demonstrated in such announcements as "if a horse does his job in this event, he faces the calf." At Cheyenne, where horse races were taking place outside the arena simultaneously with calf roping, the announcer praised a roper's horse: "He didn't even look at the race horses going by him. He knows what he is supposed to do." This indicates that the ability to concentrate, a human value, has been imposed upon the animal—a high degree of culture extending over nature. Similarly, at the Little Britches rodeo, a child, lacking expertise, looped his rope over his horse's legs. When the horse stood quietly in spite of this, the announcer pointed out "that is a well-trained horse; he is to be congratulated for not coming unglued and causing a wreck." The implication is that his animal nature has been overcome and he is in a realm of super-domestication—predictable. This is especially so since it is in a horse's nature to "spook", or shy, a characteristic that has never been successfully bred out of domestic horses.

Conversely, I was struck by the evident lack of patience with the roping horses' mistakes. One contestant at Calgary, in a rage because his horse failed to pull back on the calf, threw dirt at the horse. Such public displays are frowned upon, but it is clear that perfection is demanded of the animals. It is noteworthy that the sympathy of the audience never appeared to be with the roping horse. My observations among spectators were that they viewed this type of horse more as a kind of machine rather than empathizing with any lapses in skill of performance. For example, once when the horse dragged the calf away from the roper, spectators shouted "the poor guy," and "that makes me want to get a two-by-four for that horse." They totally identified with the man in this recapitulation of ranch life, calling out such expressions as "it's a bummer," and "get rid of that horse," when the horse failed the contestant.

The point I wish to stress here is that culture is seen as having been exerted over animal nature to a far greater extent in the roper's horse as contrasted to the bronc. The image of the bronc as essentially unpredictable (and thus closer to nature) is here reversed, for dependability is the paramount quality of the roping horse. It is constantly emphasized that to do well in this event man and horse must "know what the other is going to do, know what is expected of one another." Great advantage is believed to accrue to the man whose horse gives a consistent performance from one rodeo to the next. This quality of predictability associates the roping horse with culture, with being an instrument of man's will. In the pastoralist experience, as lived by the American cowboy, the realm of wild nature was seen as an unpredictable force that opposed man. This viewpoint relates to the association of unpredictability with nature and of consistency with the more "rational" force of culture.

Ropers are quick to point out that horses must never become "pets." Speaking of calf-horses, a roper told me "you can't treat a rodeo horse like a dog. If you pet him he will not work well in the arena. You don't have to abuse him, but he must have discipline to perform." There is a precedent among working cowboys, who felt that "the meanest, most unreliable object in cattle country was a 'pet horse' " (Rollins 1973:268). Analyzing this concern, it is obvious that a pet horse would not have the machine-like precision required of a calf-horse, and would expect to have input of its own—an intolerable condition for a roper's mount.

The most significant thing about the horse's role in the calf roping operation is that he performs his most essential function while he is not being directly controlled by a man. For he is unmounted during the critical time of the tying of the calf. This places him near the extreme tame, or culture, end of the spectrum. His status is dramatically emphasized: being free from the direct domination of a rider, he could bolt and run away, or refuse to pull the rope, but very rarely does.

HORSES IN OTHER TIMED EVENTS

In other timed events, the horse does not work in a riderless state, but nevertheless a great amount of training is evident. The steer roping event, whose details have been given previously, is sometimes referred to as "the thinking man's part of rodeo," because it requires great skill, and the horse shares in this image. With its intricate maneuvers and the great weight of the steer, contestants admit "it is very demanding on the horse; there is a lot to learn." They feel horses have to be "level-headed" and have a "steady disposition" to qualify. One participant said of this event "these horses are like race horses, they have to practice every day. You need to go slow teaching horses this event." To the spectator, however, the rider's skill is demonstrated as paramount in the arena, and the horse appears only instrumental to it.

In team roping the factor of two horses and two riders working in conjunction adds a dimension of camaraderie between the men and demands an extra measure of cooperation from the two horses. Each must maneuver his rider into position according to whether he is the header or the heeler, and both must face the steer once he is roped. But their riders remain in the saddle throughout.

Thus it is evident that in the timed events the man-horse relationships show important differences from those in bronc riding. Roping animals are far along on the tame end of the continuum I have proposed. They are servants of man and they are manipulated to show off the rider's skills. Each is an adjunct to the rider, never occupying "center stage" as an equestrian performer might.

RODEO HORSES AS COUNTERPARTS OF COWBOYS' MOUNTS

Also in the arena during much of the rodeo performance are two other classes of equines—the stock contractor's horse and the pickup men's horses. The stock contractor's mount is a quiet, responsive, and tireless animal, in which he places a great deal of confidence; he rides it continually while directing the proceedings. The horse ridden by the pickup man has to be fearless, willing, and dependable, as it must come in close contact with wildly bucking and kicking broncs. It should be agile enough to avoid the hooves of the broncs, and at the same time stay near enough to allow a contestant to jump off the still-plunging bronc and onto its back behind the pickup rider. These horses, both significantly characterized by the quality of predictability, are categorized as friends, totally domesticated partners. It is possible for them to share the symbolic, as well as the physical, realm of their riders. Thus they come to a position at the contrasting pole from that of the bronc. The stock contractor's and the pickup man's horse, though they are used to carry out the rider's will, have in addition been accepted into the human circle of domestication. The horse has become part of its rider's cultural sphere, and the man in turn has extended something of himself into the animal.

The seeming paradox in which the oppositions of partnership and dominance are at once part of the man-horse relationship is explored by Paul Bouissac with reference to

> western film narrative, in which the domination of a man over a horse is highly stressed; a cowboy, as a rodeo performer, is a mythical breaker of horses as well as an excellent rider. His horse is simply an aspect of his power and prestige; and when the horse contributes to the cowboy's survival, it is as an instrument the perfect functioning of which is credited to the owner. In some early westerns the horse played the role of the owner's best friend; that does not contradict my hypothesis, because the horse can be viewed as a psychological extension of the cowboy's domination (which humanizes his mount).

(1976:147)

The same ambivalence was noted by a chronicler of range life, who wrote that "the highly trained ponies that he personally rode" were adopted by a cowboy "into his family, and they took him into theirs. Nevertheless he at times might enthusiastically quirt them, and assuredly they frequently deserved the treatment" (Rollins 1973:55).

Tales of heroic horses bringing cowboys home through blizzards or risking their lives for them in other ways are still commonly told in range country. There can be an undeniable intimacy between them, and an admiration of a man for his horse which is not often expressed as eloquently as in the inscription one cowboy put over his horse's grave:

He had the body of a horse,
The spirit of a Knight, and
The Devotion of the man
Who erected this stone.

(Rollins 1973:56)

Particularly under the conditions of a solitary life, a cowboy's horse could become more than a servant. It was at times a partner and friend, his closest companion. It is this type of relationship which to some degree is reflected by the timed event, stock contractor's, and pickup men's mounts, rodeo's close analogues of the working cowboy's horse. Writing of this man-horse association, Larry McMurtry points out

> that the tradition of the shy cowboy who is more comfortable with his horse or with his comrades than with his women is not bogus. Cowboys express themselves most naturally, and indeed, most beautifully, through their work; when horseback they perform many extraordinarily difficult acts with ease and precision and grace. As the years pass they form very deep bonds with the men and the horses they work with.
>
> (1968:72)

McMurtry refers to these friendships as "mateships," and writes of "the sacramental relationship of man and horse" (1968:27).

THE SACRIFICIAL ROLE OF THE HORSE IN RODEO

If the man-horse relationship is sacramental, then I suggest that it may be also sacrificial. As noted previously, much of the cowboy's equipment, derived from the Spanish, is punishing to the horse. His stock saddle is heavy beyond utilitarian purpose, his spurs are designed with elaborately pronged rowels, and the bridle bit is of a type that has been described as an instrument of latent torture.

Though it does not deal specifically with the cowboy complex (except, significantly, as a symbol of freedom from parental authority), the idea of the horse as a sacrificial animal was recently explored in the play, *Equus* (Shaffer 1974). In this work the horse takes on aspects that cast him in the role of a victim of the sadistic cruelty and display of power associated with the crucifixion. Equus is referred to as "my only begotten son" (1974:50), "in chains for the sins of the world" (1974:65), and as taking a lump of sugar for his "last supper," eating them "for my sake" (1974:70). The hero in the play replaces his picture of the tortured Christ with one of a horse, and the two are transformed into one symbol. The horse's bit becomes synonymous with pain and man's domination. The archetypal horse, Equus, is "the *God-slave* (italics mine), Faithful and True," and "into my hands he commends himself" (Shaffer 1974:71). I find it particularly relevant to my study that it is the singular nature of the equine that makes it ideally suited for the sacrificial role. The term "God-slave" expresses the paradox of the horse's submissiveness, its strange willingness to do man's bidding and bear the pain he inflicts, in spite of the possession of physical power and strength far in excess of that of its human masters. There is a striking parallel here with the concepts of nature/culture which I have been relating to the horse. For it seems that it is because of the extent to which man's culture has been exerted over the horse's nature that the equine animal becomes such a peculiarly appropriate and tragic sacrifice.

The association of the horse with the crucifixion is not original with *Equus*. In a study of the horse in myth the tradition is mentioned that "the Christians of an earlier age seem to have considered the horse as a blessed animal, since our Savior was born in a manger" (Howey 1958:192). Thus in legend was the greatest possible honor paid to the horse of an emperor when the mother of the ruler obtained the sacred nails of the cross on which Christ was crucified. Not knowing how best to preserve the holy relics, she was advised by the bishop to "take these precious nails for thy son the emperor. Make of them rings for his horse's bridle. Victory shall always go with them" (Howey 1958:193). So the horse has been linked to Christ through their common pain.

Oddly enough, one of the early rodeo books refers to "that *passion play* of the West, the Round-up held at Pendleton, in eastern Oregon about which country so much of the history of the Northwest is wrapped" (Furlong 1921:xii). I found the sacrificial motif running like a thin thread throughout the deeper level of rodeo. Observing a bronc in the chutes who was missing one eye created a symbolic connection with *Equus*, in which the horses, as sacrificial gods, had their eyes put out by the protagonist. Often I noticed that rodeo men spit on the sides of the horses in the chutes, a strange act which brought to mind the treatment of Christ by the high priests before His sacrifice (Matthew 26:67). On many broncs bloody marks were visible over their forequarters, where spurs had gouged the flesh. And, to encourage a bronc rider in one rodeo to spur harder I heard the announcer urge "show the pony a lot of iron!" "Knife him out" is a rodeo term for spurring a bronc into the arena to begin a ride. Sometimes, before letting them out of the chutes, broncs are hit with a leather strap. (This is specifically allowed in the rule book.) They are often prodded, pinched, or punched while in the chutes. Rodeo people would be quick to claim that these acts are not evidence of cruelty, they are meant to "wake them up" in an effort to increase the animals' bucking potential. Yet it could be questioned whether these procedures are efficacious in making a horse buck harder, especially since they are generally done so far ahead of time. I feel they are ritualistic expressions, sacrificial in the sense that they are believed to evoke the resisting power of the animal only in order to have that power more fully oppose the rider in the arena. Through a heightening of the animal force, I suggest that man expects to gain a more potent victory in subduing it. In a sense, then, the horse's increased power would be taken as the rider's own, and would comprise a sacrifice to it.

A saddle bronc rider who ranches in Wyoming reflected the sacrificial strain of rodeo when he told me about his technique for training a horse. The mare in question, he said, had a habit of "raring up" when ridden, and he had been asked to break her of this dangerous behavior. He described in detail his procedure of deliberately making the mare rear up by jerking on the bit and then repeatedly hitting her over the head, first with a piece of pipe and then with a baseball bat, "with all my strength." What I found most remarkable was the choice of words in his narrative and his use of detail not necessary to convey its surface meaning. He laughed as he related "the blood flowed everywhere. She was a yellow buckskin mare, and she ended up covered with blood. I have never seen so much blood. The mare had started out a yellow color but you wouldn't have know this after she was covered with red blood." I felt in the relating of this episode that the horse had taken on the role of an expiatory animal, a scapegoat. In the huge muscular form of the narrator there was the overweening spirit of power that can make martyrs of the submissive. The rebellious yellow mare, at the mercy of his bit and weapon, became that sacrifice because of her bleeding head, the loss of blood denoting the ebbing of her strength to resist. The red and gold imagery is suggestive of the crucified Christ, often likened to a form of animal that becomes sacrificial. Gerard Manley Hopkins, for example, spoke of the Savior in terms of knighthood, as "my chevalier," and made the windhover, a hawk with red stripes in its wings, a symbol for the crucifixion. The downward plunge of the hawk and the death of Christ become one as they "Fall, gall themselves, and gash gold-vermilion" (1948:73).

Violence, of course, is an integral part of the frontier mystique, and, as my data have shown, finds expression within the context of the ranch/rodeo life. Richard Slotkin (1973) has delineated a phenomenon he calls "regeneration through violence" relative to the American frontier. According to this concept, as it can be applied in my study, a process takes place during violent conquest in which there is an absorption of energy on the part of the conqueror from that which is conquered. This relates to the idea that one gains more power by taming the fiercest spirit, by vanquishing something that was formerly the epitome of freedom. The more violent the struggle, the greater is the resultant invigoration. Using this thought, in the breaking of a ranch horse, in the riding of a rodeo bronc, as in the conquest of the land beyond the Western frontier, man would gain the power and energy which these ravished elements gave up in the struggle. What happens here, on the deepest level, seems to be akin to the factor underlying blood sacrifice. In the latter, according to the findings of Marcel Griaule among the Dogon, for example, through ritually killing the animal an individual believed he could take his victim's "life force" (1975:131). I suggest that the same dynamics could operate when there is no killing, but rather a vanquishing, as in the instances of man's extension of culture over nature which I have been describing, and in which man extracts power from nature.

Animals, particularly horses, possess powers which man lacks but admires—especially muscular strength, grace of motion, and speed. Blood, however, may be conceived of as something they share in common. Indeed blood is often mentioned in rodeo, and, as one looks about, is frequently in evidence. I sometimes noticed blood dripping from mouths of bitted horses ridden in the arena. Broncs often exhibited various open wounds and fresh brands. Many contestants left the arena bleeding, and their condition seemed to be taken for granted. Stock contractors, rodeo managers and helpers, as well as pickup men, were subject to bloody wounds and kicks and commonly displayed them. At several rodeos when a contestant was bucked off and seemed to be slightly hurt, the clown would ask "What color is blood?" The announcer answered "red." Then the clown called out "okay. He's okay, then," as he inspected the man on the ground. Another typical quip is for the announcer to tell the clown to "be sure to get a good seat for the rodeo, so you can see it in living color—blood red."

HORSES IN THE SPECIAL ACTS OF RODEO

From a discussion of the rodeo horse as a sacrificial animal, I will now turn to the horse as it is portrayed in rodeo as a humanized animal. In this form it occupies a position even further along the continuum from wild to tame, or from nature to culture, than is the case with mounts such as calf roping and pickup horses. I am referring here to horses which appear in special acts and individual exhibitions, and provide a contrast to the standard events. Horses in these contexts may be viewed as defying the traditional role that society assigns to this species, as another way in which the sport of rodeo further explores and comments upon the dilemma of man-horse relationships. The themes expounded in these acts sometimes contrast sharply to rodeo's overall message of the human domination of nature and the conception of nature as a force inimical to man. They seem to belong to an ethos alien to rodeo; they are counterpoints to it. It is relevant to note that true performing horses, such as those typical of early circus and the English hippodrome, for example, are rarely seen in standard rodeo. In A.H. Saxon's study of the hippodrome it is pointed out that spectators viewed the equine actors in these productions as "sagacious," and were inclined to feel more empathy for them than for the human actors in the dramas. Such audiences are described in terms unthinkable for rodeo enthusiasts, as having

> an attitude toward animals that is quite foreign to the present century. At the time of the appearance of these plays Romanticism was in full bloom. Darwinism and the theory of the indifferent universe was still some fifty years in the future; nature was viewed, with childlike simplicity, as being sympathetic to man.
>
> (1968:8)

Almost all the highly trained horses in rodeo appear in novelty acts with clowns. As the classic figure of ineptitude, the clown serves as a foil for the horse with which it is paired, making the animal appear smarter. Often this status is portrayed by means of a routine in which the blundering harlequin tries unsuccessfully to put a saddle blanket and saddle on the horse. Not only is the horse shown to be superior in intelligence by outwitting the man in this act, but he has also defied the traditional role of equine subservience by refusing to accept the symbols of human dominance. Of course in a rodeo this evokes much laughter; the general belief holds that such a situation can only occur in a mythic world—the carnival world momentarily created by buffoonery. It is soon over; the broncs are in the chutes, the calf-horse is in the box; things will return to normal.

There are several typical varieties of clown-horse acts, and the animal does not always end up in a position of control, though he may reach it at one time in the sequence. Sometimes, for example, a scene is staged whereby the horse brings the clown home safely after he gets drunk on Saturday night. In this act, the horse will push him out of the arena with his nose, as the clown staggers forward. Or the horse may come up behind the clown, lower its head between the clown's legs, and cleverly appear to put the man on his back, carrying him from the arena in a mounted position. Here there is a temporary reversal of roles—the horse is wiser, and is the "keeper" of the man. Nature is thus seen to triumph over culture, especially when "culture" has included getting drunk. It is noteworthy that at some point during a typical clown-horse performance, the horse usually rolls over on its back and the clown will sit on its recumbent body, reemphasizing human control and dominance. Then the animal will rise and again become the "superior" of the clown. Needless to say, such an act is the product of arduous training and mastery over the horse, but it is made to appear otherwise to the spectator. Cues are disguised by comic gestures and are seldom evident to the amused audience.

Typically, at the end of such a performance, the horse is "dressed" by putting a hat and a large pair of glasses on the animal and placing a pipe in its mouth. Here I find the ultimate extreme in representing culture over nature—the horse is humanized to the greatest extent possible. As a finale, the announcer typically gives a name to the caricatured horse—saying "there you have it, folks, that is Hubert Elton" (some well-known figure who is disliked). Rodeo parades, as previously described, are an integral part of the bigger celebrations, and display the prominent themes of the sport. Near the beginning of the 1978 Cheyenne Frontier Days parade, for example, this motif of culture over nature was keynoted. A famous rodeo clown walked beside his faithful companion—a horse dressed in a pair of pants— undeniable evidence of the humanization of nature.

An interesting rodeo variation on the theme of performing horses was an act which was heralded by trumpet fanfare and the announcer proclaiming that now the audience will be treated to a display of the equine brilliance of the world-famous Lippizan stallions. "Here, direct from Austria, you will see high-schooled horses perform difficult feats like the capriole." At this point, having built up the audience's anticipation, he is interrupted by the entrance of a clown, who rides two mules "Roman style," in a standing position with one foot on the back of each. With mock seriousness, the announcer calls for a "reverse!" and each mule goes in the opposite direction, confounding the clown. Here, the lowly and ungainly mules provide an ironic contrast to the vision conjured up in the minds of the observers of the precise and intricate maneuvers exhibited by the Lippizans. For

Here is the ultimate expression of culture over nature: the animal is humanized by being dressed in hat and glasses. *(Photo by Robert Ridley)*

the celebrated horses are paragons of equine expertise, and as such, I suggest, symbolize the highest degree of human culture being extended over the natural world. The Lippizans, of course, would be as out of place at a rodeo as a cowboy in a tuxedo. The message in the act just described seemed to be that such sophisticated performances are all right for cities and Easterners, but as for the West, "give me the simple life!" Let us cling to rural values, lowly creatures, and "down-to-earth" attitudes. The anti-intellectual, anti-aesthetic strain of the frontier was clearly framed in the language ranch/rodeo people best understand—through the use of horses.

Another example is relevant here, an equestrian act which I saw at an Eastern rodeo (Rhode Island), and which would never be observed as part of one of the standard Western rodeos. This Eastern rodeo was sponsored by the International Rodeo Association, a different organization from the Professional Rodeo Cowboys Association which produces the biggest and most prestigious Western rodeos, and which considers those of the other circuit to be nonprofessional. Rodeos of the International Rodeo Association seem to be slightly less ranch-oriented, and have more Easterners and Southerners as contestants. In addition, it was my observation that they are structured somewhat more heavily in favor of the performance over the contest aspect in the performance/contest ratio. It should be said, though, that the International Rodeo Association would not view itself this way. What I wish to describe as a contrast to Western rodeo acts was an exhibition of classic equestrian skills and dressage. The rider was a young woman, and as she guided her mount through its paces, her cues to the horse were carefully concealed. Dressage riders ordinarily wear pants which are loose enough to obscure their leg movements, and the more expert the rider, the more subtle are the hand and arm movements on the rein. Such a performance would be out of keeping with the Great Plains ranch/rodeo spirit in which stress does not appear to be placed on what the horse can do, but rather on what the rider can make the horse do. For an equestrian display like the one included in the Rhode Island rodeo tends to focus attention on the skill of the horse. In my experience at horse shows, the rider is specifically designated as the "exhibitor" of the horse, and the animal is afforded paramount emphasis (except in equitation classes, in which riding skill alone is judged). In a horse show, accordingly, it is recognized that it is the horse who wins the ribbon which is always pinned to the animal's bridle. Rodeo, on the other hand, makes it evident that human input is of central importance, and it is the rider who receives the trophy award—a buckle to be worn by him and not the horse.

A further factor of significance is that in an equestrian performance such as the one just described the horse and rider appear "center stage"—alone in the arena. This contrasts sharply with the mounted displays that typically occur within the Western rodeo context. In these, a horsemen's drill team with headquarters in some nearby town often puts on an exhibition at the beginning of the program. These are group affairs, demonstrating the collective skill of riders working together. They consist of various movements such as quadrilles, modified square dance routines, figure eights, criss-cross formations, and concentric circles, symbolically stressing conformity. Speed is a conspicuous part of the displays, as many routines are executed at a gallop. Unity of motion is the over-all effect, since individual riders are submerged in the whole. Riders are typically all male or all female. Men's groups adopt a title like "Cheyenne Sheriff's Posse," and wear uniforms with star-shaped badges and holsters with revolvers. Women's groups, like the "Casper Dandies" or the "Foxy Ladies," wear matching pastel or gaudily colored western suits. One announcer drew attention to the uniformity in apparel of a ladies' drill team, telling the audience the riders were all wearing Tony Lama boots, and "underneath it all—Vanity Fair."

These displays of mounted teamwork in rodeo suggest the collective power and force implicit in the conquest of the West, depict the isolation of the sexes into separate spheres of life, and also represent the role of the traditional social order in controlling behavior. By stressing conformity, they provide a stiking contrast to the individualism which is constantly extolled as being one of the most important of frontier traits, and the one which rodeo emphasizes and wishes to preserve. A similar example is given by Bouissac, who notes that the Liberty Horses in the classic circus act are manipulated in specifically meaningful ways, through which they express a paradoxical message. Being "harnessed, like domestic animals," but "unmounted and unhitched, like wild animals," they are "simultaneously controlled and free" (1976:134). Thus the decoded message of the act, symbolized by these combinations, represents the conflicting cultural values in the order "conform and be yourself!" This paradox is felt to be "at the root of moral education in Western cultures" (Bouissac 1976:136). Certainly the ranch/rodeo culture, with its emphasis on both group conformity and individualism, exemplifies this dichotomy.

THE HORSE IN THE BAR

One more outstanding example is relevant to my present topic of culture being extended over nature through the agency of increasingly "humanized" horses. This is the act of riding a horse into a building, almost always a barroom. It is a commonly occurring motif in the folklore of the American West, in which a cowboy coming off the range nonchalantly enters a saloon with his horse and orders a drink for each of them. I found that this event was often in the minds of ranch/rodeo people, and that a rodeo version of it has become a tradition. While it does not seem to be carried out frequently, due to practical limitations, the possibility of doing it is constantly considered, joked about, and discussed. Informants took delight in telling about riding a horse into the Mayflower Bar during Cheyenne Frontier Days, and said that someone usually manages to do it at Denver, Fort Worth, and North Platte during the annual rodeos in those cities. Fascinated by this idea as it relates to my theme of the horse as an intermediary between nature and culture, I wanted to be in the right place at the right time to experience it first-hand. Failing in this, I talked whenever possible to men who had accomplished the feat, and to bartenders who were undecided as to whether they dreaded or welcomed the equine intrusion.

The general procedure is that rodeo hands who are "whooping it up"—often on a dare—will "steal a pickup horse and ride it into a bar." Significantly, participants assured me "a pickup horse will go anywhere." Thus, according to my interpretation, this versatile horse is made to seem at home in both worlds—the animal and the human. It then becomes an agent which transcends its usual role in society, violates order and propriety, and extends itself into a "higher" realm. In their concern with this act, rodeo participants are imposing culture upon the horse to a degree that seems like the ultimate possibility— taking the animal into a strictly human sphere. The whiskey-drinking horse of the old Western folk narratives and tall tales does not only express the cowboy's philosophy of "what's good enough for me is good enough for my horse." For, in addition, by partaking of liquor, the horse shares in the consumption of an unnatural substance which has undergone a "raw to cooked" or nature to culture transition, a substance which has power to affect the mind. This act thrusts the animal further into an artificial and incongruous realm.

A bar in the Old West served as the center of social activity, a gathering place for men from outlying areas to exchange news and share conviviality, and was symbolic of the existing order of the group. It was a male world, with the exception of "bad" women who may have been accepted there due to reasons previously mentioned. "Decent" ones were, of course, excluded. Bars in today's ranch country have retained many of these same functions, and often serve as places of business for the cattle trade. By bringing his horse into this social setting, in reality or in a tale, the cowboy was making the ultimate statement about this animal's inclusion in the deeper aspects of his life. The horse can be accepted into the male camaraderie mystique, which finds the most fervent expression of its intimacy in the atmosphere of the bar. Today's rodeo hand, with a strong sense of identification with his cowboy predecessor, is motivated to recreate this scene under the guise of a prank.

Thus it is clear that there are many ways in which the sport of rodeo manipulates and dramatizes various categories of horses to give concrete expression to relationships existing between man and the equine species. These range from the wild (feral) horse, through the bronc, to the roping horse, the trick horse, and the pickup man's horse. I have proposed that these types of horses demonstrate progressive degrees of man's control and dominance over them, and that they represent various stages in the spectrum of wild to tame, nature to culture. The horse is remarkable in its capacity for participation in both poles of these dichotomies. Bridging the realms of nature and culture, the horse becomes a symbolic representative of the conquest of the "wild West" by man.

Feelings of ambivalence often characterize the ranch/rodeo relationship with horses. There is an apparent paradox, for example, in a man's feeling of close partnership with his horse at the same time that he experiences complete dominance over the animal. There can also be a sense of personal identification with the power and freedom represented by the horse even as the attempt is being made to master it. In addition, it often appears that the horse takes on the role of a sacrificial animal, victimized as it often is by pain and domination in the ranch/rodeo setting. This is related to the phenomenon of power accruing to the forces of culture through the conquest of nature, suggesting a process of "regeneration through violence" in which a sense of renewal emanates from the struggle between man and nature, as that which took place on the American frontier.

The oppositional contests between man and horse in rodeo are structured so that the performance of the bronc—that is, the degree of its rebelliousness toward man—is counted equally with the rider's skill in reckoning his score. Through use of varying amounts of equipment representing extensions of culture, as well as in the ordering of events on the program as to the amounts of "wildness" exhibited, rodeo manipulates and displays different facets of the culture versus nature opposition.

The wildness of rodeo broncs and their resentfulness of man are considered to be inborn traits, and at the wild polarity horses are perceived as unpredictable and undependable. This is one reason that rodeo men often categorize women with broncs, since females are felt to share these qualities. At the opposite, or tame, end of the spectrum, horses such as those used for calf roping and steer jerking are characterized as predictable and dependable—associated with "culture" as opposed to "nature." At the farthest degree toward the polarity of tame, such as when a horse is "dressed" or ridden into a barroom, the animal may be "humanized" enough to temporarily enter man's own domesticated sphere.

The bucking bronc remains as the key animal and central symbol of rodeo, and at present great effort is being expended to "breed the buck back" into these horses, thus reversing the centuries-old process of genetic selection for more docile mounts. This phenomenon illustrates the strong appeal of the Western frontier ethos and the importance attributed to keeping its wildness of spirit and mystique of conquest alive.

Other species of animals, as will become evident in the chapters to follow, occupy roles in rodeo that are very different from those of the horse and reflect man's contrasting images of them and relations to them.

6

THE ROLE OF CATTLE IN RODEO

CALVES, STEERS, AND COWS

Whoopee ti yi yo, git along, little dogies,
It's your misfortune, and none of my own.

In the Springtime we round up the dogies,
Slap on the brands and bob off their tails.
Then we cut herd and herd is inspected,
And then we throw them on the trail.

Oh, you'll be soup for Uncle Sam's injuns;
"It's beef, heap beef," I hear them cry.
Git along, git along, git along little dogies,
You're going to be beef steers by and by.

(White 1975:16–21)

TURNING FROM the role of the equine species to the role of the bovine species in rodeo, it becomes immediately evident that there are profound differences between the two. Contrasting perceptions of these dissimilar forms of livestock in the minds of ranch/rodeo people lead to differences in the treatment of cattle as compared to horses and to variation in the part each plays within the framework of the sport.

From the earliest days of trail driving in North America, the horse has been man's essential helper in the tasks of cattle herding. The individual relationship which a cowboy shared with his mount was a sharp contrast to his collective relationship with cattle. Whereas his horse was given a name and was felt to possess a distinct personality, cattle had only the group identity of the herd; cattlemen are prone to refer to them as "a bunch of cows." Much of this difference, I suggest, stems from the fact that horses, as just described, have the extraordinary capacity to bridge the gap between man and nature. They

169

become part of man's own domestic sphere, and often there is a sense of identification with them.

Beef cattle virtually never have this role. (I am considering here all classes of cattle except bulls, which will be treated separately). Cows are perceived as less intelligent, less sensitive, and less responsive than horses. They generally behave as a herd, seldom as individuals, and are conceptualized and manipulated accordingly. They remain generally remote from the realm of human culture, and are not "trained." It is expected, in the order of things, that they will totally submit to man. In the ranch/rodeo view a cow appears to occupy a rather static position. It is born with much the same traits with which it will die. The capacity to learn and respond—the imposition of culture over its bovine nature—is not considered as a possibility. Though it is a domesticated animal, the cattleman does not normally experience a taming process in connection with it, and any such process in which its wild ancestors were transformed through human endeavors are remote from him. When the cowboy refers to range cattle as "wild" he refers to their behavior, and to the fact that they are not easily handled and controlled; there is always the threat of a stampede. But because cattle are under his care and jurisdiction and are kept solely to be used for human purposes, they exist in a realm sharply distinguished from that of true native wild animals which are not in his control.

Attitudes toward cattle are reflected in the treatment they receive at the hands of men, often very different from that afforded to horses. In the rituals of the range, for example, cows were routinely dragged to the branding fire after being roped, whereas horses were not (Rollins 1973:214). The marking of cattle—cutting them with a knife in addition to burning—was a procedure not inflicted upon horses (Rollins 1973:216). Neither were horses rebranded after each sale according to the routine for cattle (Rollins 219–220). Custom dictated that "punchers often subjected cattle to two humiliating actions from which horses were spared." While horses were merely roped and thrown, and held by lariats until the work on them was finished, cattle would have their heads twisted and their legs pulled backward and forward. Ordinarily, the "officiating puncher" would sit on the calf during the proceedings, but never on the horse. In addition, cattle were often "hog-tied"; horses seldom were (Rollins 1973:227–228).

Similar practices and the same attitudes pervade modern ranching. Though horses sometimes receive harsh treatment, it is generally less evident and is less expected than the routine roughness of behavior

Above: Because cattle and horses are perceived so differently, the saddling and riding of a cow seems the height of the ridiculous.   (*JJJ Photo*)

Below: The difficult maneuvers of steer roping enable a single rider working with his horse to overpower and tie up a steer.   (*JJJ Photo*)

extended to cattle. The fact that ranch/rodeo people often refer to the capacity of horses to become partners probably accounts for much of this. Cattle seem to be most commonly placed in the category of "objects." Very few informants evidenced a perception of them as sentient beings, and they are seen as having little or no input into a relationship with man. As one calf roper phrased it, "cows are just there. Maybe they have feelings, but to me they're just there. I've chased too many of them over the hills to worry about them. Horses are dumb, but they can be your friend."

Cattle are commonly herded with whips, electric prods, and goads, are kicked, and have their tails twisted to make them move, whereas horses are not ordinarily treated this way. The difference is partly due to the reaction which would be expected from the more sensitive equine animal, but it is also related to a kind of deep-seated "respect" cattlemen feel for horses. Most ranchmen profess a great "love of cattle" and cannot conceive of a life apart from them. This means that they take pleasure in daily contact with the animals, as they manipulate and master them. As I have already mentioned, acknowledgment and prestige accrues to the range man who "knows cow," but this insight implies only that such a man has exceptional ability to control cattle.

With regard to human relationships with the bovine species, it is significant that in the eyes of the ranching culture, a cattle man and a cattleman may be identical, whereas a horse man and a horseman are not. Anyone, by buying the appropriate animals, can become a cattle man, a cattleman, or a horse man. But a horseman is one who is singled out as having not only a great deal of experience, but also special abilities in the understanding and handling of horses. Within ranch/rodeo society, a person is admired a great deal more for horsemanship than ability with cattle, though a cowman who "runs a good outfit" is respected as a business man.

A man's cruelty toward cattle is not often a cause for criticism. It is accepted as part of the ranching way of life. Cruelty to a horse, however, as Bennett also found in his study, makes a person subject to "hostile gossip" (1969:93). I talked to one rancher and rodeo stock contractor about an incident of severe cruelty to a horse, and asked if people in the community ever interfered with such behavior. His answer was that "a person has to mind his own business in the West; sometimes a person will interfere, and sometimes not." He went on to tell me "cruelty to a horse is absolutely the worst thing in the world; it makes me want to puke. It is worse than if a man is beating his wife." A cattleman said that "ranchers are much more apt to be cruel to cows than horses, even though there is more opportunity to treat horses bad because you're with them more." The best thing a rancher might say of a cow is "that old girl has been a good cow for me; she's had eight calves in a row and never gave me any trouble."

The language customarily used with reference to cattle indicates human attitudes toward them. The word "cows" seems to be used interchangeably with "cattle," and designates all classes of bovines (except bulls), including steers. This practice of referring to a group of animals collectively by the feminine term is unusual. Horses, for instance, would never be called "a bunch of mares" if both sexes were included, even if the males were geldings. Neither would a mixed herd of sheep be known as a herd of ewes. This practice suggests that the image of creatures who are conceived of as completely man-dominated, close to nature and lacking in potentiality for being accepted into the human cultural realm, causes cattle to be perceived as female. Their main purpose, of course, is to reproduce, but this is true of many animal species that are still not collectively viewed as female.

It is very important to remember, too, that in the eyes of a cowboy "a horse was a horse, but a steer was only meat" (Rollins 1973:228). The destiny of the bovine species as beef must be closely associated with its low position in the ranchman's hierarchy. The prime economic concern of range country is beef, and there is much preoccupation with it. Ranchers, considering beef their special realm, seem to use it as a sign of their identity and even their masculinity. Ordering steak for breakfast attests to strength and manhood, and "going out for dinner" is equivalent to "going out for a steak." In range country a "cattleman's cut" is always the specialty on the menu, and I noticed ranchmen were uncomfortable with the idea of eating buffalo meat.

The association of a meat diet with strength and virility is prevalent among ranchers. One northern Montana cattleman approached the subject by praising the special quality of the grass in his area, because of its high protein content. He said "that's why the best beef cattle and bucking horses come from here; they are big and strong when they come from north of the Missouri River." He explained "that's why the Indians of the Plains were the fiercest—they ate buffalo meat from animals that had fattened on northern grass, so they were tougher. There was no trouble in conquering the fish-eating Indians, but they [the government] had something on their hands here, as meat made them more aggressive. Now, what has happened is that doctors have taken away fat and red meat from people's diet. They have become weaker because red meat makes people strong. The protein is in red meat, and people need it. You notice if you hunt coyotes with dogs, they are not strong unless they are fed on red meat and fat."

Hough's influential work on the cowboy contains a similar argument, asserting that Americans have the cowboy, and the industry with which he is associated, to thank for their freedom (1923:325–329). "The beef herders and the beef eaters of history have been winning peoples"—not the "vegetarian nations," he writes (1923:327), and our diet of beef is what keeps us strong enough to defend our liberty. Thus beef and freedom are closely associated, and both are products of the grasslands—"that glorious abounding, open, manly West, where there never was a throne except the saddle" (1923:329).

Most ranchers would agree, and they complain to the management of restaurants which do not feature beef. In a small Montana town the placemat of a popular restaurant advises "Big Horn County Cow Belles say 'if you don't find beef on the menu, beef about it.' " "Sambo's" had formerly received complaints about not serving enough beef; as a result throughout Montana and Wyoming this chain of restaurants displays a card at each table reading "we've beefed up our menu," to advertise recently added beef specialties. Also in Montana and Wyoming road signs advise "This is cow country—Eat beef." In the northern Montana ranch country a sign depicts a cowboy figure with the announcement "This is beef country," and from the opposite direction the motorist is urged to "Eat beef today." Bumper stickers commonly seen in the northern Great Plains also show preoccupation with this issue:

> Beef up America.
> Don't complain about beef prices with your mouth full.
> If you can afford booze, you can afford beef.

McDonald's, whose specialty is hamburgers, gives strong support to rodeo throughout the western states. This company paid the entry fees for the contestants in the 1978 P.R.C.A. Finals in Oklahoma City, contributing a total of $12,000 for this purpose. Another fast-food chain, Arby's Roast Beef, also backs the sport. One rodeo, whose officials wore jackets stamped with Arby's name and trademark, also featured a song about their beef sandwiches.

The sport of rodeo is inextricable from its roots in the ranching industry, and various livestock events are often held in conjunction with many of the larger rodeos in the Great Plains. The Calgary

Stampede, for example, includes extensive beef cattle exhibitions. Some of these center on promoting certain breeds, and feature displays of carcasses and cuts of meat from those animals as well as live specimens. "Sir Loin" was the symbol for beef in the 1978 exhibits. This figure was depicted as a tenderloin steak anthropomorphized by means of a hat, feet, a monocle, and an umbrella. He "told" the story of ranching and gave statistics about the huge investments a beef producer must have in land, equipment, and cattle. He enlightened the passing crowds concerning the high protein, vitamin, and mineral content of beef, and concluded "Boy! Am I a bargain!" His image also appeared on free beef recipes and stickers and pins reading "Eat Beef."

In sharp contrast to such observations in the Great Plains, where the graphic emphasis on beef production merited public approval, enjoyment, and participation, was my experience at an Eastern rodeo. A beef steer had been donated for a raffle in connection with a Rhode Island rodeo, with the understanding that it would be slaughtered and butchered for the winner. But when the animal was placed on public display for the weekend of the rodeo, there were complaints about this, and requests that it be removed from the grounds. People expressed the opinion that it is not proper for children to view a live animal which is to be eaten. Such behavior, of course, would be classed as lunacy in the ranching culture of the Great Plains. There children begin as toddlers to "rope anything that moves" in preparation for a life that will be directly involved with raising cattle for meat.

Rodeo's function as a ritual of the beef empire is evident in its treatment of the many classes of bovine animals which represent their ranch counterparts. In the classic timed event, calf roping, young animals are chased and roped by mounted cowboys, then tied, reenacting the traditional range prelude to the processes of the roundup—branding, marking, and castration. Through the years the sport has received a great deal of criticism from animal protection agencies for this event. Rodeo officials are particularly bitter and defensive about calf roping, and politicians in Western states who aspire to office must speak with care if they wish to avoid the wrath of the ranch/rodeo oriented populace. In 1973, for example, a Colorado Senator, who five years later expected to become a candidate for governor in that state, introduced two bills dealing with calf roping (Brown 1978a,b). "The rodeo industry, interpreting the bills as an outright attack and an effort to ban competitive calf roping, banded together to fight the proposed legislation" (Brown 1978a:5). The issue became a major one, since both the Professional Rodeo Cowboys Association and the National Little Britches Rodeo Association have their headquarters in Colorado, and it is very much a pro-rodeo state. The politician later declared that he did not intend to outlaw rodeo, and that his only concern was "weekend cowboys who were getting together, and they'd have one or two calves and use the same calf over and over again." But the rodeo industry did not agree with this interpretation of the bills, and tried to link the Senator with the Humane Society of the United States, an avowedly anti-rodeo organization. Regretting the furor the bills created, he claims that he is not and never was against rodeo, and that "it will be a cold day in Hades" when he tries to introduce another such bill, having "lived with this horse crap for five years now," since he first introduced the controversial bills (Brown 1978a:5).

Humane societies have frequently expressed the opinion that calves suffer a great deal of stress from repeated ropings, and that far too many injuries are sustained by the young animals, especially in the delicate tissues of the trachea and esophagus. In one study of roping events it was determined that a 225-pound calf traveled approximately twenty-seven miles per hour at the moment it was lassoed and that "the resulting force exerted on the calf's body caused severe damage" (Naviaux and Miller 1977:7–8). Rodeo people and Western audiences in general, however, see nothing cruel about calf roping and assert that such complaints are unwarranted examples of Eastern ignorance and misguided sentimental nonsense. Audiences I observed at Great Plains rodeos were always enthusiastic about calf roping. They identified strongly with the man-horse team versus the calf, or with the man if the horse misbehaved. Contestants indicated that calves were just beef, and they never were perceived as possessing "rights" or deserving sympathy. Many did say that stock contractors were not anxious to injure calves, due to the dollar investment that each animal represents.

One rodeo director with a lifetime of experience in the sport brought up the subject of the prevalence of outsiders' disapproval of the calf roping event, and provided the following insights. "It's the difference between a baby and a monster. If two six-year-olds fight, no one wants to see it, because no one wants a baby to get hurt. But everybody does want to see Mohammed Ali fight because he is a monster and can take it. The difference between a baby and a monster is like the difference between a calf and a bull."

Turning now from the roping of calves to the roping of full-grown bovine animals, one finds that steer jerking, even judged within the context of an admittedly rough sport, is outstanding for roughness toward cattle. Also called steer tripping and "steer busting," the details of the event have been previously described. It is the only event of rodeo that I heard criticized by people within the ranch/rodeo group itself for being too hard on the stock. Indeed many rodeos do not allow it on their programs, and some states outlaw it. It is also the only event that I found to be in real disfavor among regular contestants in other events. At Casper, Wyoming, for example, the rodeo that traditionally follows Cheyenne by two days, the steer wrestlers complained bitterly. They resented the damage that steer jerking in Cheyenne had caused to the animals they must now use, and felt it was responsible for making them more difficult to handle. One bulldogger told me "steer tripping is inhumane. It is allowed in only a few states, and should be outlawed by congressmen. It breaks horns and necks, and many steers die a few days later of ruptured intestines." His event, steer wrestling, he said, "doesn't hurt them at all." A prominent steer roping contestant admitted his event "can be very hard on steers if it is not done right." He said it is also "rough on horses," but stressed that "it's the thinking man's part of rodeo; it requires great skill."

The steer roping event seemed especially raw and brutal in the drenching rain and mud of the Ogalalla, Nebraska, rodeo, during which I had the opportunity to study the reactions of audience members. The terrific suddenness with which the running steers were knocked down, the impact of their heavy bodies on the muddy ground, and the inevitable dragging of them across the arena seemed to stand out so clearly that the spectacle drew the audience into a much-increased spirit of participation. There appeared to be no distractions from the outside world, as the storm raged and the spectators huddled together in total absorption. The commonest audience reaction to the steers' plight was laughter. Spectators evidenced enjoyment of the panorama, and the fate of the steers, as beef animals, seemed natural to the order of their world. The audience became as one in overwhelming approval, joined in an ethos which made the event not only acceptable but desirable. A few people remarked genially about a steer who hit the ground particularly hard, making such comments as "he'll have a headache tomorrow," or "he won't feel much like eating for a while," but they neither showed nor voiced regret or sympathy.

In contrast to the standard roping events involving calves and steers, in which nonhuman implements—the rope and the strength of the horse—are used as aids in conquering the animals, is the very different event of steer wrestling. This sport features a more elemental contest between man and beast. Rodeo people consider it to have no ranch orientation; as one contestant in the event told me after describing his many injuries, "ranchers are too smart to do it." It is noteworthy that in this event nothing intervenes between the contestant and his quarry, as he grapples with the steer using only his own body. The horse's function is just to position him correctly for contact with the steer, and the mount does not participate in the actual downing of the animal.

Thus a pattern is seen, somewhat similar to that suggested for the bucking events, in which culture is exerted in varying degrees over the bovine animals in the timed events. However, the various nuances in degree and kind which characterize the reactions of the different classes of horses, the different intensities and ratios of oppositional behavior and cooperative behavior, are lacking in the structure of bovine events. The ultimate and uniform result is that cattle are effectively vanquished. Whether this is accomplished with the traditional implements of cowboy culture—horse, saddle horn, lariat, and "piggin' string" (tying rope)—or by a man's physical strength and skill alone, as in the bulldogging event, the end result is the same. The cattle are brought totally under control. And though the animals put up a natural struggle against the restraining processes, the contests are not purposely designed to give leeway to those struggles in the way that the bronc and bull riding events are. Each timed event contestant, unless something goes amiss, simply ties a bovine animal, or holds it down, in a position of helpless subjugation for the time specified for his event.

COMPARISON OF THE ROLE OF CALVES AND STEERS IN
RODEO WITH THAT OF HORSES

As compared to the horse, whose various natural and humanly altered attributes are used in different ways to express many themes, cattle in rodeo denote one concept—the total submission to man that befits a meat animal. Human culture, including the element of the partner-horse, is at all times represented as supreme over their nature. Roped, tied, tripped or jerked, or wrestled down by hand, their image is of a dominated creature, a passive instrument of man's will. Input from the bovine animals is not significantly structured into the sport. Though it is admitted that a few calves or steers possess a fighting spirit that makes them harder to conquer, such animals are looked upon as a disadvantage to the contestant, an incidence of

Above: In steer wrestling the "dogger" grapples with the animal, using only his own physical strength to throw it to the ground.   *(JJJ Photo)*

Below: In rodeo's wildest event there is grave danger of being trampled. Quick action by the clown distracts bull from fallen rider.   *(JJJ Photo)*

misfortune in "the luck of the draw," and not as possessing a special asset meriting respect. A calf may escape the cowboy's loop, a steer may dodge the header's or heeler's rope, or veer away from the tripper's most skilled maneuver, or an animal may resist being dogged by a steer wrestler. But it is noteworthy that these failures are attributed to the contestant's bad luck or mistake, not to the cleverness of the particular animal. If a bronc is especially rank, in contrast, the announcer may comment "it's no disgrace to be bucked off that one!" And I have already described the great respect that rodeo people feel for the bucking animals that oppose them most intensely. The timed events, unlike the rough stock events, provide little sporting play or give-and-take interaction between contestants and the animals and imply a virtually undisputed victory of human culture over raw nature as represented by the calf and steer.

BULLS IN RODEO

The prominence of the bull in mythology is perhaps more easily understood today because of the current questioning of Christian values and the evident revival of those inherent in most pagan faiths. Christianity is associated in men's minds with peace, humility and chastity; with the shepherd's crook and the innocent lamb. If the present age is—as is so often proclaimed—one characterized by violence and sex, then it is no longer a Christian age. It has come closer to those faiths and ages in which aggression, power, courage and sexual vigor—the admired qualities of the warrior rather than those of the saint—were most revered. It was in such creeds that the bull, as a symbol of power, fertility and aggressive courage, became equated with divinities and confused with kings. Power, irresistibility, brute force, these were the bull qualities that held the greatest appeal for the people who thought of their king as a god.

(Fraser 1972:26)

So greatly does the image of the rodeo bull differ from that of the other classes of bovine animals just described that it is surprising to think of it as belonging to the same species. The quality of its maleness is paramount—in the form of its body, its behavior, and its spirit. The way in which it is perceived by man is of a very different order from the calf, the steer, or the cow.

Though the bull represents in fact a form of domesticated animal, it is categorized in rodeo as essentially wild. As one bull rider put it, "bulls are always wild; there is no such thing as a tame bull. They're wild when they're born, and wild when they get old. They stay wild until they are ground up for hamburg." Rodeo people do not think of bulls as having a capacity to be any other way, or of going through phases of more or less wildness. Unlike the horse, which is perceived as having several aspects to its nature, the bull is believed to have one—wild. The bull riding event is traditionally heralded as "rodeo's wildest event" and the contestants as riders of "wild Brahma bulls." So wild are the animals purported to be that, in contrast to bronc riders, bull riders are not required to spur the animals. It is considered enough just to attempt to stay on the huge and powerful beasts as they buck and sometimes spin.

Next to "wildest" the commonest term associated with bulls in rodeo is "downright mean" and "really rank." Informants concurred in the opinion that they are "ornerier than hell," and always followed this description with the assertion that "they're bred to be mean," or "they've got Brahma blood, and that makes them mean." Many informants liken the innate meanness of rodeo bulls to Spanish fighting bulls which are "bred for it," but they consider their sport of riding bulls much more challenging. At the International Rodeo Association Finals in Tulsa, for example, the announcer spoke of bull riding as requiring far more skill than bull fighting. "It is one thing to fight or kill the bull," he told the crowd, "and another thing to ride it. Riding it is the most dangerous sport in America today." Most rodeo people consider the Spanish bull fight "cruel" whereas they believe their event is not. They stress the fact that there are many more bull riders than bulls injured in rodeo, and that bulls are well treated and cared for by stock contractors.

The "Bad Brahma Bull" image (which has been incorporated into a rodeo song) is reinforced by what is felt to be a "mean look" in the eyes of the beasts, by the hump usually present on their backs, and most of all by their formidable horns. A girl bull rider who said she is not scared of bulls, but that she "respects the hell out of them," spoke of the hooves looking big when you get on a bull, and the hump seeming as tall as the rider. She confided that "the size of the bulls, their horns, and the look of them freaks lots of people." In standard men's rodeo, a "coward's bull" refers to one with no horns. Girls are not supposed to ride bulls with horns pointing upward, but only those who have horns going outward or those with "banana horns"—hanging down. The horns of the bull represent a constant threat of danger, for being gored means serious injury or death. This is the reason for the immediate intervention of the clown, once the bull rider is on the ground.

Rodeo people constantly stress that this factor of continued danger is the big difference between the nature of bulls and horses. For once a rider is bucked off a bull, it is considered likely that he will be deliberately attacked by the animal—a situation which does not exist with broncs. The top rodeo bull fighter at Cheyenne told me that often "bulls are really out to hurt a man—they will get their heads down and push down on him." A very important concept continually emphasized by rodeo informants is the idea that bulls will step on a person who is on the ground, whereas horses will never tread on humans if they can avoid it. Contestants indicated that after the rider is off, "a bronc tries to get away and will not stomp on you. It's not in his nature to hurt you, so the bronc rider doesn't have to worry about the animal. The bull, though, is out to get you, and will trample you, so the rider must hustle for his life."

Bulls are perceived as "naturally having a will to buck" to a greater degree than horses. When rodeo stockmen try out animals for bucking potential, they say a much larger percentage of bulls as compared to horses are found suitable. Rarely a rodeo bull can be a "pet" as far as allowing someone to stroke it, they told me—"one out of ten thousand you can put your arms around." But such an animal still remains "deadly if you are on its back." Rodeo people say bulls are "ungodly hard to ride," and this is attributed to a different way of bucking as compared to broncs. Spinning bulls are notorious for making it difficult for a contestant to achieve a qualified ride. Also, the fact that the bull's hide is loose on its body, unlike that of the horse, is said to make it much more difficult to stay on the animal's back. For "the bull's hide rolls in bucking with the rider."

In addition to their wildness and meanness, bulls are always considered much less intelligent than horses. As one rodeo man told me "bulls don't think, whereas horses do. All forms of cattle are the same—they do not think. Some guy in a lab probably won't agree with that, but I have punched cows, and I know they haven't got much brains." Another said "a bull is not as smart as a horse; it would rather step on you or hook you. A horse will out-think you, a horse looks back all the time, watching you." Rodeo people (exclusive of bull riders) often extend this image of stupidity to include the contestants in the event. Most informants feel that bull riding takes less finesse than other events; "it doesn't require much—no balance or brains, just strength." One offered the opinion that "bronc riding requires more thinking and balance; there are more things to think about." An officer of the Professional Rodeo Cowboys Association, a former bareback bronc rider, said "though bulls are more dangerous because they come looking for you, there is more skill required in horse riding events. In bull riding, all you've got to do is hold on, you don't have to spur." Rodeo people seem to agree that "it takes much longer to be real good at bronc riding than bull riding."

There is a prevalent notion that bull riders are stupid because of the extra measure of danger and risk in their event. One veteran rodeo man at Big Timber expressed this emphatically, saying "bulls are ornery; they will kill a guy if they can. That's why there is not much sense to ride them. I say bull riders take a size six and a half hat. That's what they take because they haven't got much sense." One bull rider realized that he and his fellow-contestants are "to some extent set apart. They say we are dumb." Common speech reveals a similar concept in the designation of a man who is strong but stupid ("brawn but no brain") as a "bull." The rodeo song "Bull Rider" contains the assertion "Well I may be a fool—but a coward I'm not" (LeDoux). A bull rider's less sophisticated image is in keeping with his simpler equipment; all he puts on the animal is a bull rope and bells.

The bells are said to make the bull mad, and announcers keynote the bull riding event by asserting "the bull doesn't like anything very much—to the delight of the crowd." The rodeo bull is viewed as not just unfriendly, but as an actively aggressive enemy who takes pleasure in injuring a man. Expressing this hostility, the announcer may tell the clown as he enters the arena "that bull could make a shish-ke-bob out of you and he would like to do it." Another announcer made this more graphic, describing "chunks of clown meat on a bull's horn." At Calgary the crowd was told "this bull got a clown down a few weeks ago in another rodeo, and the clown is still in the hospital in Lethbridge. He's in rooms twenty, twenty-one, and twenty-two!" Typically the clown quips that the bull is such a mean critter that he would like to take it home to his mother-in-law. At one rodeo a bull began to paw the ground in the arena, an action that was interpreted as a sign of rage. The announcer struck the essence of what appears to be the mystique of man-bull relations when he said to the clowns "that bull wants to dig a grave for you guys!"

The bull is always viewed as an animal of tremendous power and strength. "There is no way to outmuscle a bull" contestants admitted. Announcers constantly stress the great weight of the bull and make comparisons using the man/animal weight ratio—a one-hundred and fifty pound man to a two-thousand pound animal. Frequent references designate the bull as "a ton of unleashed fury." The massiveness of the bull is a quality men identify with. One contestant told me "rodeo is still a man's sport. You take a one-

The outcome can never be predicted when a contestant pits himself against "a ton of unleashed fury" in bull riding.   (*JJJ Photo*)

hundred and fifteen pound woman against a two-thousand pound
bull, and you figure what happens!" When it was pointed out that a
man is not stronger than a bull either, he said "yes, but a one-
hundred and fifteen pound man can whip a one-hundred and fifteen
pound woman easy."

Rodeo people dwell on the tremendous strength of the bulls and
like to relate instances when bulls have escaped during shows and
totally demolished cars in the parking lot, destroying huge amounts
of property before being recaptured. Judging from what I observed
during the escapes I saw, people often carried the bull's potential for
destructiveness somewhat beyond the realm of actuality. For example, at the Calgary Stampede one year a bull broke the fence and
entered a nearby playground. The bull reportedly "attacked" a child
who was in his path there. Certainly the huge beast could have killed
her instantly, but I saw the child minutes after her encounter with the
bull, and her injuries were confined to a cut lip, probably from
falling, and severe fright. Yet an official told me right after the
incident "a bull will go after anything!" When mounted men started
lassoing the escaped bull, it was amazing how quickly the animal
tired; after a few minutes he lay down and had to be pulled to his feet.
When I interviewed the owner of the bull, he said "he was born that
way—wild," and indicated that he had gotten away before. I noticed
several times in the arena that a bull would put his head against a
man's body in such a way that his nose or the area of his head between
the horns contacted it, causing no injury to the man. To deliberately
gore someone, an animal would ordinarily have to angle its head. I
am not saying that the bull is not a dangerous animal under many
conditions, for it often causes severe and even fatal injuries, but what
I am suggesting is the prevalence and importance of the general
image held of this animal in the minds of rodeo informants as a deadly
and destructive enemy—a killer. The main point of significance
seems to be that it is not in the bull's nature to *avoid* causing injury by
deliberately altering his course or pattern of behavior. In this he is
considered to be unlike the horse, who is more sensitive to changing
conditions, and will often adapt his actions to them through his own
more flexible temperament.

Whereas broncs are viewed as the outlaws of their kind, the
exception, bulls are conceived of as representatives of a uniformly
hostile class. Their stubborn nature will never be overcome. Announcers typically say of a bull that men are trying to subdue in the chutes
"there's trouble with a big black bull down there—he's got a differ-

ent idea." When bulls escape from the arena or refuse to leave it, they are not driven or cajoled, but rather roped and dragged out. The sensitivity and responsiveness attributed to the equine nature is felt to be absent in bulls.

Bull riding is called the "roughest, toughest event in rodeo" in which "the rider has to fight to stay aboard." Bulls are treated far more harshly than horses, and are routinely given electric shocks to make them move and to stimulate them before they are released into the arena. "Horses are considered to be more delicate," a stock contractor told me, "they suffer more from rough treatment." Though technically a domesticated species, bulls seem to be excluded from man's protected sphere. I found it of great significance that their quality of wildness is often associated with the force of nature, as when the announcer refers to the moment before the chute gate opens as "the lull before the storm." Names of bulls also reflect this, as exemplified by "Tiger," "Tornado," and "Cyclone." In addition, man-created ferocity and enmity is suggested by names like "Frankenstein," "Al Capone," "Cyanide," and "Explosion." The barrel into which the clown dives in mock fear of his adversary is called a "portable bomb shelter."

A former world's champion bull rider gave much insight into the spirit and meaning of his event. He told me that "bulls are the greatest challenge; bull riding is one of the last chances today to do something individual. It is more dangerous than riding a bronc, and you still have to get away from the bull, even after a qualified ride." He added "bulls have a built-in sense of not wanting anyone on their backs. It's a heck of a sensation when a bull has been out four-hundred to five-hundred times and nobody has ridden him before, yet you can do it." The aspiration of a man to become the only person or one of the very few, to make a qualified ride on a certain bull has deep and widespread appeal within the rodeo complex. It seems to represent the ultimate test and expression of the qualities exalted by cowboy/rodeo society—aggressiveness, male toughness, individualism, and domination. I found this "myth of the unconquerable animal" to be a pervasive expression of human determination to accept the challenge to vanquish nature. In Tulsa for the Finals one year, I talked to a taxi driver who was much involved with rodeo patrons during the ten-day affair. He told me about a tie between two bull riders at the last performance. "There was a ride-off, and neither bull did much. Then they went out and got two bulls that had never been ridden before. One of the riders was then knocked all the way across the arena."

Called "one of the last chances today to do something individual," bull riding provides a challenge that appeals to frontier spirit.   (*JJJ Photo*)

INTERPRETATION OF THE BULL RIDING EVENT OF RODEO

As "America's most dangerous sport," bull riding is a unique ritual which, like the other events of rodeo, expresses a particular meaning and message. The first key to its significance is the animal itself. The sport's foremost bull fighter, in discussing the nature of the bull, focused on an essential point when he said "You see people riding a dude horse, and you know it is possible to ride them, but bulls you look at differently." (By a dude horse—a perfect word choice—he implied a foolproof, dependable, and well-trained mount that would be no challenge even to a "dude," the Western word for a greenhorn, or one uninitiated into the ways of horses and horsemen.) Thus, I feel he struck at the heart of the issue, for in the case of horses there is always thought to be the possibility of taming, of exerting culture over nature, of bringing the equine animal to the tame pole of the wild/tame dichotomy, and even of including it within man's own inner circle of domesticity.

With the bull, this is not felt to be possible. The bull remains bound into the sphere of nature, unalterably near the wild pole. As one informant phrased it according to his insight, "the bull traditionally, historically, hereditarily, has been bred not to be domesticated, whereas the horse has been. So there will never be a shortage of bucking bulls, unless fifty percent of the American population become bull riders." Thus the bull remains in the view of rodeo a perpetual challenge (and, it seems, a desirable one) to man, who, try as he might, cannot extend his culture to any considerable degree into its nature. He can capture it, rope it, overpower it by use of weapons and technology, and use it for breeding, but the one thing he cannot do is either "outmuscle it" or affect its nature by altering it with any appreciable taming or training. In this sense it is categorized as "wild," and "enemy." The structuring of the bull riding event is closely related to rodeo people's perception of the bull as resistant to human influence.

The belief that a bull will not only trample on a human form in its way, but even attack a person, keeps this animal in a sphere alien to man. The constantly emphasized point that even the wildest of broncs will avoid such injurious behavior is an important element in keeping the horse nearer to the human circle than the bull can ever be. As an unalterably hostile creature, the bull is viewed as not partaking of human culture, and having no potentiality for a willing-servant, friend, or partner role. Rather, the bull plays the part of opponent to man, and it is this role that rodeo utilizes—and indeed reinforces and enhances for its own purposes. Electric prods, noise, spurs, gestures, and often the antics of the clowns are used in a deliberate effort to make the bull buck harder—to exaggerate his "wildness."

The fact that the bull is not perceived as susceptible to inclusion in man's cultural realm is reflected in the type of equipment used for bull riding. In discussing the equine rough stock events, it will be recalled, I drew attention to the varying amounts and complexity of the accouterments used by riders. I theorized that these characteristic arrangements are used to represent gradations in the degree of culture being exerted over nature, and to allow an interplay between the human controlling force and the oppositional power of the animal, to create the contest. Relating this to the bull riding event, the equipment used on the animal is the simplest possible, and is not made of leather but of rope. Both the flank strap and the band which encircles the animal's body and is looped around the rider's gloved hand are made of rope. Nothing touches the bull's head or any other part of its body, and nothing is placed between the rider and the animal's back. This relative freedom from restraint indicates that the event is structured to allow the bull expression of the fullest extent of his wildness, and indeed to encourage it. The stark simplicity of equipment is symbolic of the very low degree of control which culture is seen as exerting over the nature of the bull. The attached bells, I was told, have a practical function in the release of the bull rope after the ride. As mentioned earlier, they are also claimed to make the bull angry. In either case they may be said to favor decrease in restraint and increase in the spirit of opposition of the bull.

A factor also of significance in the structuring of this event is that rodeo tradition dictates a bull will attack a horse. Therefore in standard rodeos (with some exceptions) no one ordinarily remains mounted in the arena during bull riding, and clowns take over the role of protecting and rescuing contestants. The alleged hostility of the bull toward the horse—the animal that man takes into his realm as a partner—still further confirms the bull as an outsider, an enemy that remains wild and dangerous. The inclusion of a traditional clown into the event of rodeo which features the bull is in itself a fascinating study. For certainly the same surface functions could be served by men dressed in cowboy or other clothing. But since death is felt to be more implicit in bull riding than in any other event, the use of clowns may, on a deep level, serve to counteract this element. Though I cannot say that rodeo audiences exhibited the "blood lust" often attributed to them during this event, certainly spectator excitement is at its height during bull riding, and polls indicate it is the event of greatest interest. Clowns act to lighten the otherwise somber tone of the event which is generated by the threat of danger. They serve to ease the tension and are ready with jokes to divert audience attention when there are delays or mishaps. Clowns are not always humorous, though, and they have a function in increasing the bull's wildness—running at the animal or waving at it to increase its bucking—and with it, the contestant's score. It also occurs to me that, although rodeo clowns are always male (women clowns are said to be prohibited in the arena unless they stay at all times inside a barrel), their classic harlequin image is rather sexless. I suggest that this "neuter" influence contrasts strongly with, and perhaps to some extent counteracts, the extreme degree of maleness symbolized by the bull. Rodeo bull fighting clowns are actually brave and skillful men, but their grotesque costumes and antics belie this. Rodeo's bull event is frequently compared to the bull fight, and I suggest that the ridiculous character of the rodeo clown represents the antithesis of the matador. For the Spanish bull fighter is elaborately dressed, an explicitly sexual figure, prepared for a serious ritual. The clown, on the other hand, as a buffoon, acts to defy and divert the deadly serious nature of bull riding.

Spectators sometimes respond to bulls with laughter, even when no clowns are present, as when the animals fall or have to be roped, or refuse to leave the arena. Audiences do not react the same way to similar situations with horses. This type of laughter seems to reflect their feeling of the bull as an outsider to human concerns, an object never viewed with sympathy. One influential rancher who is involved with rodeo told me he had just returned from Spain, where he had attended a bull fight. He said he felt sorry for the horses used in the event, but felt absolutely no sympathy for the bull.

Certainly the bull stands as the classic symbol of maleness in the ranch/rodeo conceptualization, as it has for so many peoples throughout history. For "to a pastoral people a bull is the most natural type of vigorous reproductive energy" (Fraser 1972:34). Charging bulls depicted in cave paintings at Lascaux, dating from about fifty-thousand years ago suggest this masculine image (Conrad 1957:126). And with his symbolic mural, *Guernica*, "Picasso has given modern expression to an idea almost as old as man himself—that bulls are the essence of male force" (Conrad 1957:127).

Writing of the pastoral Fulani, whose lives are intimately associated with cattle, Riesman gives insight into the male mystique represented by the bull.

If a woman's sexuality is in some way evidence of her deep-seated weakness, that of the man is the source and the symbol of his strength. Everyday language reflects this attitude when people say of a man that he is a bull (kalahaldi) to express admiration. The kalahaldi is the stud-bull of the herd, while the word ngaari, also used to express admiration, designates the male of the bovine species. Among the cattle, the bull that defeats all the others can mount the cows of the herd; among humans, one who marries a woman defeats other men. The ideas of courage and virility are mingled in the single word ngorgu, which means "evident virility."

(1977:88)

It is understandable that a pastoral people who place high value on cattle production would admire the bull for his sexual vigor and reproductive capacity. Cowboy society, with its emphasis on masculinity and its aggressive outlook, would be little prone to exalt the characteristics of the cow. So it seems natural that rodeo, with its cowboy pastoral heritage, would give a prime place to an event featuring the bull.

Whereas a meeker society might look to the cow as the central symbolic source of bovine fertility, the rodeo society's admiration of aggression, power, physical strength, and brute force makes the bull an ideal representative. The unusual prominence of the male bovine's secondary sexual characteristics and the marked sexual dimorphism peculiar to the species distinguish the bull from other animals. His legendary sexual potency and fertility make the bull a natural source of admiration for those who exalt masculinity. His massiveness, the lack of delicacy and refinement about the bull, and his essentially untamed nature may cause men to identify their own maleness, their desire to wield power and to be free and wild, with these qualities in the bull. Bull riders' trucks and trailers display signs stating "I'm lover, fighter, and wild bull rider." As one cattle authority points out "the virtues of the bull are all masculine virtues." He is "fearless, powerful, combative, proudly potent—these are the characters that most men hope for, the characters in men that most women admire." "A maiden," the writer adds, may wish for "a lover with the strength, courage, and sex-assurance of the masterful bull" (Fraser 1972:187).

Although women may be initially attracted to this type of man, it was my observation among rodeo people that many wives and sweethearts of bull riders objected strenuously to their men's participation in this event. On the surface this may be attributed to the risk involved. On a logical level, though, almost as many contestants are

Above: Simplicity of equipment symbolizes the low degree of control which culture is seen as exerting over the nature of the bull.

(Robert Ridley Photo)

Below: In fighting the bull, a clown often uses a barrel for protection against his powerful and aggressive adversary.

(JJJ Photo)

hurt in the bronc events; yet women voiced scarcely any comparable antipathy to bronc riding. Many approving bronc riders' wives told me they could not tolerate their husbands riding bulls. If their husbands were bull riders, they said, they would ask them to quit. I have already mentioned that it is a common occurrence for a woman to issue an ultimatum to a man that he must "choose between me and the bull." Women appear to sense, with underlying alarm, the deep-seated male exclusiveness implied by this event. The totally masculine unit of man and bull in rodeo seems to leave no room for even a vestige of a feminine element. Bull riders may well appear to be, in the perceptions of their women, "lost" to them.

This masculine exclusivity may explain why rodeo men object so uniformly, so fiercely—and to a degree beyond logic—to the idea of a female bull rider. Bulls are a strictly male sphere, and it is unthinkable that women should be around them, handle them, or have any interaction with them, let alone attempt to master them by riding! The aura of danger and excitement which surrounds the bull is conceived of as a totally masculine element—one which must be met and opposed by their own male force. I found that this spirit of two opposing male forces—animal and man—is very important in the thinking of rodeo men. Bull riders spoke frequently of their respect for the animals as "real athletes" in their own right. The bull riding director of the P.R.C.A., also a contestant, spoke of a special bull in this category. "He will stand in the chute, and he trembles when you put the rope on. He is not scared, he is getting psyched-up. Like any other athlete, he gets his adrenaline running. He is smarter than most bulls. Bulls are like people, they get excited, knowing they are going to perform, and they enjoy it. Like the cowboys, they don't have to do it. They don't have to buck; you can't make them buck, so this means they must enjoy it. The rope only makes them kick higher and be showier."

It is noteworthy that the sport of rodeo is structured in such a way that a man wins only on the rankest bull. Relevant to this is the deep feeling contestants have for especially wild bulls. They spoke of these animals often, particularly of a recent contender, "General Issimo," who has been bucking bull of the year three times. Contestants said they hate to see him, and others like him, get old and slow down. "As this happens to a bull who is really successful at throwing people off," they said, "there is a better chance of their being rode. You hate to see this happen when you know that in their prime they could have thrown the rider." Bull riders expressed great concern that the aging bull should be retired by the stock contractor before he begins to lose his strength, his vigor, his quality of being unconquerable. They felt it grossly unfair to use a bull beyond his prime years. The bull riders' frequent expression of such feelings indicates that they actively desire to oppose their own strength and manhood to the enduring animal force represented by the bull. The sport is structured to fulfill their desire that the bull be given much leeway to remain unvanquished. Their perceptions of the animal assume the quality of the impenetrability of the bull's essential nature to man's extension of culture over it.

For purposes of contrast, it will be useful to refer briefly to the Spanish bullfight, and to the theory of J.R. Conrad regarding its symbolism. From his study of Spanish life and the ritual of the bullfight, he proposes the idea that the bull which is tormented and killed in this spectacle represents hated male authority. This feeling of animosity, Conrad says, first develops out of the Spanish family system in which a boy grows up with a repressed hostility toward his father, and then extends this to all authoritarian forces. Overpowering strength in the bull, like great power in a man or an organization like the church or state, becomes a symbol for "restraints upon his individualism." Thus he argues that the Spanish bullfight provides a culturally approved release for repressed antiauthority feelings. Conrad refers to the idea of Clyde Kluckhohn that a ritual practiced within a culture often tends to portray a symbolic resolution of the conflicts characteristic of that society (1957:186–193).

It is clear that in the American rodeo, the bull represents something quite different. Conrad gives a key to this when he states that "the Spanish bullfight is not a sport. There are no teams, no equally matched foes. There is no question of the ultimate outcome"—the killing of bulls (1957:189). Rodeo, on the other hand, structures into the context of the man-bull encounter a sport, a contest, in which there is at least the implication of matched contenders. Rodeo scoreboards during the event record statistics, such as "bulls 4, cowboys 3," and announcers often stress the fact that "the bulls are ahead today." In keeping with the view of rodeo as a ritual of frontier values, I think that in pitting himself against the bull, riding the animal becomes a ritual of male testing, and through the challenge offered by the bull a man has the chance to become in many ways the animal's equal. Contrasting with Conrad's Spanish authority model, it might be said that the American spirit of "democracy" makes contestants give to the bull a high degree of autonomy. This is suggested in the way in which the bull riding event calls for the minimum of restraining gear on the animals. It certainly is evident that, through the "conquest" symbolized by the qualifying eight second ride (and these are rather rare at many rodeos), men do not want to destroy the bull's male force; they want to first enhance it and then equal it by opposing it with their own. Rather than vanquishing it, they pay homage to it, and come to identify with it as with a brave enemy. They indicate that they admire the quality in the bull that could be called "frontier grit." In terms of an interesting word usage, bulls, though of the bovine species, are not "cowed,"—never subdued or intimidated, but ever the male rebels and "bullies" of the animal world.

Associated with their intractable spirit is the suggestion that the bull also represents "that proneness to revert to savagery which seems to be innate in most men" (Fraser 1972:87). This mystique is prevalent among bull riding contestants, who like to think of themselves as "wild bull riders," and strongly identify with the power and masculine ruthlessness attributed to bulls. One study of rodeo explains that

> Physically, bareback bronc riding may very well be the toughest event; but psychologically, at least, bull riding is second to nothing. Perhaps this is the reason bull riding seems to attract a different man. He is almost the outlaw of the rodeo circuit.
>
> (Hall 1976:123)

A prominent contestant, whose rodeo name is "Bull," expresses his sense of identification with the stock in his process of "psyching up" for a ride: "I just walk around and tell myself I'm an animal. I tell myself I'm an animal and I get worked up to a point where I'm so aggressive that there's no way I'm going to blow it" (Hall 1973:43).

Underlying the vulgarity of the announcer's quips, the clown's jokes, and the contestants' expressions runs a thematic thread denoting a kind of unity between man and bull despite the enmity between them. Physical intimacy is evident in bull riders' frequent remarks about the bull's breath in their faces and the clowns' jokes about the men's fingers in the bull's nose. During the women's bull riding competition one announcer spoke of a sick bull, who is "throwing up cowgirls." And a female contestant who rode bulls highlighted her feeling of contact with the animal through the metaphor "kissing the bull's hump" to describe getting banged in the head when the bull bucked.

An important factor in the North American pastoral perception of bulls is the notion that this class of animals is not closely associated with the concept of "meat." This does not mean that bulls are not eaten, but only that food is not their primary image. Thus they are removed perceptually from the bovine class of beef animals—calves, steers, and cows. Again, the factor that sets them apart is their sexual element. Edmund Leach in his discussion of human categorization of animals, notes that "those who are tame but not very close—'farm animals,' are mostly edible but only if immature or castrated. We seldom eat a sexually intact, mature farm beast." Leach considers the "idea that a castrated animal produces more succulent meat in a shorter time" to be "scientifically invalid" (1964:44). (Implied here, then, is the belief that animals are castrated for other reasons.) The (male) sexuality of an animal would, accordingly, appear to be a kind of mythic protection, preventing it from having the primary connotation of meat.

Thus, although the bull's sexual role in creating beef is acknowledged and valued, his own image is not primarily that of a beef animal. This is probably a natural consequence of the fact that the ranching outlook, like that of other pastoral societies, is characterized by a male oriented value-system. The beef animal image is typically the squat and blocky form of a castrated male or a rangy stunted steer or heifer. But it is never the large, muscular, and powerful bull with his thick arching neck, his hump, his wild eye, and fearsome horn. His masterful nature, which man's cultural realm has not encircled with submission, does not allow him to be visualized in the human mind as merely our tool or meat.

In summary, the bull occupies a distinct and important place in rodeo, contrasting in many respects with the position of the horse. Bull riding is considered not only the sport's roughest and wildest event, but, due to the nature of the bull, the most dangerous. The bull is perceived as being innately wild, mean, and ferocious, with a predisposition to attack man. He is visualized as having great strength, but little intelligence and responsiveness as compared with a bronc, who will "look back" and interact with its rider. Unlike a horse, who will avoid stepping on a man, a bull will trample him and try to gore him with its horns.

The bull symbolizes an actively aggressive enemy—the antithesis of the partner/friend that is part of the equine image. Not believed capable of being tamed or trained to any appreciable degree, the bull's unalterable wildness keeps it close to raw nature, as opposed to culture. In distinction to the horse, man cannot exert control over the bull and bring it into his own sphere, transforming it from wild to tame. The bull, though technically domesticated, remains outside the human realm, lacking the delicacy of spirit which would make it susceptible to the influence of culture. The bull does not become "humanized" to a significant degree, and remains a brute, an opponent.

It is significant that rodeo informants believe pure-bred Brahma bulls are "gentle, not strong-hearted, and won't buck much." Cross-bred animals, with some Brahma blood, are regularly used for bull riding because of this prevalent concept. One informant explained the extra spirit and bucking potential of the cross-bred animals on the basis of "hybrid vigor." In this I see again the propensity of rodeo people to impute the quality of crudeness to the bull. For "pure-bred" implies refinement resulting from a long period of deliberate breeding—the influence of culture—which is felt to be incompatible with the nature of a bucking bull. Just as some genetic factor in a bronc made it an "outlaw," a rodeo bull's heredity is believed to make it necessarily "rank."

Although the bull does not enter the human sphere, it seems that in a strange and illusory way man enters the bull's sphere. For bull riders foster an image of themselves as strong, dumb, crude, and wild, tough and brutish as the animals they ride—a breed apart. Men strongly associate themselves with the exaggerated masculinity of the bull, and consider bull riding strictly a male domain. Their masculine exclusivity within its context separates them from women, and from anything considered feminine, and exalts the male force as exemplified in both animal and man. Women are warned "never make love to bull riders; they will hurt you." To man and beast are attributed the quality of being totally male, ruthless in brute force. It is felt that it takes a "real man" to ride a bull, and in keeping with this, boys in youth rodeos ride steers instead of bulls. "Old timers'" rodeos also offer steer riding to men past their prime, and very young children may sometimes enter a "wild cow riding" contest.

Bull riders respect the bull as an athlete and identify with it in the way that a warrior identifies with an antagonist. The sport is structured to encourage considerable agonistic contest between the two opposing masculine forces of man and beast. Conditions allow for the bull to demonstrate as much wildness as possible in the rodeo arena, and this is symbolized by the scantiness and simplicity of equipment used on bulls. Extra riggings or a saddle would, of course, be incongruous, for the bull does not serve man in ways signified by them. The bull's ferocity is enhanced and exaggerated in the rodeo setting. The fact that, unlike a bronc rider, a bull rider is not required to use his spurs, adds to the image of the animal's innate wildness.

Bull riding seems to represent a distillation of many of the themes of rodeo as a frontier ritual. Generally occurring last on the schedule of events, unless a wild horse race is included, it serves to conclude the standard rodeo program with a spirit of the bull's untamed force. Thereby the entire ritual of rodeo, ending on this note, leaves both spectator and participant with the certainty that wildness remains a viable entity in their world. In spite of the fact that events featuring animals such as roped calves, bulldogged steers, and subservient horses have intervened between the initial wild bareback event and the concluding wild bull event, all nature is not yet tamed. Man's dominion may yet be symbolically, if not literally, extended, in an ongoing reenactment of culture versus nature—man versus bull. The importance and value of the frontier ethos and experience is thus assured for those who need it and desire it in the ordering of their universe.

7

THE ROLE OF OTHER ANIMALS IN RODEO

ALTHOUGH CATTLE AND HORSES almost totally dominate the sport of rodeo, a few other species play minor, but illuminating, roles. Some of these "supporting actors" are the pig, dog, sheep, monkey, goat, buffalo, and yak. The mule I have mentioned as regularly appearing in the company of a clown and serving as a kind of foil to the horse. Sometimes this animal retains its classic image of stubbornness and stupidity, and at other times it momentarily becomes smarter than its master, the clown. There is certainly the implication of an analogy between the clown and the mule—the clown as a caricature of a man, and the mule as a caricature of a horse. In a typical scene in which the mule lies down and refuses to rise, the clown exclaims, "I can't get my ass off the ground!" At Casper the clowns staged a mule-riding race, and in all rodeo parades clowns are mounted on mules or walk beside them.

The pig, like the mule, invariably occurs in the rodeo setting with the clown, and in every case I have seen it has been in the form of a suckling. A classic clown-pig act is the one in which the clown shouts to the announcer "There is a mad pig loose on the fairgrounds. Yes, it is a thousand pound Russian boar hog, with tusks two feet long. It has got rabies and swine flu." Then the "dangerous animal" appears—a baby pig named "Mary" that follows the clown as he feeds it from a nursing bottle. The announcer comments, "Yes, Mary is quite a ham, and there are two hams with her" (there are two clowns in the arena). Thus the frightful monster turns out to be only an innocent baby. But the message is imparted that, though the pig shows "attachment" to her master, she still is after all meat. The pig is thereby cast in a lowly role, as is characteristic of edible animals, and in a female role, both as to her own sexual identity and the association with the nursing bottle. The pig is always the object of ridicule in rodeo, as is usual for this animal whose name, when applied to a person, constitutes "verbal abuse." Writing on this subject, Leach explains "I suspect we all feel a rather special guilt about our pigs. After all, sheep provide wool, cows provide milk, chickens provide eggs, but we rear pigs for the sole purpose of killing and eating them, and this is a rather shameful thing, a shame which quickly attaches to the pig itself" (1964:50–51).

During a country-western music show held in connection with Cheyenne Frontier Days and featuring a rodeo star as the singer, one performer came to the stage holding a baby pig he was feeding with a nursing bottle. He said to the audience "I had a blind date last night, and this [the pig] was it." He followed his remark by announcing "I've travelled with enough pigs." Then, turning to the suckling animal, he told it "come on, little pig, grow up." Here again, the pig is imputed to be female, and its name an insult.

The element of the pig drinking from a nursing bottle is often the central emphasis in short clown-pig sequences in rodeo. In a frequently reenacted scene, as the clown (a surrogate porcine "mother") feeds the piglet, he tells an audience, "This is udder cola." The announcer picks up on this, saying "Udder cola!—Yes, and that is udderly ridiculous!" In the male world of rodeo, the feeding of the nursing pig by the masculine (or neuter) figure implies that the female element, to which the ranch/rodeo spirit is often overtly hostile, is after all not essential; it can be replaced. On a deeper level, though, mother's milk is significant as representing a physiological secretion. It is one of the exudations of the body, and this places it in the category of those substances described by Leach as being "objects of intense taboo," which have special importance to an individual in the conceptual ordering of his universe (1964:38). I will refer to this theory again presently, and apply it to rodeo in more detail.

Sheep occasionally appear in special acts on the rodeo program in which the process of herding them forms the basis of the entertainment. An example of this is a sequence in which a sheepdog (a Border Collie) is ridden by a Capuchin Monkey dressed in cowboy clothes. The pair round up the sheep and drive them into a corral in the arena. The rider is advertised as a recent graduate from cowboy college who needs a job. But, the announcer adds, "woolies are getting scarce here in the West now, so jobs are difficult to come by." The punch line is that since this is the situation, they will send this "graduate" to Washington, because "one more monkey in the government won't make any difference." Within this act, several aspects of the ranch/rodeo ethos are made explicit. The traditional antipathy of the cattleman toward the sheepman finds expression in the sarcastic announcement that "the next best thing to being a cowboy is being a sheep herder." The fact that even a monkey can successfully herd sheep is, of course, derogatory, and this is carried further by the announcer's warning that the little cowboy may "get the sheep so confused he will scare the ticks off them." Additionally, the fact that sheep are becoming scarce in their territory is always pleasing to cowboys, who have a longstanding aversion to woolies and their herders. The act is also structured to give vent to ranchers' hatred of predators such as coyotes, as the announcer provides details about the dangers from the wild that make it necessary for the cowboy to safeguard the sheep. More will be said to elucidate this issue in my discussion of the relation of ranch/rodeo people to the wild.

As for the monkey in such a performance, though it is technically a wild animal, it has been partly tamed, and as a primate its resemblance to man makes it seem a part of the human sphere. Anthropomorphized by clothing, and placed in a human niche, depicted as deprived of every vestige of its wild nature, this monkey becomes the parody of a stupid and dominated person. The illusion that the monkey as a rider is in charge of guiding his mount is intended on a surface level, though this is scarcely convincing. The dog, in reality the "brains of the outfit," by being cast as an animal that is saddled and ridden, as opposed to its normal role as solo sheep herder, becomes symbolically lower in the animal hierarchy. Typically, sheep were not herded in the American West by mounted men, anyway, and this is one reason why cowboys have always felt superior to sheepmen as herders on foot. The incongruity of a "cowboy" herding sheep is an additional factor making the monkey—and by implication, the sheepman—ridiculous.

Similar acts feature a monkey riding a greyhound that jumps hurdles or rides in a miniature barrel race. Surely the exhibition of the monkey "running the barrels" conveys the same derogatory message made clear in other ways about the only event for women in standard rodeo. It is caricatured as such a ludicrous performance that even a monkey can do it. In both these cases in which a monkey rides a dog, a clown is in evidence as director of the event. These performances are fascinating instances of a reversal in the usual order of things—for here the wild exerts control over the tame.

Of all the minor animals in rodeo, the role of the goat is perhaps the strangest and most complex. As explained in the second chapter in which I presented an overview of the sport, the goat is never a participant in standard professional men's rodeo. It is generally

Symbolic connotations of goats contribute to the view that these animals are appropriate for use in girls' rodeo events.

(JJJ Photo)

reserved for girls' rodeos and the girls' events of youth rodeos, though the Little Britches circuit does include a goat tying event for "junior boys." When they pass to the senior division, and nearer manhood, however, boys no longer enter this event.

In goat tying, the goat is simply an inferior substitute for a calf; it is an animal with which no self-respecting cowboy would concern himself. Fortunately for the animals, there is no roping in this event—only tying. It is significant that the rules in goat tying state that the horse must not come in contact with the goat or the rope to which it is tethered; if this occurs there is a ten second penalty for the contestant. Thus the horse functions only to carry the rider into the arena, but does not serve as the all-important partner, as in calf roping. The event has no ranch orientation or any suggestion of ranch usefulness, and it gives the impression of being only a parody of the calf events. Neither is there any grace or beauty to it, and, at least during the times I have seen it, scarcely any challenge, for the goats are small and put up little resistance. The contestants experience it as "fun," but nevertheless they make themselves appear ridiculous. It is relevant that, though even in women's rodeo all arena helpers are male, in this event it is another girl who restrains the goat (usually astride it, holding it by the horns) until the contestant, galloping in on her horse, comes near enough to the tethered animal to try to grab it. The message seems clear that handling goats is strictly for women. Since the goat is tied by the neck, in addition to being held, all semblance of any "sporting chance" is denied to the animal. That the goat is used at all is evidence of the way rodeo looks at women and the way rodeo women perceive themselves. I can say this with conviction because at the Girls Rodeo Association Finals I saw for myself that female contestants can be highly adept and successful at roping and tying calves in the traditional manner. There may be no real necessity, then, to resort to the use of goats.

In goat tail tying, exclusively a girls' event, contestants are made to look even more foolish. The rider merely gallops into the arena, dismounts, and tries to tie a colored ribbon on the goat's tail. It is an undignified procedure, and I noted that many of the girls straddled the goat backwards in order to accomplish the aim.

Another event involving the caprine species is the wild goat milking contest, which was a feature of the women's finals in San Antonio. This was a frantic race in which teams of girls tried to extract milk from the udders of what the announcer called "fiesty range goats." The animals were more terrified than resistant, and were handled with astounding roughness, sometimes dragged by

After grappling with her quarry in a sea of mud, this contestant signals her success in tying the goat.   (*JJJ Photo*)

their horns, an ear, or a leg after being milked, to reach the finish line. A clown was present to add to the intended humor of this event, and he periodically seized a goat and pumped its tail up and down in a mock effort to obtain milk. As with the baby pig acts, the effect here was one of emphasis on mammary glands and their secretion.

The rodeo practice of making the goat the province of women seems to be related to the species being conceived of as a shoddy imitation of the bovine animal. As I have shown, the notion that women and cattle belong to mutually exclusive spheres is central within the ranch/rodeo outlook, as is the case with other cattle-complex societies. Male informants who were aghast at the idea of women bull or bronc riders approved of female participation in goat events. They grouped goat tying and goat tail tying with barrel racing, and said "these are created events; there is no reason to do them on the ranch or prairie," and so they said that they "could see women entering these types of events." It is important to remember that goats are not customarily used for meat by the ranch/rodeo culture, or indeed by many consumers in this country.

On a deeper level, women are no doubt associated with goats because of the traditional sexual connotations of the caprine animal. Regarding the goat's image in myth, it is well known that Pan, satyrs, and fauns have goat-like natures, and that the goat is an "ideal symbol of the excessive sexuality which these gods and creatures were believed to possess. When one calls a man an 'old goat,' it still refers to this lecherous nature" (Mercatante 1974:120). Folktales also stress the sexual practices of goats. Since male rodeo participants generally think that female participants are lacking in "womanliness"—and hence something is amiss with their sexuality—probably this is felt to make the goat an appropriate animal to be used by women in the sport. For both goat and girl have an image of being outside of the normal socio-sexual behavior of their group—the goat being aberrant from nature and the girl deviating from the norms of her culture.

Indeed rodeo people expressed their perceptions of goats as "miserable animals." One woman, whose children were regular contenders on the youth circuit, said she dislikes goats because "they eat everything and they walk on cars. They jump up on my Maverick and slide down it. They do their b.m.'s on our haystacks and then the cows won't eat the hay." I found that goats were felt to be coarse, indiscriminate, lewd, and mischievous. I sensed that ranch/rodeo people generally did not like goats because they could not really dominate them. Goats are notoriously unpredictable—a quality that caused much uneasiness, even enmity, among informants. One cannot control the actions of a goat, nor can one expect consistent behavior from it. The word "capricious" came into the language because of this characteristic. The unpredictability of the goat is no doubt associated in the minds of ranch/rodeo men with the same quality in women, for they indicate that they view women as rather tricky, and relate this to females having greater intimacy with nature. By allying women with this particular animal, their sharing of its trait of capriciousness has particular relevance to the idea that the female, unlike the male, is closer to nature than to culture.

Two other very different animals that occasionally appear in rodeo should be mentioned: the North American buffalo and the Tibetan yak. It is traditional at the Calgary Stampede to include as an exhibition, not a contest, an Indian buffalo riding event. Wild buffaloes, fitted with flank straps, are mounted by Plains Indian riders in native costume, who attempt to make eight second rides. The performance proceeds in the manner of bull riding, except that all animals and their riders enter the arena at the same time. This creates an effect which is quite different from the usual pattern of individual rough stock riders, each in turn occupying the arena alone. Indian buffalo riding is a popular attraction which keynotes the rodeo on successive days and imparts to it an extra measure of wildness. This enhances the spirit of the Calgary Stampede as a traditional Western festival staged by a modern city which fervently wishes to remember its origin as a frontier outpost. The event is structured so that the Indian-buffalo units in the arena are aggregate, rather than individual (as they easily could have been). The overall impression imparted by this exhibition is thereby not so much the domination of man over animal as it would have been in a solo contest. Rather, by emphasizing the performers en masse and calling attention to man and animal as quaint relics from regional history, the theme of the destruction and/or subjugation of both the Indian and the buffalo as obstacles in the taming of the West is stressed. Calgary, once a frontier cattle town, and located in the heart of a region still considered to be the domain of the cattleman, thus manages in its ritual to categorize both Indian and bison as "colorful figures of the past," which had to give way to the preeminence of the beef empire in the Great Plains.

The inclusion of yak riding in rodeo is also of great interest, especially since this species is the basis of pastoral subsistence in Tibet. The yak is an animal which is both wild and domesticated, and which has been cross-bred to cattle. Performances of this event were held on the two Saturdays of the 1978 Calgary Stampede, and consisted of attempts by two top Canadian bull riders to make qualified rides on hybrid yaks. Both failed, and it was made clear that "out of six-hundred times out in rodeo, these animals have never yet been ridden for eight seconds." It is said of the yaks used so far in rodeo that they did not establish a set pattern of bucking, and their "incredible speed and agility put most riders on the ground before they knew what happened" (Johannson 1978:120). The announcer stressed the toughness of these unusual animals as exemplified by their "being able to survive on eating bark and wood." Belonging to a species adapted to the cold climate of high altitudes and noteworthy for its ability to withstand the extremes of nature's rigors, yaks are symbolic of the hardihood that is often imputed to exist only in a creature who partakes of the wild. Considered even more unconquerable than a bull, and significantly, less predictable, they represent the ultimate in the wildness of nature, the farthest pole in the continuum of tame to wild that is possible to include within a contest event of rodeo. They are at present used in the sport only in the Canadian Northwest—which is, appropriately, the most recently tamed area of the Great Plains frontier.

Thus it may be said that the mule, pig, sheep, monkey, dog, goat, bison, and yak add wider dimensions of meaning to the sport which deals primarily with cattle and horses. These minor animals introduce themes which serve to expand and clarify rodeo's deep level exploration and ordering of nature versus culture, as expressed by the wild and the tame. Relevant to the assertion of man's mastery of nature as the central theme of rodeo is the idea of the self as it relates to the outer world. Before proceeding to a discussion of the relation of the ranch/rodeo complex to the wild—that portion of the universe which is, or is conceived to be, beyond the realm of man's direct control—the concept of the individual as it is manifested in the sport will be considered. Related to this is the phenomenon of those physiological factors which serve to demarcate the perceptual boundaries between the individual and the world beyond it and to mediate between them.

8

HUMAN RELATIONS WITH NATURE EXPRESSED IN RODEO

THE CONQUEST OF PAIN AND FEAR

ON ITS MOST BASIC level, as I have shown, rodeo represents a dramatized expression of the values of the cattle industry—the extension of culture over nature, the human over the animal, the tame over the wild, the controlled over the free. Inevitably, its scope must go beyond the domestic sphere, for the wild is the ultimate source of whatever elements remain to be conquered or subdued. Mastery is the keynote—the mastery of nature that is synonymous with the conquest of the West. Within the context of rodeo as ritual I theorize that certain relationships between people and the rest of nature are symbolically defined and ordered. These relationships involve each participant, as represented by his own individual self and its physiological extensions, in interaction with various components of the environment which are encountered at progressive distances outward from the self.

It is by reference to the concept of the human self that I am able to explain, at least in part, one of the outstanding (and one of the strangest) aspects of rodeo—the stress that the sport places upon bodily injury and pain. I suggest that this phenomenon represents a mastery of the self as the innermost component of nature—and that this mastery comprises the initial step toward control of the outer portions of the environment.

At the outset, a rodeo contestant must conquer fear. As one bronc rider told me, "I have learned how to control my fear, and to distribute fear to use it for my own advantage." And a bull rider confided that "after a bad injury you have to go back, to prove something to yourself." It is impossible to overemphasize the tre-

mendous concern of rodeo participants with injury and their preoccupation with overcoming it. Contestants are continually taping
parts of their bodies before competing. Everywhere in sight behind
the chutes there seems to be someone wearing a cast. In the arena the
judges are often previously injured contestants on crutches, and stock
contractors commonly ride with splinted legs or arms. Announcers
frequently give the audience information about a present contender
now back in the sport who was told by doctors he would never ride
again due to a broken neck or back. Typically a pickup man may be
mentioned who broke his leg at the last rodeo and who has removed
the cast so he can ride in that day's performance. A great number of
ropers have lost a finger or thumb when they have dallied their rope
around the saddle horn and caught a digit in the coil. But they take
this in stride, and one, I noted, even called attention to this condition
by wearing a ring on the stump of a missing finger. I have found that
rodeo contestants continually talk about their injuries, though they
never complain about them. One bull rider told me about having
"three major operations in sixteen hours" to repair a ruptured bladder
that "busted loose three times." He told me he had broken every bone
in his body except his back, neck, and left shoulder. It is said of the
celebrated cowboy Freckles Brown that at the time he made his
record-breaking ride on the bull Tornado "his inventory of broken
bones and fractures began at his neck and ended with his toes. X-rays
of his body looked like a jigsaw puzzle" (Krakel 1978:3).

Each rodeo event has its own special risks and hazards peculiar to
its contestants. Bareback riders, for example, suffer trauma to the
arm that holds the rigging, and steer wrestling leads inevitably to
some degree of knee trouble. Bull riders, in addition to the major
injuries resulting from falls, tramplings, and gorings, usually have
pulled groin muscles from gripping the bull. Saddle bronc riders
most freqently break their legs, either in the chutes or when they are
bucked off. Doctors say calf roping is the safest event, involving only
an occasional sprained ankle or broken leg sustained in jumping off
the horse (Smith 1976:93).

Many rodeo men refuse treatment for their injuries. A Nebraska
doctor who specializes in treating rodeo cowboys describes them as
"stoic individuals who shrug off their injuries except in the most
severe cases." A recent article in the medical journal which is devoted
entirely to sports injuries refers to the fact that in the arena

  it's obvious the cowboy is courting serious injury. But, incredibly, he
  may be making that spine-rattling ride in spite of an injury—a broken

jaw, dislocated shoulder, torn ligaments—which would sideline most professional athletes.

(Smith 1976:90)

Rodeo physicians also point out that "when a cowboy is hurt, he won't admit to pain unless it's so bad he can't stand it, so probably three-fourths of the injuries never get treated. It's a point of pride with them to show they are not concerned about injuries." Physicians sometimes see extreme cases like "the clown who fractured two lumbar vertebrae when a bull pitched him into the air and he landed on his buttocks, but refused to be hospitalized" (Smith 1976:92).

As I interpret this phenomenon, rodeo people, by evidencing indifference to pain and injury through their ostentatious lack of concern about the physical realm, achieve a very real sense of mastery over themselves. They might be said to flaunt their injuries, and seem to glory in them as badges of their conquest of fear and pain. Going further, they have perhaps come near to conquering their own mortality, for, in sustaining these wounds, they have also willingly risked death. According to my view, they have not only conquered self by their indifference to pain, but in a larger sense they feel they have conquered nature by refusing to bow to it. They have risen above it, for injury and pain are part of the natural world. By thus freeing themselves from their own bodily limitations, perhaps they are liberated to the highest degree possible from the restrictions of nature itself. This can represent the winning of a battle over nature just as does the subjugation of animals and the land.

The concern of a great number of contestants with the power of the self is also manifested by their active participation in the theory and practice of psychocybernetics. They stress that an individual can indeed accomplish whatever he sets out to do, by convincing himself that whatever is willed, if it is believed possible of attainment, can and must be accomplished. Most rodeo schools now teach this attitude, particularly in relation to bull riding, and I have already noted that many top winners ascribe to it. I see a parallel mechanism operating in certain aspects of the born-again movement as manifested by the "Cowboys for Christ." Through his subscription to this ideology, a person can receive, and take unto himself, the power of the Holy Spirit. In this process the self is glorified and greatly strengthened by this outside force which deigns to enter and merge with it. Thus the contestant is enabled to accomplish feats of conquest which lead to success through the exertion of his miraculously-

Above: Participation in spite of painful injuries attests to a rodeo contestant's sense of mastery of self—and nature.   *(Robert Ridley Photo)*

Below: Physiological secretions, like milk, often receive emphasis in rodeo, as exemplified by the wild cow milking event.   *(JJJ Photo)*

empowered self. Rodeo participants' testimonies frequently indicate that they attribute winning to such a phenomenon.

Having given this background concerning the self and its significance in rodeo, it is time to consider the relation of the individual to elements which are outside it in nature, and which ultimately relate it to the wild. I will proceed from the physical body to an aspect of that body which is at the same time of it and yet external to it. By this I refer to the physiological extensions or outward secretions (there seems to be no accurate word for these elements which Leach calls "exudations" [1964:38]) that appear to play such an enigmatic yet obviously important role in the ritual of rodeo.

THE EMPHASIS ON PHYSIOLOGICAL SUBSTANCES

> The exudations of the human body are universally the objects of intense taboo—in particular, feces, urine, semen, menstrual blood, hair clippings, nail parings, body dirt, spittle, mother's milk.
>
> (Leach 1964:38)

> Other Ndembu symbols, at their sensory pole of meaning, represent such themes as blood, male and female genitalia, semen, urine, and feces.
>
> (Turner 1967:29)

Rodeo's strange and initially puzzling emphasis on certain of the physiological substances which are excreted or exuded from the body is far too pervasive and consistent to be attributed merely to the audience's presumed appetite for vulgarity. Rodeo performances are noteworthy for the frequency and repetition of references to these excretory and exudative functions. From the simplest unsanctioned country rodeo on up through the most prestigious Professional Rodeo Cowboys Association Finals in Oklahoma City, virtually all rodeos exhibit this phenomenon in some way.

Preceding an analysis of this element of rodeo and suggestions as to what it adds to the deeper level of the meaning conveyed by the sport, some typical examples will be given. These are representative of the way in which such substances as breath, intestinal gas, feces, urine, mucus, pus, spittle, sweat, milk, and detached hair are featured in rodeo. It is essential to point out here that my treatment of these, as compared to that of Leach (1964) or Turner (1967), on whose observations I am drawing, is more complex in being concerned with these elements in animals as well as in man. This adds a different dimension to what has already been said about them in anthropological literature. It is precisely this new dimension that I will give primacy to here, in order to elucidate the underlying significance of rodeo's ritual. For it is through the blending of the animal with the human that rodeo is able to focus on the central dilemma of man's relation to the rest of nature. Does he, with his position of dominance, stand as a creature of another order—separate—or is he, after all, an intrinsic part of it?

It is not by accident that rodeo people are generally referred to as the "shitkicker crowd," and they willingly accept this epithet. At many rodeos, including the National Finals, I saw belt buckles for sale bearing the slogan "I'm proud to be a shitkicker." In a sense the entire atmosphere of rodeo is permeated by excrement; the smell of cattle and horse dung in the air is the inevitable accompaniment of the sport. This is greatly intensified by the terror of the animals in the chutes which causes virtually all of them to have diarrhea. In the pens, the runs leading to the chutes, and in the arena there is always manure, constantly tread upon by the animals, officials, and contestants. On the grounds surrounding the arena spectators commonly walk in manure, and those seated near the front may become splattered with it.

There is consistent scatalogical emphasis throughout a typical rodeo performance. A clown, for example, takes part in a dialogue with the announcer, asking him "What did you call those two men?" The announcer answers "pickup men," and the clown retorts "They're fired." To the announcer's question "Why?" the clown replies "There's a pile right there, right there, and right there!" The announcer then says (disgustedly) "They're supposed to pick the *cowboys* up." A more complicated clown routine enacted at a very prestigious rodeo involves the "little house on the prairie," an outhouse that is located by two clowns who search for it with a witching wand made of toilet paper. The outhouse is finally dynamited by the clowns, which causes the walls to collapse revealing a man inside in a very undignified position. The man comes running out with a toilet seat around his neck and is told by a clown "That's what happens if you mess around long enough—you get it in the neck!"

Conversations often follow along in the same vein. A contestant who was relaxing over a Pepsi told me about his friend, a roper, whose thumb had been torn off during a rodeo performance. The man, with his detached thumb, was flown to the nearest hospital, but the surgery performed there to reattach the digit was unsuccessful. Unconcerned, the roper returned to rodeo and declared that the only problem he had as a result of his accident was the difficulty experienced in "learning to wipe his butt with his left hand." A traditional rodeo prank is to substitute laxative gum for the candy-coated variety and pass it out to a fellow contestant just before he leaves for a long bus or plane trip.

Shirts sold and worn at some rodeos read "If God had intended that Texans should ski, he'd have made bullshit white." The word is used constantly. One contestant described as his reason for having a poor ride not being able to "get my shit together." When a girl who had been learning to rope and tie calves was leaning against a fence exhausted, and literally covered from head to foot with calf dung, her friend had an opportunity to tell her "you know something—you're full of shit," and no one could argue. Behind the chutes a helper would tell a contestant who was mounting a bull or bronc how to keep from "getting the shit kicked out of you."

A clown-donkey act features the related theme of intestinal flatulence. The donkey lies on the clown with its rear end near the clown's head and refuses to move. The clown begins to dig in the dirt in a frantic effort to move the animal off him. While digging, the clown calls out "There must be oil here," and the announcer asks "Why?" To this the clown replies "Because there's a gas leak!"

Urine, too, receives its share of attention from the clowns. They may, for example, sneak up behind someone in the arena and pretend to urinate on him. A story about the witnessing of a "miracle" is told at many rodeos. The narrator describes his experience of waiting to use a phone booth in which a fat lady was making a call. "A little-bitty mouse came down the street and ran into the phone booth, up the fat lady's legs under her dress. The lady screamed, jumped up and down, and clapped her knees together. That's when I witnessed this miracle—that lady squeezed a half a gallon of water out of that little-bitty mouse!"

Spittle has already been mentioned as a bodily secretion that is much in evidence in rodeo. Almost all rodeo people chew tobacco, and there is constant spitting in all directions. Saliva receives emphasis too, by the many ways in which the mouth is used in the sport. Biting a bronc's ear has been mentioned. In addition, the rope used to tie the calf, the "piggin' string," is always carried in the contestant's mouth until it is used. One world's champion all-around cowboy is even pictured in his official photograph with this rope in his mouth. Barrel racers inevitably carry their whips in their mouths while riding around the barrels. And contestants in the rough stock events tie on their all-important glove by pulling the strings with their mouths.

Horses in the arena frequently drip saliva from their bitted mouths, and there is common reference to "bull slobber," as in the song which relates

That dirty old bull slobbered all over my face.

(LeDoux)

Nasal discharge is often mentioned, as in the pronouncement that the clown needs a doctor because he put his finger in the bull's nose and "the boogers bit him." During a typical bull fighting act, after the bull has been goaded to butt a dummy, attention is called to the fact that now the "man" (dummy) has "the bull's boogers on him." In the song "Bull Rider," the contestant complains that his animal "blew snot in my face" (LeDoux).

The exhalations of the bull are referred to either as foul breath or as giving someone hay fever by coming into contact with it. Odors from bulls are frequently a topic of conversation among contestants, and a song calls attention to their "stinking hair" and contains the descriptive lines

Well, the dust and the hair and flys from off his hump
Whipped to my nose as he made another jump,
And the stink of it all was more than I could stand.

(LeDoux)

Sweat is commonly in evidence in rodeo, both on animals and men. The announcer will likely allude to it at some time in the performance, as when he calls a certain animal "as rank as a sheepherder's winter underwear in the spring." Clowns play it up by lifting the arm of the dummy they prop in the middle of the arena during the bull riding and fanning the underarm area while they make a gesture of repulsion. Later there is a reference to this same dummy as "dead" after it has been struck by the bull. The clown explains to the announcer that he can tell the "man" is dead by the smell given off from the corpse.

The clown "cries" over the death of his friend, the dummy, sobbing and dabbing at his eyes, ostensibly shedding tears—another type of bodily secretion. Also, in a remarkable sequence involving feigned death, one clown shoots another with a shotgun, causing water to spray out in all directions from the "wounded" man's body; the water represents his "insides." A relevant form of real-life "clowning" was an incident I observed among a group of ranch/rodeo people who took part in a wagontrain expedition for recreation. One of the participants had a glass eye, which he repeatedly removed from its socket and then reinserted, much to the amusement of his fellow riders. There was continual mention of this and joking about it throughout the several days of the affair: the eye was to be awarded to the best rider, best lover, the winner of a lottery, and so forth, on the last day. I found this episode a remarkable example of the strange phenomenon of preoccupation with those elements which are part of the body (in this case a prosthesis as a substitute)—yet at the same time are, or can be external to it.

Blood, as mentioned, often drips from open wounds on both man and stock. Serum oozes from raw brands on cattle and horses, and several times I noticed pus dripping from the infected horns of bulls—an exudate that flew in all directions when the animal tossed its head. Medical treatment would not have been impractical.

"Hair clippings," mentioned in Leach's list of "exudations" (1964:38), play an interesting part in rodeo. I found that saddle bronc riders habitually pull some of their horse's mane out to use as a marker for positioning their hand on the rope rein. Needless to say, something else could be used as well for this purpose. I have already drawn attention to the use of a piece of mane or tail in a rodeo contestant's belt loop for good luck, and to the rodeo song that commemorates horse hair as a talisman. The hair motif also receives emphasis in the song about a bronc called the Yellow Stud, for when

The wooden gate flew open, the stud bailed out high;
An explosion of yellow hair seemed to fill the sky.

(LeDoux)

Chicken feathers, as a variant of animal hair receive emphasis in the rodeo clown joke about the man who had a chicken and wanted to shave its feathers. He sent a request to the Schick razor company for a razor to use for this task. The corporation wrote back "We have men's Schicks, we have women's Schicks, but we have no chicken Schicks." One of the most noteworthy uses of human hair in rodeo involves a celebrated bull fighter, who, at the moment of greatest danger, when he has attracted the bull away from the contestant and the animal is charging at him, instantaneously jerks off his "hair" (wig) and tosses it in the air. This dramatic scene from Cheyenne Frontier Days was captured on film and shown on television in connection with advertising. The wig worn by this particular man, unlike that of a true clown, is a short crop of gray hair that appears to be his own, so the effect of this action is quite startling to the observer.

The secretion of milk, already alluded to, is one of the commonest themes in rodeo. There is occasionally on the program a colt race involving nursing mares. Quite frequently there is a wild cow milking contest or a wild goat milking contest, and sometimes there is explicit reference to the physiology of milk secretion. One team in goat milking got ahold of a goat which the announcer said "wouldn't 'let down her milk,' " a term dairymen use for the hormonally regulated release that allows the milk flow to begin. He added "maybe the goat isn't even wet, it's dry. But we've got to get the pump working. It's hard to do, especially with one that doesn't want to be milked!" Invariably, at almost every rodeo someone refers to the "tornado that struck at milking time." This storm "blew the barn away, blew the cow away, and left the little old lady holding the bag." Then, of course, the announcer has another chance to retort "udderly ridiculous!"

Women's breasts are frequently the subject of rodeo humor. I have already mentioned the "rawhide bra" and "Vanity Fair" references. In a typical sequence the clown points to the grandstand and says "There is Raquel Welch!" The announcer asks "Where?" and the clown quickly changes his mind: "Oh, no, it is two bald-headed men sitting together." At each performance of the Calgary Stampede Rodeo when a particularly large breasted country-western star appeared as a featured entertainer, the singer's upper anatomy was alluded to as "a pair of forty-fours."

THE MEANING OF BODILY EXUDATIONS AND EXCRETIONS IN RODEO

It is clear from the frequency and consistency of reference to them in rodeo that the bodily substances I have been describing are of considerable importance to the central issues which the sport manages to explore and discuss by means of its structured events. Let us see how the basic question of what is the relation of man to the rest of nature may be elucidated by reference to this class of elements.

Edmund Leach's essay (1964) in which he discusses the connection between animal categories and verbal obscenities offers insight on this matter of the function of bodily exudates in man's logical ordering of his universe. Leach's theory is that a child first perceives his physical and social environment as a continuum, not as something which is made up of separate things. He has to be taught to distinguish the world as composed of individual items with names. Thus one of the fundamental human concerns comes to be that of determining the boundaries between the self and the external world. Our perceptions are trained to do this, Leach says, by a "simultaneous use of language and taboo. Language gives us the names to distinguish the things; taboo inhibits the recognition of those parts of the continuum which separate the things" (1964:35). In this way, he points out, language "places each individual at the center of a social space which is ordered in a logical and reassuring way" (1964:36).

"All scientific enquiry," Leach reminds us, is concerned with " 'discovering' those parts of the environment that lie on the borders of what is 'already known.' " He argues that those elements which "fill the interstices" between the "separate things" of our environment become "the focus not only of special interest but also of anxiety"—that is, they become taboo for us because we have suppressed the recognition of them as "nonthings" (1964:37). The exudations of the human body which, Leach says, are "universally the objects of intense taboo," fit this category. These substances, according to his theory, are "ambiguous in the most fundamental way," as they relate to the basic human problem of determining initial boundaries between the self and the environment. In trying to answer the dilemma posed by "what am I, as against the world? Where is the edge of me?" the bodily exudates represent substances that are "both me and not me" (1964:38).

This notion that such tabooed elements serve to separate the self from the world external to it (acting as a kind of bridge by partaking of both), has much to recommend it in elucidating rodeo's stress on these substances. For it strikes the heart of what I interpret as the essence of rodeo—namely, its primary concern with relations between man and animals and the profound dilemma as to what is the boundary that separates them. Leach, as I have said, believes that we are only able to perceive our environment as composed of separate entities through a process of suppressing our recognition of the nonthings which occur between them (1964:37). This, then, is the reason that such intermediary substances as urine, mother's milk, spittle, hair clippings, and the like become taboo. My idea regarding this is that rodeo, by continually emphasizing these substances and bringing them out into the open—in other words, by *not* suppressing them as the "interstices"—makes the reverse point that after all we are essentially one with the animals. Thus I suggest that rodeo's use of bodily exudates partially removes the conditioned barriers which have been imposed within the universe of each self, and tends to return the environment of that self back to an original continuum. Thus both animals and man can be considered part of nature viewed as a continuous world. This motif, of course, runs counter to the explicit overall theme of rodeo which places man, as the ultimate master of animals, in a world apart—the world of culture as opposed to the world of nature. Thus is the universal dilemma of man's place in nature, with all its attendant contradictions, deeply explored within the context of rodeo.

It is noteworthy that the work of Victor Turner on Ndembu ritual also deals with bodily substances in a manner which is in some ways relevant to the rodeo context. In his discussion of ritual symbols, Turner says that one of their characteristics is "polarity of meaning." One pole of meaning, the ideological, contains references to "the norms and values that guide and control persons as members of social groups and categories"; the other pole of meaning, the sensory, "is associated with natural and physiological phenomena" (1967:28–30). Turner mentions "such themes as blood, male and female genitalia, semen, urine, and feces" as symbols at the sensory pole which also have ideological poles of meaning (1967:29). His theorizing is suggestive of an application to rodeo, in which bodily substances are used to represent strong sensory symbols which are in opposition to the "ideological" frame of reference. For the ideological, Turner says, stresses the "harmonious and cohesive aspects of social relationships." In rodeo, these relationships would be those encompassed by the accepted ranch/rodeo ethos, which asserts that man is separate from the rest of nature and is master of it. It would include man's categorization of nature as consisting of a hierarchy of discontinuous forms ranking below him in a graded series. This is the traditional social outlook embodying culture over nature, an attitude reinforced by the dominant religion. This ideological pole involves a prescribed way of behaving toward animals and toward the land in the light of shared certainty regarding man's supremacy over all of nature. At the sensory pole, however, the indications are that humanity and animality are close—almost indistinguishable in the by-products of their physiological mechanisms. Thus the motif of man as part of nature runs counterpoint to the ideological theme of the separateness of man and nature.

Though dirt is not properly classified with the bodily substances just discussed, its close association with them in rodeo makes it worthy of mention here. Contestants are seldom free from it, as they work in the earth-filled arena for their particular event. It spatters their clothes and clings to their bodies, seeming to represent a badge of membership, a sign of belonging. When a rough stock rider bucks off, he has a special way of rolling on the ground (away from danger) which puts him in intimate contact with the dirt. Bulldoggers "dig in" to the earth for their tussle with the steers, as do calf ropers to a lesser extent. Clods of mud and dirt are kicked up from the hooves of animals, flying into the faces and laps of rodeo spectators as well. It is possible to sense the presence of a special shared sensory delight when a rodeo is held in the rain. The arena becomes a slick sea of mud which only adds zest to the spirit of the performance. A contestant whom I heard sing at rodeos made reference to a rider who "jumped off in the mud, blood, and beer"—thus summing up the strange mud-mystique in rodeo and its association with the body. It is noteworthy that clowns frequently come out into the arena and try desperately to sweep it with a broom. The dirt and refuse they attempt to remove is made to seem impossible to pick up, and the illusion is given that it "disappears" by means of movements of a spotlight, thus completely frustrating the efforts of the clown to clean up the trash.

Dirt represents the next farthest removed substance from the self and its bodily excretions, and is often taboo in its own right. It is not only an intermediary element between the human body and the environment outside it, but also, in rodeo, it is a common meeting ground for man and animal. Horses, cattle, and men leave their exudates there, the bull paws the ground in anger, the contestant rolls in the dirt for safety, the bulldogger wrestles in it, and the disappointed roper throws it at his disobedient horse. It seems to unify the diverse elements of rodeo and blend the elements of man and animal. At times, representing earth, it may stand for nature, much as Riesman (1977) found that for the Fulani "bush" stands for nature, and that "going to the bush" means a kind of merging with nature within the framework of a village/bush dichotomy that is somewhat comparable to the culture/nature opposition. Going to the bush for one's bodily functions represents a kind of analogue, Riesman points out, to the Anglo-Saxon expression "to answer the call of nature" (1977:276). This idea fits in with my assertion that the oneness of man with nature is the meaning symbolized by rodeo's stress on physiological functions.

In summary, regarding the self in rodeo, it may be said that individual stoicism toward injury and pain signifies a conquest of the body which is consistent with the theme of human mastery over nature. Physiological exudations and secretions receive marked emphasis within the context of rodeo, both in their actual presence as perceived by the senses and by verbal and gestural references. It is significant that the total effect is one of intermingling between human and animal elements, so that they become hardly distinguishable. My own theory about this phenomenon is that it acts to assert man's oneness with the animal world, and thus with nature. I suggest

Fallen bronc pins rider beneath him. Dirt is often the common meeting ground for man and beast in the arena.

(*JJJ Photo*)

that just as certain extensions of culture in the events of rodeo make animals seem human, so these exudates are elements of nature that make humans appear like animals. Turner's, Riesman's, and particularly Leach's ideas about bodily substances can be appropriately used to substantiate my concept. Leach's notion that body exudates serve to demarcate the border between "me and it," "we and they," (1964:35) or "here and out there," seems particularly applicable to the rodeo situation. I believe it is inescapable that though man sets himself above nature through his continual attempts to master it, he senses he is yet also within it, and rodeo relies on vulgarity for a mechanism to express this essential contrapuntal theme. So far this study has been concerned with the self and with the totality of what I call man's inner circle of domesticity and control. Now it is time to consider various relationships to the sphere that is beyond this—the realm of the wild.

9

RELATIONS OF THE RANCH/RODEO COMPLEX WITH THE WILD

I have been a rancher and stockman all my life, and I have also been a dude rancher as well for the past fifty-five years, for my Dad crossed a dude on a mother cow in 1922; and a fine cross it has proven. Anyhow, I think I can qualify as having a fair sagebrush knowledge of "recreation." However, it looks to me like, in the long run, there'll be damn little time, nor inclination, for recreation if people are short of food, building materials, metals and energy. I just don't agree that the United States can afford to lock up a huge scope of country and let it go back to wilderness. That's what this country all was originally, and it wasn't worth a damn until it was made into something productive. Made by enterprise, initiative, hard work and a lot of guts, and paid for in blood.

(Krakel 1977:72)

ON ITS DEEPEST LEVEL the ritual of rodeo expresses a set of beliefs concerning the tame and the wild and the human relationship to them. In ordering their world, ranch/rodeo people appear to divide the various forms of nature into separate realms which determine the character of interactions with them. Included within the human sphere of influence are those creatures that are conceived of as either directly controlled by, or as having some degree of close relationship to, or identity with themselves. These are animals that can be subjugated for useful purposes and those which are potential friends or partners, such as cattle and certain classes of trained horses, domesticated forms that share the everyday human world. Some living things may partake of the tamed sphere only partially or sporadically, moving back and forth between the inner circle and the realm outside of it. Certain pleasing songbirds, for example, or a few

223

gentle and appealing deer who come to his property in winter, may receive the approval of a rancher and thus merit his protection as a temporary part of his domesticaed sphere.

Previous chapters have revealed the nature of the principal animals which have been taken within this inner circle and explored the interrelationships between those animals and the people who control them. Now I will focus on the realm that lies beyond. Because the pastoral life specifically necessitates dependence upon that realm which is outside of human control—the alien world of the wild— pastoralists have traditionally been deeply concerned with their relations to that world.

As a result of constant association with the natural world, cowboys and their descendants, the ranchers and rodeo men, tend to categorize the elements of their universe and sharply divide them into two spheres. Thus they conceive of them as either "here"—under my control and domination, and having relative predictability—or "out there"—of the wild, alien, virtually uncontrollable, unpredictable, the enemy. There is an ongoing process of striving to bring these elements under human control. This phenomenon had its origin in the earliest days of cattle trail driving, when wild nature was so often the enemy. The inhospitable plains wilderness, harsh extremes of weather, indigenous wild creatures who were, or were thought to be, inimical to man, as well as to his property and the animals under his protection, instilled fear and fostered antagonism. Hostile reaction between the two disparate spheres thus became ingrained into the way of life of the early cattle herders and was forged into a characteristic outlook which was handed down to their descendants, the ranchers. Rodeo, as a ritual of cattle ranching, serves to dramatize these same tensions and interrelationships. It is important to remember that the cattle frontier was reflecting the spirit of the American westward movement in general. Its exploitative and aggressive attitude toward nature and the wild were implicit in the whole process of "the taming of the West."

Cattle ranching developed into an industry which has continued to deal intimately with the issues involved in a war with the wild. Its concern with the man-nature struggle has not only been retained through the present day, but has become exacerbated. Dating from the close of the golden era of open-range ranching when sudden climatic extremes were only one component of a series of disasters including the influx of homesteaders and farmers, the use of barbed wire, and the encroachment of "civilization," all of which brought infringement on their previously unchallenged rights, cattle ranchers became defensive. There resulted a strong tendency to blame the forces of the wild for the problems inherent in their particular way of life. Faced with the frustrations which are inevitable in a mode of livelihood like cattle raising, which involves in such great measure the element of risk, and which even in modern times remains essentially at the mercy of nature, ranchers seem to vent their anger upon the wild forces beyond their control. They lash out at nature even in those instances when the causes of their problems might be attributed more accurately to culture. For economists say that world and domestic trade conditions, widespread manufacture of synthetics which lower the demand for animal products, difficulties in obtaining labor, and dwindling resources, are factors which lead to increased expenses of operation and a consequent higher cost of beef production, and thus profoundly affect the ranchers' success.

These humanly created factors, however, are outside the personal concrete experience of the cattlemen, and foreign to the strong traditions which have been handed down to them through their forebears. The wild as enemy is something they still face in their daily life, and they focus on it in distinction to more complex, intangible, and remote issues. This explains a large share of their concern with the elements of wild versus tame and their evident fierce antagonism toward a great many parts of the natural world of the wild. It helps to account for the ranchmen's fury over being denied access to an existing wilderness which they so earnestly desire to bring under control and use for profit. Thus they strike out against the wild and against the forces that they feel oppose them—the environmentalists and the government.

Rodeo reflects these attitudes and antagonisms. As an outgrowth of the cattle industry and as a sport which is sustained and perpetuated by cattlemen, it expresses the ranchers' orientation toward the outer realm of the wild as well as the inner domesticated sphere. Since the ritual of rodeo represents, as I have indicated, a dramatization and intensification of the process of conquering the wild—the extension of culture over nature—it must necessarily include within its context a consideration of the untamed elements of man's environment. Reference to the wild is a recurring motif throughout the sport, relating it to the herders' world.

Though the pastoralist lifeway is primarily concerned with animals in the sphere of the domesticated, it also involves a relationship to those sharply contrasting forms which are outside of it—in the wild. Writing of a Spanish Asturian mountain cattle complex in his essay on the importance of metaphors in anthropological inquiry,

James Fernandez suggests that "the intimate contact these villagers have with these animals (cows) has an impact upon them. In a sense, those we domesticate have domesticated us and those we have not domesticated are still useful in measuring the achievement or excesses of our domestication. If life becomes too much a following about of cows, men may be excused for turning a bit bearish" (1971:39). Significantly, then, it is not just the realm of domestic animals with which such societies are concerned that become the measure of their existence. For, as Fernandez goes on to say, "one remembers that there are other animals men study to situate themselves." There are, for example, "the bears in the forests" and the rats from which, in addition to cows and calves, "men are wise to draw the appropriate lessons that each nature has to teach" (1971:40–41). Fernandez concludes that "however men may analyze their experiences in any domain, they inevitably know and understand them best by referring them to other domains for elucidation" (1971:58). He cites the example of "I (a man) am to you (a woman) as hawk is to dove" as exemplifying a set of associations occurring within and across domains, stating that it is in these formulae that "we begin to get a sense of order in culture" (1971:59). It is just such "metaphoric cross-referencing of domains" of which rodeo often makes use, expressed in words or implied by symbols.

Throughout my study I found that the domain of the wild was consistently used as a frame of reference for clarification of the ranch/rodeo position with regard to the various components of nature. In the Professional Rodeo Cowboys Association Reference Book, for example, which contains a description of each of the sport's standard events, the spirit of steer wrestling is elucidated in terms relating to the wild. The reader is advised by use of a predator-prey analogy to "watch how top horses run for the steers like hawks swooping in for field mice" (Rodeo Reference Book 1977:32). In another instance, to augment and make more vivid the author's comparison of a Mexican fighting bull with an American rodeo bull, a clarifying metaphor was again chosen from the wild realm. "Frijoli Chiquita's size and proclivities," we are told, "were as much like those of his bovine American brothers as the same characteristics in a wildcat and a chipmunk" (Hanes 1977:99).

Imagery involving the rattlesnake as arch-enemy in the wild appears frequently in the rodeo, as in the ranching, context. In an introductory book on the sport of rodeo, a section on bull riding explains "the bulls are mostly cross-bred Brahmas—powerful, fast brutes, mean as rattlesnakes" (Rounds 1949:125). Another rodeo writer employs the same metaphor with regard to the "bad woman" whom the rodeo hero is about to marry. Describing this deplorable situation in snake terminology, his buddy says "Rita's been closing in on Pierce for a year, just like an old diamondback easing up on a field mouse, so slow and deliberate you can't tell he's moved at all till you see the trail he's left behind him." When another friend of the hero asks the speaker why he did not interfere in the romance, the answer carries out the same metaphor: "I tried, I did everything I could to bust it up. But Rita had me figured out and sidestepped every trap I laid for her" (Crawford 1965:64–65). I observed that rodeo people found reference to rattlesnakes peculiarly apt in expressing their feelings and attitudes about the wild. Illustrating this, a former bull rider, in describing his event, focused the extreme fear of the bull that a contestant experiences after his ride into a most revealing expression. He told me "a cowboy would rather French-kiss a rattlesnake than find himself alongside a snorting bull after he is bucked off!" There could hardly be a more precise way to symbolize the very essence of danger than by this vivid verbal and sensory transference to the least tame and most lethal creature of the wild.

All popular rodeo contestants are given nicknames, and one man had been dubbed "Sidewinder" because of his particular style of riding a bull. Once I became aware of the snake theme, I found allusions to this form of wildlife to be rather prevalent in rodeo, indicative of a preoccupation with the fearful rattler. Snakeskin hat bands, sometimes even including the rattles, were in evidence on a few contestants' hats. Rattlesnake belts were also worn. In fact, I noted that a new and popular style using rattlesnake pelts is developing among rodeo as well as ranch people. Intrigued by the implications of this, I investigated Western stores in cattle ranching areas where rodeos were held. I learned that, in addition to the major items such as belts, boots, and hat bands, such shops sell rattlesnake hide wallets and purses. Pen holders and ash trays feature the entire rattlesnake embedded in plastic or just the rattles. Ear rings and key holders are made of the rattles alone. Belt buckles are fashioned from snakeskin as well as from the serpents' deadly fangs and rattles preserved in plastic.

Clerks said, "we sell tons of it to ranchers and rodeo people. It is very popular." Salespersons and buyers were willing to share their concepts of rattlesnakes with me. These revealed an overwhelming hatred and deep fear of the creatures as representatives of the wild realm. "People here kill them any time they run into them," was a typical statement. "I hate them; they are so dangerous it is unbelievable. They come right at you, ready to do battle. When you grow up on a ranch, you feel strongly about rattlesnakes." One saleswoman told me "the people who buy and wear these rattlesnake items live in the country like I do, and find rattlers on their doorstep." Almost all informants singled out for retelling, with marked disgust, instances in which rattlesnakes had appeared at their very doors. Penetrating the sanctity of their own domesticated realm brought special dismay. A woman told me she feared them because she has "two little girls five and six years old." But men evidenced a fear of the rattlers equally strong and deep-seated as that of the women. Interestingly, almost every rancher or rodeo man with a ranching background related a story from the past about a rattlesnake appearing at his doorsill. And without exception it involved a time "when my daughter was a baby," or when "my wife was just a new bride." As the epitome of an evil enemy it seemed that the rattlesnake had to be visualized as opposed to the innocent, and, usually, the female element. The snake was generally perceived as a male figure, even in those cases in which it was used to symbolize a woman's actions.

Ranch and rodeo informants felt (contrary to what zoologists say about the species) that "rattlesnakes will strike at anything. They're naturally mean and will strike whether startled or not." Significantly, one mentioned that the actions of the snakes "depended upon their mood, the weather, and the time of year." Here, again, as I have noted previously, the quality of unpredictability is a prime attribute distinguishing the wild from the tame. Invariably those who discussed the rattlers gave vivid accounts of killing them on sight, usually with a shovel, rock, stick, or gun. "You just get him before he gets you," a Montana rancher explained. A rodeo stock contractor and cattleman said "rattlesnakes are pretty cruel; they hypnotize little birds and animals so they can't fly or get away, and they die a terrible death." One woman told me it was necessary to "run over them with a car two or three times in order to kill them," so tenacious are they of life. A widely distributed advertisement for Nocona boots depicts a man wearing this brand of cowboy boots stomping upon the neck of a rattlesnake whose body is twined around the upper portion of the boot. At the moment captured in this scene the hand of the cowboy—on whose third finger appears a ring bearing the words "Let's rodeo"—wields a sharp Bowie knife with which he is about to cut off the head of the snake. The rattler's jaws gape under the impact of the cowboy boot, revealing its lethal fangs and other anatomical features of its mouth cavity.

Several informants mentioned that cats were immune to the at-

Rodeo man metes out violent death to his arch-enemy, the rattlesnake, in
a scene symbolizing conquest of the wild. *(Courtesy of Nocona Boot Company)*

tacks of this deadly species, and could "hypnotize the snakes." A ranchwoman revealed that she habitually kills rattlesnakes that her cat "brings in the house to play with." It is fascinating that a domestic cat would be afforded this capacity. It suggests that the feline species, with its dual status as half wild and half tame, is perceived in this case as a bridge between man's domestic sphere of which it is an accepted part, and the extreme wild realm represented by the snake as enemy—totally beyond human control except in death. Relevant to this notion, the Indian medicine man, Lame Deer, in his description of how the white man has altered and tamed the wild, says disparagingly to the dominant culture, "You can't do much with the cat, which is like an Indian, unchangeable" (Lame Deer & Erdoes 1972:120).

Other related forms of life share the rodeo spotlight with rattle-snakes by becoming trophies—symbols of the conquest of the wild. One year, for example, alligator-tooth necklaces were chosen as gifts to be presented to all rodeo queen contestants by the National High School Rodeo Association. Needless to say, numberless alternative gift-choices could have been made instead of the teeth of this beast with the archetypal image of being fearful and monstrous—a vicious enemy to man. The aspect of the alligator being an endangered species would occur to a conservationist, but, as I will be discussing in more detail, virtually all ranchers expressed the general feeling that such beasts have no right to live irrespective of some possible utilita-rian value to man. Speaking of African elephants, for instance, one ranch/rodeo informant declared incredulously that "some nuts are even trying to save them from extinction." He found this fact deplorable, referring to elephants as "dangerous animals," and relat-ing it to his own cultural and regional disdain for anyone concerned with the possible value of preserving bears, eagles, or coyotes.

Yet in an ambivalent way some of these same people seem to identify with the wild which they seek to destroy. In keeping with this mystique, wealthy ranchers may now buy boots made of almost any type of "exotic leather" they may choose. Built into advertising for these items is the idea that their owner must have "made it," for there is an implied relationship between the work ethic, prosperity, and purchase of them. A recent ad by a boot company shows a rancher with a pretentious house and an expensive car in the background. He says "nothing ever came easy for me. I worked hard for everything I got and it paid off. Now I can enjoy the things I want out of life, like these Laredo lizard boots. Sure they're expensive, but I deserve 'em. Maybe you do too." This seems to be another (though more subtle) way of saying that all life must yield and make way for human interests and material advancement. The same message was expressed repeatedly by ranch/rodeo informants who oppose wilderness preservation because it would cut down on economic profits from cattle grazing, timber, and mining. They justify destruction of the wild by claiming that the numbers of people who would make use of and enjoy it are so small in comparison to the huge numbers who would benefit from utilization of the derived resources.

Cowboy boots of New Zealand crocodile now sell for $1,250. The Justin Company's latest boot style features vamp and trim made of python, with a belt to match. Boots with "genuine anaconda vamp" are featured in a Nocona advertisement in which a cowboy, identified by his cattle in the background and a "Let's rodeo" ring, is shown in the act of using his fingers to flick off a scorpion that has landed on one boot. Also in demand are boots made of ostrich, sea turtle, and elephant hide. Leddy adds shark, and a noted Western supplier custom makes boots to order from anteater, caribou, hornback lizard, water buffalo, and leg of ostrich. One rodeo official brought about a dozen different pairs of boots with him when he travelled to the national finals. When the pair he was wearing was recognized as ostrich leather, he said "I bet you think it's mean to kill those poor animals!"

Most contestants on the rodeo circuit, unable to afford exotic leathers, nevertheless have ways to reach out to the wild realm and position themselves symbolically in relation to it. One of the commonest ways to do this is by use of feathers in one's hat—either in the form of a band of feathers around the crown, or, more frequently, by a large feather stuck jauntily into one side of the hat band. The latter style has recently come into vogue, and is now seen in rodeos everywhere. It was first popularized by a flamboyant champion saddle bronc rider who bears the nickname of "Hawkeye." His rodeo companions say they gave him this epithet because of his skillful shooting of a certain hawk which others had been unsuccessful in killing. But, probably for the sake of possible environmentalists among his fans, he now tells people that his nickname refers "to my nose which is shaped like a hawk's beak." However this may be, he always wears a golden eagle feather in his hat band, and this custom is imitated by many other contestants. One wearer of such a feather told me he did not have it for luck "for it certainly didn't bring the eagle any good fortune." Hawk feathers are often seen in hat bands, and I have noted a few peacock plumes. A band of feathers around the hat is less conspicuous but frequently seen. At the women's finals a very long red feather from a mawcaw was worn by one bull and bronc rider, who told me it was "a good luck piece." She said "the pickup men don't like it, and are always threatening to bite if off." The feather drew a great deal of attention and comment; whenever the contestant wearing it was in the arena, the announcer spoke of her "red feather from an exotic bird that cost twenty-five hundred dollars."

A bull rider, the same man who christened his buddy "Hawkeye," drives a pickup truck that displays on its rear window a scene symbolic of the wild. It depicts a bald eagle flying over a snow-capped mountain. This, again, seems to represent the sense of identification with the wild which is so frequently encountered among rodeo people. Motivated by this feeling, they would tell me "we should try to save some wilderness and wild animals so that our children will be able to see something without going to a zoo." But as indicated previously they recognize the value of and a human need for only "limited amounts" of wild country, and generally are not willing to place a priority on preservation of wildlife or wilderness. They are quick to point out that, as one saddle bronc rider phrased it, "people have to realize that we can't make the whole country into a wildlife sanctuary; we need the resources." In general their world and interests are pragmatic and their values concerning the wild are measured in terms of economic usefulness. They expressed disagreement with recent proposals to set aside huge areas of wild country in the northern Great Plains to save the grizzly bear from extinction. It is significant to note, however, that informants who were interviewed strictly as rodeo contestants, as opposed to ranch informants with an interest in rodeo, were slightly more in favor of a certain amount of wilderness preservation than working ranch people. For example, some rodeo contestants, with an evident flair for the wild, indicated that they want the government to save some of the wild mustangs, while ranchers are almost unanimously against it. One bareback rider reflected his appreciation for the wild when he told me "there should be some wild areas and game preserves. It would be a hell of a country if we didn't have any of these things." But his opinion is not typical of most ranch/rodeo people of the Great Plains.

A female country-western singer who is closely associated with rodeo was chided by contestants during her performances about her admitted interest in "saving the seals and the whales." But she was a match for her tormentors. "No, I won't forget the seals and the whales," she told them, "or the donkeys either." Many rodeo songs give expression to this theme of the wild which is found as an underlying motif throughout the sport. Noteworthy among these is the ballad often sung at rodeo gatherings, to which I have already referred. Answering the question as to why the cowboy "rides for short pay," the lyrics stress the strong appeal of the herder's relation to the wild in terms of a "hawk on the wing," the "northern lights," and "spring" on the "Great Divide" (Durton). Thus specific references are made to images in nature which connote the freedom and vastness of the Western wilderness, and a cowboy's feeling for them. It is significant that these elements are remote ones—things the cowboy cannot touch. They are rather "out there," in the distance, and I suggest they are symbols for the sphere which is not controlled by man. In fact, these particular elements tend to dwarf the realm of man, either by power, as in the case of the flight of the hawk, or by virtually infinite expanse, as in the night sky and the mountainous domain where rivers flow toward opposite seas.

Other rodeo songs, too, feature a sense of human identification with forces of the wild. One contains the line "I'm a wild raging stallion in a race with the wind" (McGinnis), and another tells of the man who "rode broncs like a brother to the wind" (Crockett). In the song about "rodeo gypsies" there is mention of going to "see if we can't catch the wind" (McGinnis). Such lyrics reflect the rodeo spirit of reaching out to the wild as the ultimate source of the tameable—the challenge which still exists.

Rodeo parades, which offer invaluable insights into the meaning of rodeo, also show the importance of the theme of the wild. At the Cheyenne Frontier Days, for example, universally acknowledged as the most important of all American cattle-country rodeos, it was fascinating to find that the 1978 parade revealed this concern. Featured as the keynote of this long presentation was a clown riding a scooter and pulling a cage. Inside the cage was the skin of a bear, arranged to hang within the enclosure like a "bear rug." There could hardly have been any more blatant expression of man's dominion over nature than this strange display, ostensibly designed to amuse children of all ages. The bear, which, as I shall be pointing out, is a symbol of the very wilderness itself, was here shown as not only captured, but dead—its life and spirit gone, only its crass utilitarian function remaining. The animal was further derided by its association with a clown, and by the unfulfilled expectation of seeing a live animal in the cage and finding only a pelt in its place.

The second attraction of the parade was remarkable also. This consisted of an automobile towing a large circus cage in which appeared a "gorilla"—a very realistic representation, though obviously a man dressed as the beast. Here again, the rodeo theme of man's dominion over all forms of nature received emphasis. For this showed that even the primate most closely resembling man in outward form was nonetheless subjugated by being confined, while he strained at the bars of his prison, roaring all the while. On another level, too, since there was a man beneath the furry suit, this figure symbolized "the beast in everybody" in its concrete form. Thus it expressed as well the paradoxical strain in rodeo of a sense of identification with creatures of the wild. Other rodeo parades, I noted, also demonstrated this theme. In Casper, Wyoming, for example, people who were dressed as gorillas, chipmunks, and ducks gave exhibitions of dancing on a truck platform.

Further along in the Frontier Days parade was a float sponsored by a railroad company, consisting of a live caged buffalo and a group of Plains Indians in native dress. The sign on this display gave testimony to the conquering of both these wild forms in the taming of the West by designating them as

Our predecessors on the plain—
The oldest inhabitants on the
line of the Union Pacific.

The participation of an authentically outfitted mountain man on his horse also gave the spirit of man's historic penetration of New World wilderness. In conversation, this picturesque old man, who carried with him on his mount a live dog and fox in addition to a great deal of equipment, told me about his lifestyle. He said he "really lives the life of a mountain man, trapping beaver and coyotes, whichever there's too much of, in the Yellowstone during the winter." In the summer, it is his practice to appear at rodeos, not only in parades but often in the grand entry of the performance as well.

Once, near the end of my field work, when my ideas about the wild and its relation to the ranch/rodeo complex were already firmly outlined in my mind, I had a remarkable experience. Passing by a Western store in a ranch town during the annual rodeo, I was astounded by a window display of objects put together especially for the annual rodeo; they seemed to echo my themes concerning the tame and the wild. Very carefully arranged were Western shirts, bridles, boots, saddles, and all manner of accouterments for man and horse. It was evident that much time and thought had gone into creating this array of objects, for it was tastefully and appropriately done. As props for their wares, rustic items such as fences and wagon wheels were used. Rodeo records and tapes were intermingled with many types of gear for the working as well as the competing cowboy. In one corner was a men's perfume, labelled simply "Sex." But what arrested my attention was a huge poster which had been strategically and artistically placed amidst the other items. It depicted the head of a bald eagle, its black and white image a brilliant contrast to the vibrant color of a blue sky. Its keen eye and open yellow beak had been caught in a moment of fierce action, and it epitomized the spirit of the wild. Truly this magnificent raptor was the scene stealer. Upon inquiry I was told, "we had a whole bunch of posters of all kinds, and the person who arranged the window picked that one." Indeed the effect of this eagle, familiar image of the unrestrained power of a wild predator, was overwhelming. Set among the tools and symbols of man's domination over domesticated species like horses and cattle, its implications were clear: the opposition between the wild and the tame and the human position with regard to them were demonstrated to be central concerns of the ranch/rodeo world. Use of such images is a way to reflect upon the process of domestication, to measure, as it were, the extent of man's conquest of nature by comparison to the uncontrolled world of the wild that lies beyond.

SOME EXAMPLES FROM OTHER PASTORAL CULTURES

Due to the closeness to nature that characterizes their lifeway, it is common for pastoral people to perceive a division between their own domesticated realm and that which exists outside of it in the wild, and to assess their own relation to it. It is easy to understand the urgency of the pastoralist to situate himself with regard to the wild, for whether he is an American cowboy or a Tibetan or African herder, he must oppose the wild as a force not only "other" than himself and his realm, but often inimical to it. Yet because he is directly or indirectly involved with some facet of the transforming process from wild to tame, there is at the same time a strong propensity to appreciate the wild and to identify himself with it. Certainly the possession of the sense of freedom and independence, boldness, and aggressive spirit that often characterizes members of pastoral societies creates admiration for similar qualities which they see reflected in the wild.

Exemplifying this attitude are the Tibetan nomadic pastoralists, who have a "self-image projected by a complimentary term in common use" which is "unconsciously revealing," and "sums up the ideal man." This way of addressing someone is "son untamed" and can also

be translated as "not subdued" or "like high pasturage not domesticated." It is the criterion by which men are judged, the universal sign
of admiration, and the most apt expression of what the culture hero
should be (Eckvall 1968:92–93). Thus, with the same ambivalence
to which I have previously referred, Tibetan pastoralists, whose
lifeway brings them in opposition to the wild, nonetheless see
themselves as ideally partaking of it and identifying with it.

Even when some feeling of identification with the wild is part of a
pastoralist's ethos, however, there is a perceptual division which
sharply separates the realm of the wild and makes it of a different
order from man's inner circle of domesticity which includes those
parts of nature under human control. The work of Paul Riesman
dealing with the pastoral Fulani of West Africa illustrates the
phenomenon of this perceptual division. His findings show that the
dichotomy of village/bush is conceived of by these cattle-herding
people in a way which is roughly analogous to the way in which I have
been using tame/wild. For the Fulani the bush represents that which
surrounds man but which he is never able to grasp fully in his
imagination (1977:254). In Fulani thought Riesman says "the bush
(or nature) is a force truly other than and independent from man as
intelligent being" (1977:257).

As in the case of the Tibetan pastoralists' expression "son untamed," linguistic usage helps to elucidate certain concepts of the
Fulani herders regarding wild and tame. To the Fulani mind the lion
represents the bush (or the wild), and in the language of these cattle
people, there is no existing word for "lion." Riesman interprets this
fact as an indication of the "absolute otherness" of this wild animal of
the bush. In other words, for the Fulani, the lion is unclassifiable.
The creature has been given no name with which to "grasp" it because
the lion itself, and all that it stands for, escape the control and
mastery of man. "When represented by the lion," Riesman concludes, "the bush appears as an aspect of the world on which man has
no grip." In addition, "the lack of a real name seems also to express
the lack of preexisting bonds between man and the lion" (1977:250).
The lion and the bush both represent the unknown to the Fulani. The
bush, as the wild, is "at once near and far," since it surrounds each
village and yet "extends to infinity." Thus no man can truly com-
prehend it, and Riesman attributes the absence of a word for lion in
Fulani to the fulfillment of a need for an image to signify the
unknown (1977:251).

The Fulani look upon the cow, in contrast to the lion, as being of
the bush and of the village at the same time. "It is not of the bush in

the same way as the lion, because man has a certain hold on it; all the same, it is from the bush that a cow gains its subsistence" (Riesman 1977:255). Since man subsists from the cow, and thus has some control over it, the cow may be thought of as an intermediary between man and the bush. Through his cattle, a man establishes a relation to the bush, for he must enter it to look after his herd. This entry into the bush signifies to a Fulani his separation from society (Riesman 1977:256). So in this sense it seems to correspond to leaving the domestic for the wild, the two realms representing the culture/nature opposition as I have been using it. The bush is a Fulani metaphor for solitude (Riesman 1977:31), and a man's going into the bush symbolizes not just his aloneness, but also "the individuation of the person" (Riesman 1977:256). This concept suggests a correlation between the emphasis that working cowboy herders have always placed on solitude and the "rugged individualism" that is felt to be their hallmark. It is likely that through the same kind of mystique cowboys, and their rodeo inheritors, are attracted to the wild and find a sense of personal fulfillment through relating to it.

Turning now to the Nuer, the African pastoralists who have become noteworthy to anthropologists by being so greatly absorbed with their cattle, we find again that cows are thought to act as a bridge, though of a different kind from that of the Fulani. For cattle are to the Nuer, according to E.E. Evans-Pritchard, "the means by which men can enter into communication with God." He goes on to explain

> they are, as Father Crazzolara puts it, "the link between the perceptible and the transcendental." In fulfilling this role, his cattle shield a man and his family from disaster, and he conceives of them also collectively as a herd which from the beginning of time has helped his fathers in distress, performing in each generation the same sacrificial service. In the time of the ancestor of his clan the "cow" gave her life for his salvation and so it is today. Whence springs the identification of man with ox, of lineage with herd, and of men with cattle.
>
> (1956:271)

Thus, unlike the Fulani, the Nuer do not conceive of their cattle as an intermediary between man and the wild. Apparently the Nuer mind is so much attuned to the human and bovine sphere that it hardly sees the wild as of much direct concern:

> the Nuer mind is turned inwards towards his own society of men and cattle. He is not unobservant of nature but he sees it with a contemplative and not with a predatory eye that seeks to destroy and exploit. He

sees wild creatures as something in their own right, and his disposition is to live and let live. His folk-stories reflect this attitude and the feeling that killing, like death, is something which has come about almost by accident and is not in the original nature of things.

(Evans-Pritchard 1956:267)

These insights help to explain the Nuer interaction with nature and the wild, which provides a clear contrast to the aggressive spirit of the American cowboy and rancher, who, even though at times they identify with the wild, view it essentially as enemy. Evans-Pritchard found that the Nuer have little inclination for hunting wild game, and that any killing of animals outside sacrifice is rare (1956:267; 1974:72–73). The Nuer "do not go out to hunt lions, leopards, and hyenas unless they molest the flocks and herds." Their domestic animals supply them with meat, and hunting holds little interest. In fact, the Nuer feel that hunting is beneath their serious attention—a pursuit of foreigners or men who are without cattle (Evans-Pritchard 1956:267).

Although Evans-Pritchard does not phrase it in these terms, it is evident that for the Nuer the wild also represents a quality of "otherness" from their own sphere. It has occurred to me that this may account for the significance of the "leopard-skin chief" so often referred to in descriptions of Nuer society (Evans-Pritchard 1956; 1974). This figure, who is the only person in that society to wear the skin of a leopard across his shoulders, does not have great political authority but rather is a ritual specialist. His main function is to act as arbiter or mediator in disputes, and through him it is possible that "defilements of a certain kind can be effaced" (Evans-Pritchard 1974:173). It is believed that this wearer of the leopard skin has a "sacred association with the earth" (Evans-Pritchard 1974:172), and this substantiates the idea that his role symbolizes a certain special relationship to the wild. The Nuer made it clear to Evans-Pritchard, however, that though leopard-skin priests respect the leopard, it is only in the sense that they will not kill the animal; there is no spirit, they respect only its body (1956:78). There is evidently a complete absence among the Nuer of any belief in a powerful spirit of the wild such as that espoused by American Plains Indians, for example, by which wild animals are held to be innately superior in many ways.

The leopard-skin chief comes across as a neutral figure, and I suspect that it is the characteristic "otherness" of his office in relation to the human societal realm which is represented by his wearing of the wild animal skin. To a people so greatly concerned with the domestic sphere which includes their all-important cattle, the wild represents something alien. Thus the man who wears it can be set apart—not personally involved—and fulfill his role of mediator without prejudice or partiality. This exemplifies a use of the concept of the wild as something removed from the ordinary human sphere, a realm which is very different from it, but not necessarily inimical to it.

WILD CATS AT THE RODEO

As the domain of the leopard is foreign to the inner world of the cattle-oriented Nuer, so the sphere of wild cats, perceived in terms of remote "otherness," is felt to be alien to the domesticated realm of the ranch/rodeo people. Active hostility generally characterizes the cowboy's and rancher's attitude toward those creatures they term "varmints" and, in particular, wild predators. Once in my field experience the separate realms of domesticated horses and cattle as opposed to wild cats in the form of a tiger, leopard, and jaguar came together briefly, and the results afforded meaningful insights into relationships between the two. This revealing episode came unexpectedly in the form of an act involving exotic cats and their trainers which was a grandstand attraction at one of the large prestigious Great Plains rodeos. Through observation and analysis of their act and interviews with the man and woman who performed it, I had a unique opportunity to focus on the sharp contrasts between the relationship of these wild cat trainers to their animals and that of the rodeo people to theirs.

From the very outset, when I went to the rodeo publicity office to arrange for an interview, I encountered the antagonism of everyone in the ranch/rodeo world toward these performers and their animals. Plainly evident in word and gesture was the cattle country's disgust with the act. The answer given to my request for an appointment was "Okay, but I wouldn't think you would like that act." Regarding the performers and their routine, one rodeo official told me, "I don't think there's much relationship there. I wouldn't like to be the tiger all cut up in pieces." When I met the couple, who said they had not previously appeared at a rodeo, they were severely distressed about having received their "first bad review" in that day's local newspaper. The article featured a huge photograph of the woman trainer triumphantly astride her tiger, with the caption "The lady and the tiger had 'em just a little worried." The writeup referred to the couple's "inept dancing with leopard and tiger," and went on to say that "about the most you can say for them" is that the woman "wore the least the situation permitted." The first part of the act was termed "a kinky little scenario." As though this were not enough of a put-down, the writer went on to say

> Meooo-ow, went the beast that lurks under even the blandest of cowboy hats. But they didn't even get a meow out of the tiger who was to provide the capper to an exceptionally average routine. The big cat was lively enough in his cage, but once let loose, refused to even begin performing.
>   (Hepher 1978:26)

The message that, in the judgment of cattle country, even the dullest of cowboys is wilder than these cats is unmistakable, and is a most interesting expression of the cowboy's ambivalence between hatred of the wild and identification with it. The ranch/rodeo people's disdain for this act was, as far as I could determine, universal, and the rodeo officials in particular felt it was an unbearable nuisance. Throughout the ten-day show the performers were continually at war with the rodeo producer. They indicated to me that they had never before worked under such difficult conditions, and had frequently threatened to break their contract because of the lack of consideration of the rodeo people, whose horses were in close proximity to the area assigned to their cats. They felt strongly that "the horse people resent the cats," and complained that "these people don't have eyes for our cats. Their horses are everything—their horses are their gods!" There were repeated arguments between the performers and the rodeo horsemen, and when the cat owners told them to get the horses out of their way, the horse people would not comply. The woman cat trainer explained "finally I had to use reverse psychology to get what I wanted. They wanted our cats on the rail, near the horses. I told them 'the cats will spook,' and they paid no attention to me. They would not let us move the cats. But when I said 'your horses will spook if the cats are there,' and one did just as I was talking, they gave me what I wanted."

Wild cats, of course, are the natural enemies of the equine species, and the couple admitted "our cats would love to chase those horses, not because they're hungry, but because of instinct." An evident sense of oneness with their cats seemed to imbue their owners with hostility toward the rodeo horses and their masters. "If you treated our cats like they handle those rodeo animals, they would kill you," the couple confided. "These cowboys expect cats to stay when they say 'stay,' but they won't do it like a horse or a dog would." The couple revealed their own perceptions of the domesticated versus the

wild by stressing the fact that their German Shepherd dogs, if told to
"stay," will "actually do it for ten hours, and have proven this," while
"the wild cats will only stay for a half a minute, and will not stay at all
if you go out of the room." "Our wild animals," they said, "are not as
truthful and sincere; they are more independent and unpredictable."
Thus the familiar attribute of unpredictability as a distinguishing
trait of the wild again came to the fore. The male trainer was very
explicit on this point. "Our cats are unpredictable," he reiterated.
"They're like Doctor Jeckyl and Mr. Hyde," he explained, illustrating this with a gesture in which he stretched his hands out in front of
him and turned the palms first up and then down. "They're not like a
dog. Cats would kill their owners if we took away their food. We
always leave them alone after giving them their food. The cats always
have their wild instinct; they are not tame. We respect them, and the
one thing we know is that we don't really know them, and that they
are not predictable."

Several significant themes illustrated in the performance of the
wild cat act itself are relevant to this study. The opening routine, for
example, is a dance in which the man, dressed in black leather and
boots, with a fierce air of macho snaps a whip to subdue and "train"
the woman, who is dressed as a cat and whose slithering gyrations are
unmistakably feline. After she has been "tamed," and put into a cage,
"miraculously," through the "magic" of an unexplained mechanism,
she is replaced in the enclosure by a real leopard. In the context of this
strongly sexual performance the man emerges as completely dominant over both the woman and the wild cat. In fact the female and the
feline are made to seem as one; they are interchangeable. Made
explicit here is the concept of woman as closer to nature—indeed, in
this case, as an inseparable part of nature. This theme is carried even
further during the next sequence, in which a huge silver ball has been
placed on stage, and the man opens it, revealing it to be flaming
inside. One could interpret the presence of this fire as symbolizing
"culture." The man extinguishes the fire, and suddenly the woman
emerges from inside the ball. This is followed then by another
surprise—a very small leopard that appears to be a cub also comes out
of the huge sphere. Thus the impression is given to the audience of
the woman having given birth to the cat.

Throughout the entire performance, in which both trainers carry
out routines involving a leopard, a jaguar, and a tiger, while the man
is depicted as "master," it is the woman who accomplishes all the
important feats of taming the cats. For example, it is she who makes
the large male tiger sit up on his hind legs. In the highlight of the

show, assuming a pose of complete victory over the cat, she straddles
the sitting tiger. It is significant, though, that immediately after
executing this maneuver, she lies down on her back on stage, and the
tiger in turn straddles her body, standing over her in a completely
dominant position.

The woman described her feat of straddling the cat as "the most
unnatural thing to make a tiger do." Reminiscent of the calf roper's
attitude toward his horse, whose act of backing up also represented to
him the most unnatural thing an animal could do, this scene symbolized in the context of the cat act the greatest possible exertion of
the force of culture over nature. The female trainer explained the
numerous difficulties involved in teaching the tiger to perform this
routine. "He bucked like a bronco at first," she said, taking her
metaphor from the alien realm that was now near at hand, "and I
went flying!" In describing her feelings about this act, she confided
"my proudest moment is when I straddle Hercules. It's not a macho
thing. It's not a matter of 'look what I can do!' But I'm happy to have
the power to do it." It seemed that she considered her momentary
subduing of the huge cat a personal achievement, but at best a
temporary one. I saw a contrast between this state of mind and that of
the ranch/rodeo people, whose dominance over their creatures is felt
by them to be decreed in the order of things. For the cat trainer, her
act of supremacy over the beast brought her a not-always-predictable
moment of triumph and glory.

By their conversations as well as their actions both cat owners
confirmed the belief that the woman is far superior as a trainer. "If
there is anything difficult to teach them," the male performer said,
"she is the one to do it. What takes me six months to get across to
them she can accomplish in three. If they are frightened, it is she who
must coax them out of the cage; it is her voice they respond to." The
woman told me "only I could get the tiger over his height phobia, a
man couldn't do it." The male partner related this superior ability to
a woman's "motherly instinct," and conceded "we men do not have
it." He said "the cats submit to a female because she has instinct. I am
a warrior," he went on, "their equal. I challenge them, where she is
like their mother. She is friend and mistress to them as well as
mother. When she has her period, the jaguar hugs her more aggres-
sively, is stronger in his passes, and wants to mount her." The woman
agreed: "I'm much more likely to get bitten at that time." When the
male trainer hugs his wife, he told me, "the male cat gets jealous. He
puts his ears flat down and his whiskers against his face, and his tail

swishes as though he were stalking. Then I have to give him some meat and assure him 'you know she is yours.' "

Because she is "like their mother," the woman feels strongly that the cats' affection and kisses should be reserved for her. Following one performance she called attention to the lipstick marks all over her jaguar's face. She said that when audience members come to look at the animals and want to be kissed or caressed by them, she feels indignant. She asks "what have you done to deserve that privilege? That is due only to the trainer, who has spent so much time and has given so much to them." "We are very possessive of them," she added.

In direct contrast to the ranch/rodeo people, in whose ethos human beings are seen as the most important element on earth, this couple confided that they "shy away from about ninety percent of people." The man told me he now admits his disillusionment with people and his feeling that animals, in contrast to humans, are not hypocritical, and he admires them more for this. The woman told me of her observation that many people who come to see their cats "hate the leopard because she is aloof and they can't touch her. But strong independent people always have a preference for that leopard." It was important to her to determine which of her animals different individuals liked best.

Unlike ranchers, the couple strongly identified with the wilderness. They considered it wrong to use fur from endangered species, and wanted everything possible to be done to preserve such animals. Whereas most stockmen indicate they do not want any appreciable wilderness to be preserved at the expense of mining, lumbering, and grazing interests, and rodeo people specify they want it only "to a limited extent," these wild animal performers unequivocally espoused wilderness values. Ranchers, even as regards strip-mining, told me "people should come first; they are more important than scenery. We can't afford to leave resources untapped; it is not economically feasible." The cat trainers were, in contrast, "very much in favor of saving the wilderness." They said "we are afraid there will be nothing left. The worst enemy is man. It will be a computerized zero world without wilderness. Thinking of the buck is what is destroying nature. The world will be computerized, too far from nature. We won't be able to communicate. What we are doing to the wilderness is a sacrilege." They said they knew a man who "boasted about shooting a cougar with three little ones. If people think that way, there will be no more—only those bred in captivity.

There will be no more wilderness; we will just see it in the movies."

It is no wonder that these performers with their wild cats did not feel at home in the cattle domain of a rodeo town surrounded by cowboys and their horses. Nor is it surprising that they were not welcomed there. For it was evident that two opposing value systems were exemplified. Though mastery is part of both attitudes, they nonetheless seemed to have little in common. It was as though the natural antagonism which exists between predator and prey species became crystallized into a mutual hostility. Thus the cat act people and the rodeo community of horsemen took on the symbolism of the wild versus the tame. In as valid a way as possibly could occur within the context of rodeo, the owners of the exotic cats were spokesmen for the wild, some portion of which they had transformed into "family." Of course, a captive and partially tamed wild animal cannot be entirely representative of a truly wild animal in its native state. Nevertheless, study of this act helped to bring into relief many important factors regarding the wild and the tame. It allowed the attitude of sympathy toward the wild, and attempted understanding of it, to be sharply contrasted with the attitude of aggressive hostility toward the wild. The utilitarian exploitative view toward wild nature which generally characterizes the ranching ethos was brought more keenly into focus by its opposite—the quality of an aesthetic appreciation of the wild as it was expressed by the cat trainers.

THE RANCH/RODEO VIEW OF THE WILD

One of the best ways to determine the attitudes of people toward the wild, I found, was to assess their feelings about the wildlife refuges which have been established by the government in various parts of the Great Plains. These refuges have been set aside in an attempt to protect and preserve certain forms of wildlife that would otherwise face destruction and eventual extinction. In order to learn first-hand about Great Plains ranchers' views of wildlife and wilderness, I not only interviewed them at their ranches, but visited wildlife preserves which are located in strategic cattle areas. (I made certain that rancher informants were strongly involved in, or supportive of, rodeo, in order to establish a firm ranch-rodeo connection.) The refuges at which I made studies are in the heart of ranch country, and thus are focal centers for the clashing of opposed attitudes toward the wild. Agents who administer or work in these areas are well-versed in many aspects of ranchers' views of, and relations with, the wild and were cooperative in this phase of my study.

Predominant in the typical rancher's response to the wild is his unqualified hatred of those creatures classified as predators. I want to make clear that it is not my purpose here to discount the real economic problems posed by these animals, but rather to deal with the cattleman's perception of them and the way in which human interaction with them illustrates concepts of the tame/wild dichotomy. Predatory species are generally viewed by stockmen as their arch-enemy, hostile to the human realm and its domesticated associates and dependents. Today, when major predators of the past, such as wolves and mountain lions, have been virtually exterminated except in a few remote areas, most of the ranchers' vindictiveness seems to be directed toward the coyote and eagle. (Logically, this should include only the golden eagle, since the bald eagle is a fish-eater, but most ranchmen indicated that they do not differentiate between the two species.)

PREDATORS—COYOTE, EAGLE, AND BEAR

Though in a practical sense, coyotes and eagles are of far more economic concern to sheep ranchers, most cattlemen nevertheless look upon them as hated enemies. Typically, very soon after one enters into a conversation with a Great Plains rancher or ranch-oriented rodeo participant, the subject of coyotes is brought up. Feelings are strong and emotion-charged, and anecdotes abound with what zoologists and naturalists often claim are exaggerations and unfounded fancies. An uninitiated observer is astounded at the depth of the stockmen's anti-predator reaction as well as the extreme importance with which these people imbue the subject. Everywhere they meet, ranchers discuss the "coyote situation" almost as often as the weather. Their mutual aversion seems to identify them—first as cattlemen, and then as "Westerners," and bonds them against the common enemy. They constantly petition the local and federal governments for funds with which to carry out extermination campaigns, and for stronger poisons with which to arm themselves against the wily canines. This is noteworthy because in most cases ranchers say they want to be independent of the government. But predator-control is the exception; they want politicians to side with them and to back up support with substantial funds.

The anti-predator stance of the ranchers is often felt by other people to be beyond the bounds of logic, and those on the outside who must deal with it call it the "Little-Red-Riding-Hood syndrome." According to many of the wildlife-control officials who investigate predation, the rancher's attitude is usually "I've got a problem; solve it, but my mind is made up; don't confuse me with facts." Wildlife experts point out that although coyotes eat prairie dogs, for example, ranchers kill both coyotes and prairie dogs—a completely illogical practice, they maintain. Those who deal with rancher-predator relationships usually agree that, as one ecologist phrased it, "predators are a scapegoat for all the problems inherent in making a living from livestock in the West."

The hatred engendered by predator species is a powerful and pervasive phenomenon, and in the ritual of rodeo the cattlemen's views receive reinforcement. For example, in the monkey and dog sheep-herding act at the 1978 Calgary Stampede, reference was made to the "coyote, wolf, and mountain lion" as enemies which might get the sheep if they were not properly corralled. At each performance it was stressed that protection was needed from the "mangey coyotes whose number one meal is the old woolies." Conversation among rodeo participants often turned to some mention of their plan to go hunting in order to take advantage of the bounty on coyote pelts. A rodeo stock contractor recently told me he "knew a man who skinned thirty-five hundred coyotes on his land in Montana last winter. We need predator control here badly," he went on, "and we must have it. People from back East have destroyed the land there, and now they want to come out here and tell us to keep the coyotes. Coyotes will never disappear. People live off the land here; there is no way to make a living if we have coyotes. They kill sheep, calves, and horses, and a person cannot raise them if coyotes are around." He explained that he believes in destroying coyotes even though he once owed his staying alive to money earned from hunting them. "I had no other income, so I am grateful to them. They are smart; they will always be here. There is no danger of eliminating them all."

Their emotional response to coyotes, I found, prompts ranch/rodeo people to see the animals as symbols of the unreasoning, evil, and ruthless qualities they often attribute to the wild. One Montana rancher assured me that "the coyotes around this area got so bad last winter that they killed antelopes just for the fun of it. They killed several at a time, not just one, and only ate one of them." Another said "we want all coyotes gone. But man cannot wipe out coyotes and mice. Coyotes can even survive in cities. They can raise their pups in culverts in towns and eat cats, like the ones in Los Angeles. In New

Mexico, coyotes attacked two little girls in sleeping bags. They do no good; they kill just to kill. The coyote is nothing but a killer. The 'bleeding hearts' put out propaganda about coyotes killing only mice and rodents, but really they are like humans or dogs, they will not eat a mouse if they can get a steak—like deer, lambs, and calves." He went on to say "the reason people think coyotes are scarce is that they are pretty slippery; they hear you coming and slide off into the brush. They are sneaky and hard to see, and this causes trouble. The dudes drive down the road and if they don't see them they think they are extinct. If they ever get that thick, they will eat people."

A rodeo official told me "you are around nature in rodeo; it is kin to you. Without nature—the animals—where would you be?" Nevertheless, he was convinced that wild nature could be malevolent, for he said "coyotes will pull the tongues out of living calves so they can't suck. The calves would starve and then must be hand-fed until they can chew. It is strange that an animal will do this. Coyotes will eat from a mother cow that is lame. They will just eat her udder and she will starve to death. It is similar to something in nature that makes a shark or seal go only for the liver of a tuna fish. These parts are a delicacy."

A Great Plains rancher indicated in an angry tone that "no such thing as 'the balance of nature' is possible. A stockman cannot make a living with interference from people who say there is. We must get rid of predators." He declared "there are a lot of coyotes around here now." Later in the day, he took me along with a horse trader out to his ranch to see his favorite stallion. As we drove over the ranch, we saw literally hundreds upon hundreds of gophers, swarming in every direction. There was scarcely a patch of ground not covered by the animals, and it was a strange, unnatural sight. Seeing this, the horse dealer remarked that the overabundance of gophers was due to the lack of coyotes in the area. The stockman was visibly embarrassed. "Oh," he said, "I heard there were a lot of them around."

One rodeo participant whose home I visited displayed two coyote skins hanging on the wall—evidencing not just conquest but pride in it. It is relevant to note that the desolation of the "lone prairie" in the song about "The Dying Cowboy" is epitomized as the place "where the coyotes howl and the wind blows free" (Sackett 1967:49). Interestingly, there is also a ballad about the death of a cowboy in which these animals have a more intimate role, for one of its lines specifies that "the coyotes mourn their kin." Other poems that romanticize the cowboy's life also portray these predators in a more benevolent light. One of these notes "And the coyotes sing their

248   RODEO

lullaby" (Lane 1976: 1), and another associated the animals with the
good life on the open plains:

Give me the prairies free,
Where the curlews fly and the coyotes cry.

(Lane 1976:21)

Thus beneath the surface there seems to be a strain of identification
with this creature of the wild, a feeling of reluctant admiration. But
this is far overshadowed by the vindictiveness evidenced in day-to-
day interaction with the coyote.

The eagle, which is almost universally regarded as a symbol of the
wild and the free, is nonetheless viewed by ranchers with the same
sort of hatred. Again, eagle predation would be expected to be mainly
the concern of the sheep industry, but cattlemen are deeply concerned
about it and many are convinced that, contrary to wildlife zoologists'
and naturalists' assertions, "an eagle can carry away a calf." Everyone
interested in the status of the wild will remember the photographs
which appeared a decade or so ago in conservation magazines. These
revealed hundreds of eagle and hawk carcasses strung up along
Western ranch fences as mute testament to the enmity with which
such creatures were regarded. Though this practice has been curtailed, the hate remains. One bronc rider from a Wyoming ranch
believes unquestionably that eagles kill healthy calves in spite of
biologists' evidence that such animals, rarely taken, are first diseased
or weakened. "Eagles are not an endangered species at all," this rodeo
ranchman said, against all government and conservation association
tallies to the contrary; "there are plenty of them in my area, and they
are doing well. College-educated wildlife officials say eagles don't
take many ranch animals, but I know better. A person has to shoot
them on a ranch. You are trying to make a living and they take your
profits."

A Montana cattle rancher declared "eagles are even worse than
coyotes because they are airborne. They are a bad thing, and can even
kill a full-grown antelope. They drop from the sky, double over their
claws like a fist, and grip an animal over the kidneys. They peck out
their eyes, and then the animal is done-for. They can do this to any
size antelope or fawn and can pick them up and pack them off to their
nest. They are a tremendous problem, and the only good thing they
do is to kill rattlesnakes."

"In truth," the government ecologist for a national forest in the
Great Plains told me, "the rancher's ills are caused by the economy of
the times. The eagle and coyote are scapegoats. They do minor,

negligible damage, and ordinarily feed on carrion. Eagles can't carry
away anything bigger than a jackrabbit. But stockmen see eagles
eating carcasses of larger animals and accuse the birds of killing them.
They may feed on weak and sick stock, or may kill fawns or lambs
when especially hungry, but it is not their usual habit. Programs of
destruction are being carried out far in excess of need." But he was
resigned: "people are not known to be logical; they are not convinced
by facts, but believe what they want to believe." He said: "I have
found their thinking is almost one-hundred percent emotional; there
is rarely any objective consideration or enlightenment." In one such
case, I was told, a biologist presented evidence to a group of ranchers
that an animal they believed to have been killed by an eagle was, as
proven by autopsy, starving to death at the time eagles were seen
feeding on it. "The stockmen," he said, "refused to listen, and their
response was to petition the government to fire this man. If the
government did not get rid of him, they threatened, they would not
open their land to hunting that year." This reminded me of a radio
broadcast I had just heard in Montana, announcing that the government grant of $40,000 had just been raised to $80,000 for predator-
control, due to pressure from stockmen. "High ransom," said the
commentator, "as ranchers threatened to close their land to hunters if
their price was not met."

I found that mere mention of the emotionally charged and politi-
cally involved issue of eagles provoked a storm of rage among
ranchers. The full seriousness of their hostility is clearly shown by two
recent incidents. In 1971 the slaughter of about 770 eagles took place
in Wyoming ranch country (Krakel 1973:10–16). The birds were
gunned-down from a helicopter, at great expense, and though controversy surrounds the issue of just who was responsible for the
killing—a wealthy cattle and sheep ranch owner or his ranch-
hand—the fact that it happened at all demonstrates the extremes of
predator-hatred on the part of stockmen. It is relevant that the man
who was accused of instigating and financially supporting the eagle
destruction "had built a ranching empire," and is described as a man
who "loved to hunt, fish, and observe wildlife. In his youth he guided
hunters into the rugged northwestern Wyoming mountains, and
many years later enjoyed hunting safaris in Africa and India. His
trophies included a rhinoceros and the cape buffalo" (Krakel II
1977:58).

The second incident to which I refer is a series of eagle-killings in
Texas during 1975, 1976, and 1977, in which about one-hundred
eagles were shot. Although the men directly involved were sheep

ranchers, cattle ranchers expressed support and sympathy for their fellow stockmen accused in the case, and were generally in agreement with the action taken against eagles as their common enemy. Again, the office of the man whose ideology was thought to be behind the slaughter was full of trophies from the wild. "There are three bear hides on the floor," wrote the reporter for the case. "The walls bristle with mounted heads, antlers, horns of cape buffalo, moose, deer, and mountain sheep. The man explains he has 150 others displayed elsewhere, including two rare African bongo, mounted whole." Though he was a man of evident wealth, he complained about severe economic losses caused by eagle predation (Schueler 1978:49). One accused eagle-killer is quoted as saying he "feels that Texas sheep are important to the world's food supply, that the eagles are taking the food out of the mouths of needy children." He does not realize, writes the conservation advocate, "that the grain needed to help carry cattle and sheep through the Texas winter would surely feed more hungry people than the same grain translated into meat—meat that really hungry people could not possibly afford" (Schueler 1978:51). Such thinking illustrates the lack of logical reasoning which conservationists and other "outsiders" often attribute to the stockmen's war on wildlife. The trial and conviction of several eagle-shooters in Texas left much bitterness in its wake; few were convinced of the wrongness of defending themselves against the wild predators from the sky. One of the chief government witnesses was murdered shortly after the trial. The general feeling regarding the decision was that the judge in the case upheld the federal law (there are no state laws in Texas to protect eagles), but not its spirit. The underlying significance of the eagle killings is summed up by one investigator who describes the difficulties ranchers face today in trying to hold on to "the kind of life that ranching in the old way requires," with the gradual decline of the requisite toughness and dedication. He points out that "ranching is a lifestyle and not an occupation or profession," and involves many difficulties unrelated to predators.

> For all of this—the mismanagement of the land, the vagaries of fashion, the blandishments of the real estate people, the arrival of "new people" with their unfamiliar ways, the departure of sons and daughters, and above all the subtle failure of will that overtakes an insular society when its way of life is undermined—for all this the eagle gets blamed.
>
> (Schueler 1978:72)

At the present time a third animal in the predator category is also in the spotlight of the rancher-versus-the-wild controversy. The grizzly bear, whose remnant populations (exclusive of Alaska) now exist mainly in small portions of Idaho, Montana, Washington, and Oregon, and whose habitat parallels ranch country, embodies many qualities which make it the object of intense feelings. For it can be said that this species truly symbolizes the wilderness. To insure its continued existence the grizzly bear needs land untouched by man, land that has escaped technology and maintained its natural integrity (Schneider 1977:xii). The bear is considered by ecologists to be a "barometer" of environmental quality, because it cannot survive where man has upset the ecosystem, and thus it represents the harmony of the wilderness world (Schneider 1977:178). To advocate the destruction of the grizzly is then tantamount to advocating the annihilation of the remaining primeval wilderness ("parks" and "recreation areas" are not the issue here).

Ranchers as well as their antagonists, the champions of the wild, realize this, and so the huge bear is a focal point in the controversy. Although zoologists maintain that in the natural situation of the wild the grizzly rarely preys on livestock, conditions at present, in which grazing land in bear habitat is leased to ranchers, are responsible for incidents of predation. Like other carrion-eaters, it too is probably wrongly accused of killing the stock it is observed to feed upon. The point of significance for this study is that the animal seems to represent not only the age-old conflict between domestic stock and the wild; it is also in a broader sense symbolic of man's war against all in nature that is yet untamed. Opponents of grizzly bear preservation back up their antipathy to the wild by referring to statements about the country's resources that have been subsequently seized upon and quoted by ranch/rodeo people. Editorials about the bear controversy like the following show how the instruments of exploitation signifying economic "progress" are marshalled for use in opposition to the wild.

> The high stakes for which the two factions are at odds happen to be some of the very best timber producing lands in America, the finest summer grazing, and land which contains rich oil and mineral deposits, has electrical power possibilities and energy resources which, if placed on the inaccessible list behind the iron bear curtain, could affect every American young and old, both now and way into the unforseeable future.
>
> (Krakel 1977:73)

The dilemma clearly has historical roots. It has been traditional for American frontier heroes such as Davy Crockett, Daniel Boone, and Jim Bridger to conquer a bear early in their careers, not for food but to prove their strength and manhood—their supremacy over nature. This theme from American pioneer experience finds articulate expression, for example, in William Faulkner's story, *The Bear*, in which the killing of a bear signifies coming of age for the youthful protagonist (1967). The bear is noteworthy for its upright posture, standing like a man when in an attitude of threat and menace, an image of power, and indeed revered by Indians for this very quality as well as its bravery and ferocity. In Hal Borland's rodeo novel, *When the Legends Die* (1969), the Indian hero's friendship with a bear symbolizes his attunement to the wilderness which is in sharp contrast to the white culture's obsession with destroying it. Bear-man battles have come to stand for a classic test of who shall be master of the West—nature or man. The grizzly bear's present plight, like the stockmen's ritual of rodeo, recapitulates America's conquest of wilderness and wildness. On a surface level, of course, the prime issue is grazing. Ranchers resent the turning over of grazing land for what they regard as the useless purpose of preserving a creature they perceive as fierce and dangerous to humans and domestic animals. But on a deeper level there is the ranchers' resentment of all that is wild, the ethos that views it for conquering.

The proposed wilderness for bears in the West has stirred stockmen to a fever pitch. Since the ranchers in the areas of my study were mostly located a long way from the grizzly's range, they have negligible personal or practical stake in its elimination. Yet they seem obsessed with their opposition to the bear. One rancher with strong rodeo affiliation told me "some people want to set aside huge wilderness areas of thirteen million acres as critical habitat for the grizzlies. Ranchers have grazing permits there, and lumbermen have used it for years. But now they want to make it a primitive area. By God, we're not rich enough and big enough to afford to do it. We need the minerals, lumber, and grass. Most environmentalists haven't had to work for a living; they have bureaucratic jobs and don't know what it is to work for a dollar." In an editorial entitled "Western Points of View" a Montana rancher who was against the bear wilderness preservation wrote:

> "critical habitat" and "endangered species" are common catch-words nowadays and invariably used in connection with the "need for Wilderness Areas." If all these studies and plans I have mentioned come to pass, then, boys, the rancher will damn sure join the "endangered species" and his "habitat" will be about as "critical" as they come!
>
> (Krakel 1977:73)

In conversation, ranchers invariably bring up the danger to humans which the grizzly represents in parks or wilderness areas. As Schneider points out in his book on the great bear, there is a strong desire on the part of ranchmen to believe in the animal's ferocity. People killed on the highway receive little news coverage in comparison to those rare instances of bear-caused deaths or maulings (1977:169–170). When two young women camping in Glacier National Park in 1967 were killed by a grizzly, stockmen went into an uproar which has not yet died down. Most called for complete extermination of grizzlies. Yet as one ecologist who discussed the issue pointed out, "a person in bear country is safer than a man in motorcycle country. People choose their own form of danger." The ranchers make it plain that they do not want to choose their danger from the wild. They cannot understand the feeling of a person who seeks the wilderness as a value in itself and does not wish it to be made free of all risk.

Once again, as I have noted for other species in this study, the qualities of uncontrollability and unpredictability are imputed to the bear as the epitome of wildness. One rancher expressed this mystique: "We don't aim to save the bear. Bears will survive unless they are shot. The conservationists claim we need millions of acres for the bear, and those inmates of that asylum on the Potomac will believe them instead of us. But the bear will go wherever he damn pleases and we must get out of his way or he will eat us. We don't have to stop the mining or timbering. The cockeyed bear will roam in the mountains where he wants to go. He won't need legislation to make him go." Bears are always described by informants as "very smart," as well as "big, strong, and not afraid of man." It is said "they tolerate you going ahead and doing your thing as long as you don't interfere with them." People see bears as a species not amenable to man's domination, and this helps explain the ranch/rodeo aversion to them as a part of the wild that continues to escape from human control.

A striking contrast to the stockmen's views is the attitude toward the wilderness and the wild expressed by a forest ranger. Revealing a diametrically opposed ethos to theirs, his feelings give valuable insights into the meaning of the tame/wild dichotomy. He shared with me his sensation that "if the grizzly bears are around, it makes you more alert. It is an exciting place to be; it changes the whole atmosphere. I am happy in their presence, it makes me wide awake. You shouldn't fall asleep there, as the bear might be around. It is really living. You are more alive there than when in a protected environment. It really makes you live. The bears are something to be wary of. Their unpredictability is what makes it interesting. The grizzly has the power to do whatever it feels like doing." The ranch/rodeo people, on the other hand, generally seem to obtain their feeling of aliveness from the conquest of the wild, from the taming and controlling process itself. For the rancher, I observed that the wilder the species, the more remote from man, the more independent and clever, the less predictable and controllable, the more it is hated and persecuted. Thus the coyote, the eagle, and the bear, exemplifying these qualities and being predators potentially dangerous to domesticated animals, earn the stockman's wrath to the highest degree.

DEER, ELK, WILD SHEEP, AND PRAIRIE DOGS

Other species of wild animals are perceived and categorized by Great Plains ranchers in various ways which also shed light on their views of the wild and the tame. Examples of these are herbivores such as deer, elk, wild sheep, and prairie dogs, animals whose habitat overlaps the Great Plains cattlemen's domain and with which the stockmen have specific and unique relationships.

Ranchers invariably "love deer," both by their own admission and the observations of wildlife personnel, who call this mystique "the Bambi complex." Deer seem to be closer to the ranch/rodeo people's inner circle of domesticity than any other part of the wild. Deer are gentle, sometimes approachable, and far less remote and aggressive than most wild species; they are at the opposite pole from bears, eagles, and coyotes. Most ranchers put them in a category with domestic stock as needing protection from dangers such as harsh weather and predators. Cattlemen are very proud of the fact that in winter they willingly let deer eat from their haystacks, "even with the high price of hay." They claim that the wildlife people do not give them the credit they deserve for having kept many deer alive during the harsh winter of 1977 and 1978. Ranchers identify strongly with the deer against the coyote. One Montana rancher expressed it this way: "The reason deer stay on my deeded land instead of the wildlife refuge is that coyotes don't stay around where people live. The game stay here for protection." This is a revealing statement, demonstrating the cattlemen's habit of sharply categorizing animal species, and is important in showing their attitude toward predators as "antisocial." And it again expresses the concept of the rancher as extending his protective arc to encircle a small portion of the tamer part of the wild realm beyond.

It is significant that, though they like deer, most ranchers indicate they do not like elk. This is probably related to the fact that while deer are browsers, elk are grazers like cattle, and are thus considered to be more competitive with domestic stock. In a region of the Great Plains where a large wildlife refuge comes in contact with many cattle ranches, for example, there is an area of especially favorable elk habitat. Government officials there told me that as soon as the elk cross from the protection of the game preserve onto private land, the ranchers kill them. "As soon as the elk get there," they said, "we can't hire enough law enforcement people to police it." Thus elk are placed in an entirely separate category from deer by the ranchers. I suggest that this may be related to their very different image—bigger, more powerful, more "masculine," above all less prone to seek human habitation, and more unpredictable. Thus they are perceived as being more intrinsically a part of the wild realm.

Big horn sheep, whose range is confined mostly to mountainous country, are considered to be even more of a truly wild species. It is noteworthy that almost every rancher I visited displayed a mounted head from this animal as a trophy on his wall. Each man elaborated on the details of making a special trek into its remote habitat to shoot a specimen—always a large male with huge curving horns—and took great pride in this accomplishment. A northern Great Plains wildlife refuge manager told me that "when some of these wild big horn sheep were transplanted into the federal preserve and released, ranchers hired killers to shoot them all. They took matters into their own hands, even though it was a wildlife refuge." The reason for this, he explained, was that stockmen felt that the wild rams were interbreeding with their domestic ewes, and the results of such crosses would be detrimental to the herds. Ranchers wanted to prevent, at all cost, the introduction of "wildness" into their stock. It is interesting that the objections were always made to wild males mating with domestic ewes, not the other way around, an indication that "wildness" in this case is a quality associated with masculinity. Cowboys had the same idea about their mares, believing that

> elusive wild horses were undesirable neighbors, because they displayed a habit of enticing ranch horses, particularly mares, away from their accustomed range, away from all willingness to be subject to man's dictation, and of "running them off" beyond the edges of the local map.
>
> (Rollins 1973:54)

Ranchers' relations to prairie dogs also reveal much about their attitude toward the wild. Usually when this species is mentioned the first thing that comes to the stockman's mind is the danger to a man on horseback should his mount step into a prairie dog hole. By pursuing the subject further, one finds, however, that the little herbivores are viewed as serious competitors to the stock for grass. From the earliest days of the settlement of the West, the extermination of the animals who would prey upon this species made their numbers increase. Ranchers universally seem to possess an obsessive hatred for prairie dogs, whose "towns" were once so numerous on the Great Plains. In addition to their grass-consumption, a field naturalist explained another relevant reason for the ranchers' enmity. He said they believe that prairie dogs actually remove extensive amounts of vegetation not just for eating, but also for "visual assistance." That is, the animals are said to "mow it down and leave it, wasting a certain amount of it, so that they can see predators." This alleged "waste" of grass they could be using for stock infuriates the ranchers. "As is so often the case," wildlife officials pointed out, "their vindictiveness goes far beyond what is warranted, and the cost of programs of destruction far exceeds the benefits obtained. In one area, the control operation against prairie dogs cost $2,000 for about $200 worth of forage that would have been eaten."

"VARMINTS"

Ranchers are traditionally involved in a war against a part of the wild they categorize as "varmints." Several stockmen admitted that they always kill such animals as badgers, marmots, and the like "because they are in my way." Pests are creatures not considered useful to the purposes of ranchers and in some way they have come to represent "enemy." This attitude may be a hold-over from several generations back, when all wild animals were understandably regarded as a menace to pioneers in their attempt to gain a foothold in the inhospitable environment of the Great Plains. The ethos of the present day is made clear in a recent issue of the vacation guidebook for Montana by a paragraph outlined in black for emphasis:

HUNT VARMITS YEAR-ROUND!

Hunting never closes down in Montana. With a long list of varmits and predators, from coyote to small ground squirrels, you can hunt anytime you can visit. No license is required, no limits on caliber, and plenty of diverse country makes varmits a prime sport. Sharpen your skills on mountain roaming marmots and squirrels. Hunt cottontails (yessir) and jackrabbits at will, even at night. Call coyotes and fox, or run coons and get ranchers' thanks. Practice on crows and magpies, the tricky pests of the west.

(Browning 1975:33)

BIRDS

Some species of birds too come in for a share of the rancher's enmity toward the wild. Foremost among them is the magpie. One rodeo participant who owns a ranch referred to magpies as "dirty little buggers," and a prominent rodeo official expounded on his views of these common birds. He said he hates them because "a couple of magpies will get together and kill young rabbits and squirrels. I hate to see them kill anything little. They are getting rougher and rougher all the time, as their natural feeding ground is invaded by mining, so they are getting more common on ranches. Four or five magpies in one place I know of killed some blue heeler pups. They maim them first, and they peck at their eyes." A rodeo stock contractor, also a rancher, said "we kill all the magpies around here, we tear apart their nests and break their eggs. Magpies are clever, they will come whenever you are in trouble on the prairie. If you are weak they come from miles around and peck at you. They are uncanny, and hard to shoot. It is as though the Lord was protecting them. Magpies will not let an animal alone when they find it weakened, but will stay with it all day. If a cow has a warble on its back they will peck at it, and finally make a big hole right into its intestines. They peck out the eyes of a weakened sheep or cow." He went on "they can kill a horse or a cow," and showed me the body of a magpie he had killed and tacked up on his barn door "as a warning to keep the others away from here."

Another rancher spoke of magpies as "pecking right into the kidneys of a cow, further each day, until the victim goes down." Many accused the birds of "picking on the open brands of calves." Quite a few informants had hunted magpies during their youth, in order to receive the bounty of 1¢ to 3¢ each paid by ranching communities for magpie legs or eggs. Cattlemen do not accept biologists' testimony that magpies are carrion-eaters, consuming dead tissue and maggots from the wounds of animals, or meat from those already dead, rather than healthy flesh from living creatures they have maimed or killed themselves. One wildlife official explained that "ranchers see magpies perched on the backs of their stock and blame the birds for injuring them, when in reality they are eating the flies and helping the animal." A national forest ecologist commented "in Salem they burned witches; here the ranchers blame their troubles on the magpie as a scapegoat." He had once kept some birds of this species as pets, and said "they are very intelligent, and can even be taught to talk."

When I tried to probe into the hatred engendered by magpies I was often told "they're just bad." But I was able to identify specific charges made against them by ranchers who like to hunt. "Magpies occasionally prey on pheasant and game birds' nests, and these are desirable birds for sportsmen to shoot, especially for gourmets," I was told at one wildlife refuge. "People want to be able to hunt these birds." It was also revealing to learn that stockmen perceive of magpies as "attacking song birds' nests and eating eggs of species like robins which are found around the house." Thus one can understand why magpies have earned the intense hatred reserved for the outer realm of the wild. They are categorized as enemy to the species which ranchers take into their innermost circle of domestication, like garden birds.

Song birds seem to enjoy a place within the cattleman's ordered universe like his own stock, and are often well-regarded. Once, listening to a ranch family expound upon the evils of coyotes and bears, I spotted a flock of cedar waxwings in a nearby tree. The ranchers recognized this species of garden visitors and showed appreciation for them. But many birds which remain remote, totally in the wild realm, and which, because they are of no special "use," would be enjoyed only in an aesthetic way, are ignored. In the heart of the northern Great Plains ranch country, for example, there is a refuge for the spectacular white pelicans. Local ranchers do not seem to be aware of them at all, though the huge birds often fly overhead where they are easily seen from the open rangeland. Wildlife officials said of the cattlemen in the area "they don't know they're here, or even that the refuge is here, for that matter. Most people who come to see the birds and animals are from the East. The ranchers wouldn't drive twenty miles to see wildlife, though they think nothing of going two-hundred miles to go shopping."

Wild turkeys, however (once almost exterminated in the United States, but now more abundant due to restocking), are a species that ranchers do notice. The reason for this, as one Montana stockman whose land abuts a national wildlife refuge told me, is that "wild turkeys come on to ranchers' land because they like our grain and stuff. This past winter was a terrible one. It takes quite a winter to kill wild turkeys. They will even eat pine cones. This year the only ones who survived were around homes. The rest in the hills died. We get no credit for that. We are still (to the government) those terrible people who have cattle out on the range. Twenty-one turkeys fed here during the winter on a hundred pounds of ground grain a day and what they cleaned up after the calves. Every rancher around here fed them. The Fish and Game poeople didn't do one thing toward keeping them alive; the ranchers did it all. Turkeys are usually hunted twice a year, but we wouldn't let 'em hunt this spring. They are a nice bird, they don't hurt anything, and we want to keep them around." His comments were indeed revealing, for of course turkeys are domesticable, and thus fit into the rancher's inner sphere. Being to some degree tame as well as nonaggressive, they do not challenge his interests or his domination, and do not seem part of the remote wild.

Such categorizations as ranchers are continually making can influence the fate of a species. An example of this is the mourning dove, which in some areas is known as a game bird and in others is classified with song birds. A wildlife official told me that in the ranching area where he had formerly worked, the proposal to hunt mourning doves was turned down. He said that "biologically, there is no reason not to hunt them, but, due to the 'Bambi complex' being applied to the species, the decision was made to prohibit hunting them. People hear the dove cooing and so they put it in the same light as a robin, rather than as a game bird. So hunting it was wholehcartedly voted down." He added that "information was given to people by the Fish and Game as to the fact that hunting would not hurt this species, but the general attitude was 'don't confuse me with facts.' " With insight he observed that "if a dove were as ugly as a vulture and did not sit in the backyard and coo, they wouldn't care." Again, by becoming part of the ranch country's inner sphere, doves are sharply separated from the rest of the wild, and removed from the status of "enemy."

PLANTS

Ranchers seem to lash out at the wild almost instinctively, aiming to control every element. Even the plant world becomes involved in their complex of domination. This is exemplified by an incident that occurred while I was visiting a ranch/rodeo family, sitting out by their animal pens and cattle chutes. This was not a garden area or a pasture, and there was old machinery scattered around. It was obviously a work area, and no pretense was made that it was maintained for attractiveness. The grass was trampled and sparse from the activity that habitually occurred there. Suddenly one of the ranchers reached out and pulled up all the wild carrots within reach, saying "I hate these. I just hate weeds anyway! What it needs here is to be sprayed." Through such apparently casual actions informants often revealed antipathy to uncontrolled forms of nature.

Rodeo at times also makes reference to the plant world. A noteworthy instance of this is the clown act in which a bull knocks down a stuffed dummy in the arena. When asked the name of the "fellow" thus butted by the bull, the clown responds "Euell Gibbons! We'll give him some more hickory!" As he shouts this, the clown props up the dummy again with a broom. When I talked to the clown about this extremely popular act, he confirmed that its purpose was to make fun of people who show concern for wild plants.

WILDLIFE REFUGES

Ranchers generally deplore the existence of government refuges for wildlife, and dislike the personnel who administer them. Typically they give the staff officials no cooperation, feeling that, as one man whose acreage closely paralleled a national refuge expressed it, "they [the Fish and Game men] make it as inconvenient for us ranchers as they possibly can." Entering this man's property, one encounters a sign which reads

> Enter at your own risk! You are trespassing. No gov't. trained parasites. No coons. No labor goons. No hippies or other cannibals. No reds, college pups or other dead beats. All Indians and decent white folks welcome.

It must be explained that many Great Plains ranchers are strongly "anti-Indian," but this man, though he said "Indians are drunken, lazy, dirty, and rough on horses," felt that "the government made them that way, and now the ranchers are getting the same treatment." He identified with Indians because of the "government taking our land like they did to the Indians. Our deeds are now not worth the paper they're written on." By this he referred to the fact that cattlemen's grazing rights are presently curtailed in the wildlife sanctuaries whenever the presence of the stock is deemed to be detrimental to the maintenance of the wild species for which the refuge was set aside. "Those federal employees let on they are doing a great job looking after the wildlife, but we are really the ones who do it," he insisted. "The government men are a joke, a big waste of money, bureaucrats who try to let on they are needed badly. We call them government parasites, glorified reliefers."

A former rodeo stock contractor who is a cattle dealer in an area near a large refuge said, "I'd like to put poison into the coffee of the refuge officials." He indicated ranchers in his region were incensed because "wildlife men burn off the grass instead of letting stockmen use it for grazing." They make fun of the refuge men for "letting blackbirds loose all over the place with yellow ribbons tied to their tails. No one knows what they are doing." Cattlemen want to govern the game and wildlife themselves, and bitterly resent government intervention. "Ranchers are the best game wardens," they maintain. "There is nothing over there in the refuge that wouldn't be there anyway without the government taking over. We know more about wildlife than the game wardens do. The Fish and Game men don't know the first thing about it. They are really cruel, and won't feed the antelope in winter." Such conversations were very revealing. They explicitly expressed the ranch/rodeo trait of an almost obsessive desire for control over the wild. Their aim always seems to be to extend the limits of human mastery beyond the domestic world which they already dominate. Their continual and insistent emphasis on feeding the wild species in winter epitomizes their attitude of striving to bring these into the inner sphere of the tame. This characteristic attitude is the opposite of that of the traditional Plains Indians, for example, who admire and extoll the virtues of those creatures of the wild who possess the ability to survive in the wilderness alone, unaided by man. The ranch/rodeo view, in contrast, places highest value upon those species which will enter man's sphere and become dependent upon it, and engenders greatest antipathy toward those that remain furthest from the human realm and independent from it.

Thus it is that battles rage at the borders where wild meets tame—where wildlife sanctuaries extend the untamed domain right into the very heart of the cattleman's domesticated empire. "The Department of the Interior is the worst menace and danger to the livestock industry in the eleven Western states," one irate ranch-owner in such an area declared. "Every time they take a few million acres out of production for grazing, timber, and mining, it hurts the economy. They will get you hungry and broke, and then the Communists can take over, for it is no trouble to whip a hungry man. Groups like the Wilderness Society, Sierra Club, and Friends of Earth are Communist-infiltrated groups and will not be satisfied until they get all deeded land away from the ranchers. This is why our deeds are worthless."

The officials at these large refuges in cattle country communicated their views regarding the clash between ranchers and wild life. It should be made clear that these agents are native Westerners who are ordinarily sympathetic to ranching. In fact most of them told me "I would like to be a rancher, and would be if I could afford it." They are also supportive of rodeo, and often indicated that members of their family, usually young sons, participate in the sport. At the largest national refuge in ranching country an official explained: "The federal agency administers these sanctuary areas in which decisions are presently, according to recent policy, made in favor of wildlife. Ranchers want grazing rights to have primacy over the interests of wild species, the way it was in the past. Ranchers want to be independent. For years they ran the refuge like it was their own property. They ran their cows on government land whenever and wherever they wished, and in the numbers they wanted. Now they fear loss of grazing land due to fencing of boundaries and enforcement of policy that favors wildlife over domesticated animals. They fear government control, and they are against wilderness which they perceive as a total lock-up of land." The manager of all refuges located in a large Western state summed up his observations about the controversy: "Ranchers have fears about things they don't understand—the unknown—and they manufacture ideas about the things the wildlife agencies are going to do to keep them from grazing. They won't accept the truth and believe things with no foundation."

RANCH/RODEO ATTITUDES TOWARD THE WILD: A SUMMARY AND COMPARISON TO PLAINS INDIAN VIEW

Cattle ranchers, in the total fabric of their lives and outlook, are intimately associated with the elements of tame/wild, and this over-riding concern is made explicit in the sport of rodeo. The ranch/rodeo outlook toward the wild is characterized by marked antipathy for certain species, a feeling which is said by their opponents to be far in excess of practical or economic factors involved—though it may have been originally based on such considerations. Evils imputed to certain groups of animals are frequently claimed to be exaggerated, and animal-control agents point out that a whole species is often condemned for the unusual depredations or alleged killings of stock perpetrated, perhaps, by one individual or group of individuals of that species.

It is highly significant that the further outward from the circle of the rancher's own world a group of animals is categorized, the more bad qualities characterize the rancher's perception of that species. This is carried to the extreme with coyotes, eagles, and bears, since the historic battle against wolves, cougars, and the like has for all practical purposes been won. Virtually all stockmen in the Great Plains favor programs of extermination against those animals they class as predators. Control over animals is a prime concern in the ranchers' ethos, as manifested in rodeo; they seem obsessed with bringing the untamed under their yoke. As ranch/rodeo people are involved in asserting domination over creatures in the domestic sphere, so they are attempting to institute the same regimen of mastery over the wild. Those species which resist, which are the most remote and least controllable—again the predators—come in for the greatest share of enmity. Those animals with the greatest share of "intelligence," are subject to greater villification by ranchers. "They particularly hate the coyote," said one wildlife ecologist, "because it can outwit them. Ranchers can't overcome the coyote—he usually wins." So, too, it seems that the eagle is resented for its power of flight, and the bear for its elusiveness, qualities which make them quintessentially a part of the wild.

It is noteworthy that the Plains Indians, far from despising the clever coyote, admired him for his wisdom, and frequently made him the hero of tales in which he embodies both human and supernatural traits (Linderman 1932; Lowie 1918). The eagle, too, was highly regarded for its unusual power and keenness of vision, and even into the present day possesses important religious significance. The bear traditionally was, and still is, highly respected for its strength, ferocity, and bravery, and the possession of mysterious abilities.

A brief consideration of the attitude of the Plains natives toward the wild is relevant at this point because it makes that of the ranch/rodeo complex stand out more clearly. Plains Indians generally feel that there is special power in the wild, for which they have great respect and awe. During field work on the Crow Indians' relationship to the horse, for example, I found that these tribesmen still follow the tradition of admiring the ability of their horses to get through the winter on their own, without human aid. They consider it a sign of their respect for this remarkable strength and endurance not to interfere with nature by providing artificial winter protection for their mounts. They identify strongly with the special quality of hardihood they attribute to Crow horses as evidenced by their capacity to survive in the wild. Local white ranchers indicate that they consider this "neglect" on the part of the Indians to be "irresponsible" and "cruel."

Traditional Plains Indian ethos, in contrast to that of the cattle-men, does not include the desire for control and domination over nature. The Sioux attitude toward the wild and the process of domestication, for example, is explained by Lame Deer, who accuses the white man of changing the animals "in a horrible way so no one can recognize them." He states his people's view, which contrasts so strongly with the ranchers': "there is power in a buffalo—spiritual, magic power—but there is no power in an Angus, in a Hereford. There is power in an antelope, but not in a goat or sheep, which holds still while you butcher it." He says "there was great power in a wolf," and that "a partridge, a grouse, a quail, a pheasant, you have made them into chickens" (Lame Deer & Erdoes 1972:120). He speaks of the power of such wild species as the bear and the badger (Lame Deer & Erdoes 1972:130–132) and extolls the eagle as having "all the wisdom of the world," pointing out "that's why we have an eagle feather at the top of the pole during the yuwipi ceremony" (Lame Deer & Erdoes 1972:136).

Lame Deer laments that

> the state of South Dakota has pest-control officers, they go up in a plane and shoot coyotes from the air . . . The stockmen and sheep owners pay them. Coyotes eat mostly rodents, field mice and such. They are our natural garbage men cleaning up the rotten and stinking things. . . . But their living could lose some man a few cents, and so the coyotes are killed from the air.
>
> (Lame Deer & Erdoes 1972:122–123)

He goes on to relate this to

> the terrible arrogance of the white man who determines "I will let this animal live because it makes money"; saying "This animal must go, it brings no income, the space it occupies can be used in a better way. The only good coyote is a dead coyote." They are treating coyotes almost as badly as they used to treat Indians.
>
> (Lame Deer & Erdoes 1972:123)

The sense of identification of Indians with the wild expressed here with regard to the coyote is a frequently encountered association, and has historical roots as a prime factor in Indian-white relations on the Plains. Many ranchers who evidence low opinions of the native Americans still classify them as "wild, uncivilized, useless." This attitude, of course, has precedent dating to the frontier past, when pioneer thinking categorized Indians with the wild, as elements to be cleared away, or possibly tamed, in the course of the civilizing process represented by westward expansion. The evil imputed to Indians who were regarded as "savages" became a rationale for conquering them, just as an exaggerated belief in the deliberate malevolence of animal predators is used to justify elaborate programs of extermination. Both phenomena are part of an all-inclusive war on the wild.

It is relevant to note that it was the New England-bred historian, Francis Parkman, journeying West in 1846, whose own love for the wild and its contrast to his native Boston gave him the necessary insight to appreciate the unspoiled land of the frontier. Parkman saw that civilization had a destroying as well as a creating power, and drew attention to the fact that the Indian, the buffalo, and the frontiersman would soon be eliminated in the "civilizing" process taking place. As one of the earliest observers on the frontier, whose Eastern perceptions threw his Western experience into bold relief, Parkman wrote sensitively in *The Oregon Trail* of the difference between the still wild Indians of the Plains, whom he admired, and the "camp" Indians who had been "tamed" and were in his eyes already degraded by contact with civilization.

Indians have generally retained their wild image for many Great Plains ranchers, and it is significant that this concept is extended to Indian rodeo. A recent issue of the P.R.C.A. official magazine urges readers to attend the Indian National Finals by stating that the affair will "guarantee a more exciting rodeo than you would expect." It goes on to explain that

> the action in the arena is just not matched anywhere. No better bucking horses and bulls are to be found anywhere and a lot of 'em are outlaw rejects from P.R.C.A. rodeo strings. The fact is that a bronc that has been kicked out of the draw elsewhere because of his dangerous habits is welcome at an Indian rodeo. Indian cowboys have a different attitude. They just don't give a damn, and that makes for a rodeo that's mighty good watching.
>
> So, you'll see a combination of classic rides and terrible wrecks. You'll also see the same sort of reckless attitude in the timed events, with some real world-class events . . . and wrecks.
>
> (Searle 1978:3)

"Enemy" to cattle ranchers, which once included "wild Indians" who now ride broncs instead of war ponies, has been traditionally identified as those elements of the natural world that they cannot control. Weather, for example, is a constant source of anxiety and concern in the Great Plains, and an endless topic of conversation in the stockmen's world. Every change in the wind is noted, every prairie fire dreaded, every rainstorm measured and either praised or cursed for its timing, intensity, or quantity. Hail, snow, cold, and heat are determinative variables of the pastoralists' universe, and as such, pose a constant threat. Above all, the animal world of wild nature which exists beyond the fringes of his own domesticated sphere is perceived as a menace which must be controlled. Intimately concerned in his lifeway with the wild-to-tame process, as made explicit in rodeo, the rancher attempts to extend his ethos of domination outward toward the more uncertain and less predictable world of the wilderness.

10

SUMMARY

THE COWBOY CONTINUES to occupy a preeminent position in the American consciousness as a unique figure from our history which has never lost the power to evoke the past and also to symbolize those qualities which remain important to the present. Our fascination with him (and indeed that of many parts of the world) seems only to increase with time. Perhaps, in an age when personal autonomy is rare, and as the earth becomes increasingly over-civilized, we visualize the cowboy riding over the range in a world uncluttered by the restraints that have tamed and domesticated us. For, as A. L. Kroeber noted, while the cowpuncher was never totally isolated from the rest of American society, but rather lived in complementary relation to it, nevertheless "in his social consciousness" he was "free, separate, and proud" (1963:86).

In spite of the inordinate amount of attention devoted to the cowboy in history, literature, and the media, his identity as a herder and the effect of this occupation upon him have been largely ignored. This neglect is evident quite early in the development of the cowboy image, for by 1902 Owen Wister, in the most popular "Western" ever written, had created the archetypal cowboy hero stamped with particular qualities that virtually all his successors would perpetuate. As J. Frank Dobie has aptly pointed out, Wister's Virginian was a "cowboy without cows," a "hero [who] does not even smell of cows" (1969:124). Over time, the figure of the cowboy seems to have traversed a path further and further from cattle, even to the point of becoming an "urban cowboy" today.

Yet the cowboy of the Great Plains *was* first and foremost a herder. It was his life with cattle and horses that originally molded him, and I feel it is to this life one must refer in understanding the cowboy and his counterpart, the rodeo participant. Influenced by his pastoral

267

experience, the American cowpuncher came to possess many of the qualities also observed among other stock-tending peoples. The cultures of societies which herd large livestock virtually all extoll masculinity and stress the overt expression of male sexuality (see especially Bennett 1969; Bogoras 1975; Eckvall 1968; Edgerton 1974; Evans-Pritchard 1956, 1974; Leeds 1970; Riesman 1977; Pelto 1973). Typically pastoralists exhibit a willingness to take chances, and show self-containment and self-control, especially in facing danger. They are noted for "bravery, fortitude, and the ability to withstand pain and hardship." Proud, arrogant, and tending toward aggressive, often hostile, sometimes violent behavior, herders generally possess what is called "a realistic appraisal of the world" (Goldschmidt 1965:405). They demonstrate a consistent lack of social stratification.

A key characteristic of herders is a high degree of independence of action. No doubt this developed because "in a world where man and his animals are vulnerable to so many threats, life without independent decisions, rapidly made and carried out, would be fragile indeed" (Edgerton 1974:367). The ideology of herders generally reinforces values relating to the image of the "strong man," the "good herdsman," such as physical strength, competitive physical accomplishment, and violence—"all of which are useful assets for the enormous physical labor of herding" under difficult conditions. Among such pastoralists "feats of strength, acts of prowess, violent and heroic behavior, excessive endurance and expenditure of energy" are highly valued and are stressed within the context of sports events and games as well as in traditional tales (Leeds 1970:107). It is suggested that "some of the extreme individualistic, aggressive, and competitive traits" of the herders "are connected with the necessity for individual competence in dealing with these large, half-wild animals aggregated into herds which are immensely difficult to maintain, handle, and utilize" (Leeds 1970:126).

Significantly, it is the essence of these very qualities fostered by the cowpunchers' life as herdsmen which receives emphasis in rodeo. Such traits as intensified masculinity, strength and toughness, endurance, stoicism, bravery, propensity for risk-taking, aggressiveness and violence, a pragmatic outlook, egalitarianism, independence, and rugged individualism within a code of group conformity are highlighted in the cowboy sport.

Of all the cowboy characteristics related to his particular experience as a stocktender, the most important one is his relationship to animals and the world of wild nature which comprised his environment. Seldom, if ever, in previous works on the cowboy, has this aspect received serious or indepth attention. I have suggested the way in which the trail and range cowhand's conceptual universe became divided into an inner, protected, and domesticated sphere of the tame, and a more remote, inimical realm of the wild. The American cowpuncher's views of his cattle, of the wild, and of his own status in regard to both, have been compared here with the views of two other cattle-herding peoples, the Nuer and the Fulani. The differences between them serve to clarify the cowboy's own particular outlook, and help to elucidate the conditions of the Great Plains cowboy-cattle-horse complex which made it unique. This I consider to be a prerequisite to an understanding of rodeo which recapitulates the dynamics of that complex as it interacts with elements of the wild and tame.

Such qualities as the cowboy evolved and which were stamped indelibly upon the American cattle frontier, continue to be highly valued in Great Plains ranching, and are perpetuated and intensified with dramatic clarity by the sport which reflects its pioneer heritage. The events of rodeo afford an opportunity for members of the contemporary society which supports it to bring out and set forth for display and exploration the various themes still central to their occupation and ethos. The marked tendency of these people to categorize and align the components of nature, particularly animals, in certain characteristic ways which give order and meaning to their lives is thereby provided with a valid and socially sanctioned means of expression.

Through the mechanism of challenges that are structured to measure and exalt the supporting society's values, rodeo acts to test and retest these qualities. As a representation of the spirit of American westward expansion, the sport serves to revitalize the sense of exhilaration arising from the past conquering of a formidable wilderness. Thus, though the Western frontier, which continues to hold such a profound and universal grip on the human mind and imagination, is closed forever, the ethos associated with it is invigorated and given heightened value.

Rodeo is an outstanding example of the ways in which the concepts and value-system of a society can be expressed through the context of its sport as performance. In the way events are composed as to equipment and rules as well as details of the man-animal alignment, differences between various species of animals, and society's view of them, are highlighted. Messages are conveyed by the order of events as well as in the action they contain. Traditionally, the program begins with one of the wilder events—bareback riding—and closes with the wildest—bull riding or a wild horse race. The opening sets the keynote and the finale acts to leave the impression of a yet unconquered and unconquerable realm in the minds of those who value this prospect. It is significant that the oppositional force expended by each animal in the rough stock events is given meaning and importance equal to that of the rider by means of scoring procedures. Hence it is only by pitting himself against the resisting force of the wildest or "rankest" bull or bronc that a contestant will win.

On its deepest level, rodeo is essentially a ritual addressing itself to the dilemma of man's place in nature, exploring the boundary lines between people and other forms of life. It deals with the major theme of human supremacy over nature, and specifically with man's relationship to the animals which he conceives of as existing both within and beyond his sphere of control. Ritual has been defined as a mediator between nature and culture, and my analysis of rodeo has revealed the sport's implicit exploration and manipulation of varying relationships between these two polarities. In almost every aspect of rodeo it is possible to identify the strain of certain oppositions which can be expressed in terms of the nature/culture dichotomy. These take such forms as animal/human, female/male, nondomesticated/domesticated, country/city, and predator/prey, as well as wild/tame.

Through performance and contest rodeo intensifies, dramatizes, and glorifies the taming of the wild. Yet at the conclusion of each event the bronc is not "broke," the bull is not defeated; ordinarily the "dogged" steer and the roped calf spring to their feet and run free out of the arena. In a sense, then, the wild have not been tamed. There is a future assured in an ongoing process of conquering. For in the "winning of the West," of which rodeo is a metaphoric reflection, wilderness attributes exerted both attraction and repulsion. There was admiration for the wild and the free, and yet a contradictory desire to tame the wild, transforming it into something no longer evoking admiration. Ambivalence toward the wild and the tame is central to the American Western experience, and is expressed in such phenomena as the desire to tame a wild mustang while simultaneously empathizing with its freedom and intractability; the compulsion to ride a bull while yet identifying with the power and defiance of the animal; or the stockman's act of shooting a coyote while attesting to the great cleverness of that species. Such contradictions are an important part of what makes possible rodeo's assurance that the wild-to-tame transformation which is its central concern will be a continuing process involving two opposing forces, not simply a human conquest that will ultimately come to an end.

As a blend of both performance and contest, the sport of rodeo is far more expressive than it would be through either aspect alone. Its performance level provides leeway for the inclusion of pageantry and ritual which serve to revitalize the spirit of the Old West. At the same time, through its contests, there is a particular focus on the central issue of the transformation of nature. This is specifically articulated through the various animal-man oppositions of rodeo which may be seen as representing nature and culture, and which dramatize and perpetuate the conflict between the wild and the tame.

REFERENCES CITED

Abbott, E.C. (Teddy Blue), and Helena Huntington Smith
  1939 We Pointed Them North: Recollections of a Cowpuncher.
  New York: Farrar and Rinehart.
Adams, Andy
  1903 The Log of a Cowboy. Boston: Houghton Mifflin.
Adams, Ramon F.
  1946 Western Words: A Dictionary of the Range, Cow Camp and
  Trail. Norman: Univ. of Oklahoma Press.
  1961 The Old-Time Cowhand. New York: Macmillan.
  1967 The Cowman and His Philosophy. Austin: Encino.
  1968 The Cowboy and His Humor. Austin: Encino.
  1969 The Cowman and His Code of Ethics. Austin: Encino.
Amaral, Anthony
  1969 The Wild Stallion: Comments on His Natural History. In
  The Westerners Brand Book Number XIII. William F. Kimes,
  ed. Pp. 36–45. Los Angeles: Westerners.
Barker-Benfield, G.J.
  1976 The Horrors of the Half-Known Life: Male Attitudes Toward Women and Sexuality in Nineteenth Century America.
  New York: Harper and Row.
Bennett, John W.
  1969 Northern Plainsmen: Adaptive Strategy and Agrarian Life.
  Arlington Heights, Ill.: AHM.
Billington, Ray Allen, ed.
  1977 The Frontier Thesis: Valid Interpretation of American History? New York: Krieger.
Bogoras, Waldemar
  1975 The Chukchi. New York: AMS.

Bois, Thomas
   1966 The Kurds. Beirut: Khayats.
Boorstin, Daniel J.
   1974 The Americans: The Democratic Experience. New York:
   Random House.
Borland, Hal
   1969 When the Legends Die. New York: Bantam.
Bouissac, Paul
   1976 Circus and Culture: A Semiotic Approach. Bloomington:
   Indiana Univ. Press.
Bowen, Elenore Smith
   1964 Return to Laughter. New York: Doubleday.
Branch, Douglas
   1961 The Cowboy and His Interpreters. New York: Cooper
   Square.
Brown, Barbara
   1978a Will Calf Roping Be Banned in Colorado? World of Rodeo
   and Western Heritage 2, 17:5.
   1978b Will Calf Roping Be Banned in Colorado? Part Two.
   World of Rodeo and Western Heritage 2, 18:5.
Browning, Bill
   1975 A Guest Guide to Montana. Helena: Montana Chamber of
   Commerce.
Buffalo Bill's Wild West and Congress of Rough Riders of the World
   Historical Sketches and Programme, Greater New York.
   1897 New York: Fless and Ridge.
Cawelti, John G.
   n.d. The Six-Gun Mystique. Bowling Green: Bowling Green
   Univ. Popular Press.
Cholis, John
   1977 John Wayne, Cattleman. Persimmon Hill 7:28–35.
Conrad, Jack Randolph
   1959 The Horn and the Sword: A History of the Bull as Symbol of
   Power and Fertility. London: Macgibbon and Kee.
Crawford, William
   1965 The Bronc Rider. Oxnard, Calif.: Racz.
cummings, e.e.
   1978 100 Selected Poems. New York: Grove.
Dobie, J. Frank
   1941 The Longhorns. New York: Bramhall House.
   1969 Guide to Life and Literature of the Southwest. Dallas:
   Southern Methodist Univ. Press.

Dodge, Colonel Richard Irving
    1883 Our Wild Indians. Hartford: Worthington.
Dupree, Louis
    1970 Sports and Games in Afghanistan. American Universities
        Fieldstaff Reports. South Asia Series, XIV, 1.
    1976 Kessel's "The Horsemen": The Culture, The Book, The
        Movie. American Universities Fieldstaff Reports. South Asia
        Series, XX, 6.
Dyson-Hudson, Neville
    1972 The Study of Nomads. In Perspectives on Nomadism.
        William Irons and Neville Dyson-Hudson, eds. Pp. 2–29.
        Leiden: Brill.
Eckvall, Robert B.
    1968 Fields on the Hoof: Nexus of Tibetan Nomadic Pastoralism.
        New York: Holt, Rinehart and Winston.
Edgerton, Robert B.
    1974 Pastoral-Farming Comparisons. In Culture and Personality.
        Robert A. Levine, ed. Pp. 345–370. Chicago: Aldine.
Evans-Pritchard, E.E.
    1956 Nuer Religion. New York: Oxford Univ. Press.
    1973 Where the Women Are, the Cattle Are Not. In Rules and
        Meanings. Mary Douglas, ed. Pp. 38–44. Baltimore: Penguin.
    1974 The Nuer. New York: Oxford Univ. Press.
Faulkner, William
    1967 The Bear. In The Portable Faulkner. Malcolm Cowley, ed.
        Pp. 197–320. New York: Viking.
Fernandez, James W.
    1971 Persuasions and Performances: Of the Beast in Every Body
        . . . And the Metaphors of Everyman. In Myth, Symbol, and
        Culture. Clifford Geertz, ed. Pp. 39–60. New York: Norton.
Forbis, William H.
    1973 The Cowboys. New York: Time-Life.
Frantz, Joe B., and Julian Choate
    1955 The American Cowboy: The Myth and the Reality. Norman:
        Univ. of Oklahoma Press.
Fraser, Allan
    1972 The Bull. New York: Scribner's.
Freeman, James W., ed.
    1959 Prose and Poetry of the Livestock Industry. New York:
        Antiquarian.
Furlong, Charles Wellington
    1921 Let 'er Buck: A Story of the Passing of the Old West. New
        York: Putnam.

Geertz, Clifford
  1974 Deep Play: Notes on the Balinese Cockfight. *In* Myth, Symbol, and Culture. Clifford Geertz, ed. Pp. 1–37. New York: Norton.
Goldschmidt, Walter
  1965 Theory and Strategy in the Study of Cultural Adaptability. American Anthropologist 67:402 408.
Gregg, Josiah
  1966 Commerce of the Prairies. Two Volumes. New York: Readex.
Griaule, Marcel
  1975 Conversations with Ogotemmeli: An Introduction to Dogon Religious Ideas. New York: Oxford Univ. Press.
Haley, J. Evetts
  1949 Charles Goodnight: Cowman and Plainsman. Norman: Univ. of Oklahoma Press.
Hall, Douglas Kent
  1973 Let 'er Buck. New York: Dutton.
  1976 Rodeo. New York: Ballantine Books.
Hanes, Colonel Bailey C.
  1977 Bill Pickett, Bulldogger. Norman: Univ. of Oklahoma Press.
Hanesworth, Robert D.
  1967 Daddy of 'em All: The Story of Cheyenne Frontier Days. Cheyenne: Flintlock.
Haynes, Bessie Doak, and Edgar Haynes, eds.
  1967 The Grizzly Bear: Portraits from Life. Norman: Univ. of Oklahoma Press.
Hepher, Paul
  1978 Stampede Grandstand Show Holds Firm. The Albertan, July, 10:26–27.
Hopen, C. Edward
  1970 The Pastoral Fulbe Family in Gwandu. London: Oxford Univ. Press.
Hopkins, Gerard Manley
  1948 Poems of Gerard Manley Hopkins. New York: Oxford Univ. Press.
Hough, E.
  1923 The Story of the Cowboy. New York: Appleton.
Howey, M. Oldfield
  1958 The Horse in Magic and Myth. New York: Castle Books.
Hunter, J. Marvin, ed.

1963 The Trail Drivers of Texas. Two Volumes. New York: Argosy-Antiquarian.

Irving, Washington
1971 A Tour on the Prairies. Norman: Univ. of Oklahoma Press.

Johansson, Gwen
1978 Yaks in Rodeo. The Western Horseman 43, 3:120–121.

Krakel, Dean, ed.
1977 Western Points of View. Persimmon Hill 7,4:70–73.

Krakel, Dean
1978 Requiem to a Bull. Rodeo Sports News 26, 8:3,7.

Krakel, Dean II
1973 The Wyoming Eagle Controversy. Persimmon Hill 3, 4:10–16.
1977 Wyoming's Herman Werner. Persimmon Hill 7, 1:50–61.

Kroeber, A.L.
1963 Anthropology: Culture Patterns and Processes. New York: Harbinger Books.

Lame Deer, John Fire, and Richard Erdoes
1972 Lame Deer, Seeker of Visions. New York: Simon and Schuster.

Lane, Baxter
1976 Cowboy Songs and Poems. Amarillo: Lane.

Larkin, Margaret
1931 Singing Cowboy. New York: Knopf.

Lawrence, Elizabeth Atwood
1976 Centaurs of the Plains: The Horse in Crow Indian Culture, Past and Present. Unpublished Master's Thesis. Providence: Brown Univ.

Leach, Edmund
1964 Anthropological Aspects of Language: Animal Categories and Verbal Abuse. In New Directions in the Study of Language. Eric H. Lenneberg, ed. Pp. 23–63. Cambridge: Massachusetts Institute of Technology Press.
1965 Political Systems of Highland Burma. Boston: Beacon.

Leeds, Anthony
1970 Reindeer Herding and Chukchi Social Institutions. In Man, Culture, and Animals. Anthony Leeds and Andrew P. Vayda, eds. Pp. 87–126. Washington: American Association for the Advancement of Science.

Lelyveld, Joseph
1979 Texas Says 'Howdy' to Teng with a Big Rodeo and Hoopla. Providence Sunday Journal VCV, 5. February 4: A–10.

Lévi-Strauss, Claude

1969 The Elementary Structures of Kinship. Boston: Beacon.

1975 The Raw and the Cooked. New York: Harper.

Lienhardt, Godfrey

1976 Divinity and Experience: The Religion of the Dinka. London: Oxford Univ. Press.

Linderman, Frank B.

1932 Old Man Coyote. New York: Junior Literary Guild.

Lowie, Robert H.

1918 Myths and Traditions of the Crow Indians. Anthropological Papers of the American Museum of Natural History XXV, 1. New York: American Museum of Natural History.

McMurtry, Larry

1968 In a Narrow Grave. New York: Simon and Schuster.

1974 It's Always We Rambled. New York: Hallman.

Medicine Crow, Joseph

1939 The Effects of European Culture Contacts Upon the Economic, Social, and Religious Life of the Crow Indians. Unpublished Master's Thesis. Los Angeles: Univ. of Southern California.

Mercatante, Anthony S.

1974 Zoo of the Gods: Animals in Myth, Legend, and Fable. New York: Harper and Row.

Milton, John R.

1971 The Western Novel: A Symposium. In The Literature of the American West. J. Golden Taylor, ed. Pp. 22–46. Boston: Houghton Mifflin.

Naviaux, James, D.V.M., and Robert Miller, D.V.M.

1977 Is Rodeo Cruel? Horse Lover's National Magazine 21: 7–10.

Ortner, Sherry B.

1974 Is Female to Male as Nature is to Culture? In Woman, Culture and Society. Michelle Z. Rosaldo and Louise Lamphere, eds. Pp. 67–87. Stanford: Stanford Univ. Press.

Parkman, Francis

1950 The Oregon Trail. New York: New American Library.

Pelto, Perti

1973 The Snowmobile Revolution: Technology and Social Change in the Arctic. Menlo Park: Cummings.

Professional Rodeo Cowboys Association, Inc.

n.d. What Is Rodeo? Denver: P.R.C.A.

Radcliffe-Brown, A.R.

1965 Structure and Function in Primitive Society. New York: Free Press.

Riesman, Paul

1977 Freedom in Fulani Social Life. Chicago: Univ. of Chicago Press.

Robertson, M.S.
1974 Rodeo: Standard Guide to the Cowboy Sport. Berkeley: Howell-North Books.

Rodeo Reference Book
1977 Denver: Professional Rodeo Cowboys Association, Inc.

Rollins, Philip Ashton
1973 The Cowboy: An Unconventional History of Civilization on the Old-Time Cattle Range. New York: Ballantine Books.

Rossi, William
1976 The Sex Life of the Foot and the Shoe. New York: Dutton.

Rounds, Glen
1949 Rodeo: Bulls, Broncs and Buckaroos. n.p.: Holiday House.

Rudolph, Alan, and Robert Altman
1976 Buffalo Bill and the Indians or Sitting Bull's History Lesson. New York: Bantam Books.

Russell, Charles
1927 Trails Ploughed Under. New York: Doubleday.

Russell, Don
1960 The Lives and Legends of Buffalo Bill. Norman: Univ. of Oklahoma Press.
1970 The Wild West. Fort Worth: Amon Carter Museum of Western Art.

Sackett, S.J.
1967 Cowboys and the Songs They Sang. New York: Scott.

Savage, William W.
1975 Cowboy Life: Reconstructing an American Myth. Norman: Univ. of Oklahoma Press.

Saxon, A.H.
1968 Enter Foot and Horse: A History of Hippodrama in England and France. New Haven: Yale Univ. Press.

Schatz, August H.
1961 Longhorns Bring Culture. Boston: Christopher.

Schechner, Richard
1970 Approaches. *In* Public Domain: Essays on the Theater. Pp. 55–105. New York: Discus Books.
1973 Performance and the Social Sciences. The Drama Review 17, 3: 3–4.
1973 Drama, Script, Theater, and Performance. The Drama Review 17, 3: 5–36.
1976 From Ritual to Theater and Back. *In* Ritual, Play, and

References 279

Performance: Readings in the Social Sciences/Theater. Richard Schechner and Mady Schuman, eds. Pp. 196–222. New York: Seabury.

Schneider, Bill
1977 Where the Grizzly Walks. Missoula: Mountain Press.

Schueler, Donald G.
1978 Incident at Eagle Ranch. Audubon: The Magazine of the National Audubon Society 80, 3: 41–72.

Searle, Walt
1976 Hoofbeats: Gonna Be Hell to Beat 'em. Hoof and Horn: The Magazine of Ranch and Rodeo 46, 2: 3.
1977 Hoofbeats: Hats Off to the Cattleman. Hoof and Horn: The Magazine of Ranch and Rodeo 47, 3: 3.
1978 Hoofbeats: Indian National Finals. Hoof and Horn: The Magazine of Ranch and Rodeo 48, 4: 3.

Seidman, Laurence Ivan
1973 Once in the Saddle: The Cowboy's Frontier, 1866–1896. New York: Knopf.

Serven, James
1972 Horses of the West. Arizona Highways 48: 14–39.

Shaffer, Peter
1974 Equus. New York: Atheneum.

Siringo, Charles A.
1950 A Texas Cowboy, or Fifteen Years on the Hurricane Deck of a Spanish Pony. New York: Umbedenstock.

Slotkin, Richard
1973 Regeneration Through Violence: The Mythology of the American Frontier, 1600–1860. Middletown: Wesleyan Univ. Press.

Smith, Henry Nash
1971 Virgin Land: The American West As Symbol and Myth. Cambridge: Harvard Univ. Press.

Smith, Lorraine
1976 Sportsview: Cowboys Court Injury in Battle of Survival. The Physician and Sportsmedicine 4, 12: 90–93.

Spence, Clark C.
1966 The American West: A Source Book. New York: Crowell.

Standing Bear, Chief
1933 Land of the Spotted Eagle. Boston: Houghton Mifflin.

Steele, Rufus
1941 Mustangs of the Mesas. Hollywood: Murray and Gee.

Stuart, Granville

1925 Forty Years on the Frontier: Journals and Reminiscences. Two Volumes. Cleveland: Clark.

Taylor, George Rogers, ed.
1972 The Turner Thesis Concerning the Role of the Frontier in American History. Lexington: Heath.

Thorpe, N. Howard
1966 Songs of the Cowboys. New York: Bramhall.

Tinkle, Lon, and Allen Maxwell, eds.
1976 The Cowboy Reader. New York: McKay.

Towne, Charles W.
1957 Cowboys and Herdsmen. In This Is the West. Robert West Howard, ed. Pp. 72–81. New York: Rand McNally.

Turner, Frederick J.
1894 The Significance of the Frontier in American History. Annual Report of the American Historical Association 1893. Washington: Government Printing Office.

Turner, Victor
1974 The Forest of Symbols. Ithaca: Cornell Univ. Press.

Vanggaard, Thorkil
1972 Phallos: A Symbol and Its History in the Male World. New York: International Universities Press.

Vernam, Glenn R.
1972 Man On Horseback. Lincoln: Univ. of Nebraska Press.

Webb, Walter Prescott
1936 The Great Plains. Boston: Houghton Mifflin.

Westermeier, Clifford P.
1947 Man, Beast, Dust: The Story of Rodeo. Denver: World Press.
1955 Trailing the Cowboy: His Life and Lore As Told By Frontier Journalists. Caldwell, Idaho: Caxton.
1976 The Cowboy and Sex. In The Cowboy: Six-Shooters, Songs, and Sex. Charles W. Harris and Buck Rainey, eds. Pp. 85–106. Norman: Univ. of Oklahoma Press.

White, John I.
1975 Git Along Little Dogies: Songs and Songmakers of the American West. Urbana: Univ. of Illinois Press.

Wissler, Clark
1914 The Influence of the Horse in the Development of Plains Indian Culture. American Anthropologist 65: 355–369.

Wister, Owen
1902 The Virginian. New York: Macmillan.

INDEX

Abbott, E.C. ("Teddy Blue"), 56, 57, 58, 60, 61, 64, 65, 67, 68, 71
Adams, Andy, 53, 56, 60, 67, 69
addiction to rodeo, 92, 101–102
alligator, 230
animals: boundaries between, and man, 218, 219, 220; cat trainers and, 243; rodeo, participants' views of, 123–27, 128; unity with, 218, 219, 220, 222
announcer, role of, 16
arena, description of, 12
audiences, 23–24, 154, 176, 177, 189, 190

barebac bronc riding: compared to saddle bronc riding, 144–45; description of, 27–28
barrel racing, 23, 110–11, 112, 113, 115, 119, 201; description of, 37–39; male attitude toward, 111
bears, 63, 70, 76, 226, 230, 233, 250, 254, 258, 263, 264; see also grizzly bears
beef, 173–75, 176; Americans and, 52; image of bulls and, 196; steers as, 177; associated with strength and virility, 173–74
Bennett, John, 58, 59, 68, 71, 116
birds, 223, 257–59, 261; see also

birds (cont.)
doves, eagles, hawks, magpies, turkeys
books: cowboys' attitude toward, 68–69, 72; rodeo contestants' attitude toward, 96
boots. See cowboy boots
Borland, Hal, 252
Bouissac, Paul, 6, 156, 165
boundaries between man and animals, 218, 219, 220
Bowen, E.S., 73
branding, 62, 77, 78, 115, 170, 175
breakaway roping, 40, 120
breasts, female, 113, 217
broncs, 132, 143–51; perceptions of, 145–51; symbolism of, 144; verse about, 139; violence and, 146; see also horses
brotherhood: between cowboys, 67–68; between rodeo contestants, 91
bucking: breeding program for, 148–49; in bulls, 182, 189; as inherent, 146, 148, 149, 150, 151; style of, affected by flank strap, 150–51
bucking strap, 26; see also flank strap
buckles as rodeo trophies, 18, 95, 108, 165
buffalo (bison), 51, 70, 173, 206, 264, 265

281